STUDIES IN ENGLISH LITERATURES

Edited by Koray Melikoğlu

Zeynep Zeren Atayurt

Excess and Embodiment
in Contemporary Women's Writing

STUDIES IN ENGLISH LITERATURES

Edited by Koray Melikoğlu

ISSN 1614-4651

7   Bianca Del Villano
    Ghostly Alterities
    Spectrality and Contemporary Literatures in English
    2nd, revised editon
    ISBN 978-3-89821-714-9

8   Melanie Ann Hanson
    Decapitation and Disgorgement
    The Female Body's Text in Early Modern English Drama and Poetry
    ISBN 978-3-89821-605-5

9   Shafquat Towheed (ed.)
    New Readings in the Literature of British India, c.1780-1947
    ISBN 978-3-89821-673-9

10 Paola Baseotto
    "Disdeining life, desiring leaue to die"
    Spenser and the Psychology of Despair
    ISBN 978-3-89821-567-1

11 Annie Gagiano
    Dealing with Evils
    Essays on Writing from Africa
    ISBN 978-3-89821-867-2

12 Thomas F. Halloran
    James Joyce: Developing Irish Identity
    A Study of the Development of Postcolonial Irish Identity in the Novels of James Joyce
    ISBN 978-3-89821-571-8

13 Pablo Armellino
    Ob-scene Spaces in Australian Narrative
    An Account of the Socio-topographic Construction of Space in Australian Literature
    ISBN 978-3-89821-873-3

14 Lance Weldy
    Seeking a Felicitous Space on the Frontier
    The Progression of the Modern American Woman in O. E. Rölvaag, Laura Ingalls Wilder, and Willa Cather
    ISBN 978-3-89821-535-0

15 Rana Tekcan
    The Biographer and the Subject
    A Study on Biographical Distance
    ISBN 978-3-89821-995-2

16 Paola Brusasco
    Writing Within/Without/About Sri Lanka
    Discourses of Cartography, History and Translation in Selected Works by Michael Ondaatje and Carl Muller
    ISBN 978-3-8382-0075-0

Zeynep Zeren Atayurt

EXCESS AND EMBODIMENT IN CONTEMPORARY WOMEN'S WRITING

ibidem-Verlag
Stuttgart

Bibliografische Information der Deutschen Nationalbibliothek
Die Deutsche Nationalbibliothek verzeichnet diese Publikation in der
Deutschen Nationalbibliografie; detaillierte bibliografische Daten sind im
Internet über http://dnb.d-nb.de abrufbar.

Bibliographic information published by the Deutsche Nationalbibliothek
Die Deutsche Nationalbibliothek lists this publication in the Deutsche Nationalbibliografie;
detailed bibliographic data are available in the Internet at http://dnb.d-nb.de.

Cover illustration: Jennifer Saftler, *The Carnival* (1994). © Jennifer Saftler.
Reproduction with kind permission.

∞

Gedruckt auf alterungsbeständigem, säurefreien Papier
Printed on acid-free paper

ISSN: 1614-4651

ISBN-13: 978-3-89821-978-5

© *ibidem*-Verlag
Stuttgart 2011

Alle Rechte vorbehalten

Das Werk einschließlich aller seiner Teile ist urheberrechtlich geschützt. Jede Verwertung
außerhalb der engen Grenzen des Urheberrechtsgesetzes ist ohne Zustimmung des Verlages
unzulässig und strafbar. Dies gilt insbesondere für Vervielfältigungen,
Übersetzungen, Mikroverfilmungen und elektronische Speicherformen sowie die
Einspeicherung und Verarbeitung in elektronischen Systemen.

All rights reserved. No part of this publication may be reproduced, stored in or introduced into a retrieval
system, or transmitted, in any form, or by any means (electronical, mechanical, photocopying, recording or
otherwise) without the prior written permission of the publisher. Any person who does any unauthorized act
in relation to this publication may be liable to criminal prosecution and civil claims for damages.

Printed in Germany

Contents

Acknowledgements	ix
Introduction Difference of the Different: Challenges to the Homogenisation of 'Fatness' in Contemporary Western Culture	1
1 'A comic turn, turned serious': Reading the Female Embodiment in Romance, the Trickster and the Cyborg in *The Life and Loves of a She-Devil*	35
2 'I still think it was poetic': The Poetics and Politics of Hyperbole in *Sexing the Cherry*	63
3 Mothers, Daughters and 'Excess' in *Lady Oracle* and *Sweet Death*	95
3.1 'The outline of my former body still surrounded me like a mist': Traumatic Resonances of 'Excess' in *Lady Oracle*	100
3.1.1 'Obesity', Trauma and its Manifestations within the Mother-Daughter Dyad	105
3.1.2 From 'Fat' to 'Thin': Reversals, Reconciliations, and Confrontations	124
3.2 'I know what I look like. It's all planned, calculated, willed': The Revenge Narrative of 'Excess' in *Sweet Death*	146
3.2.1 Accessing the Private through Writing of 'Excess'	150
3.2.2 Tensions in the Mother-Daughter Dyad and Desire for Power	155
Conclusion 'I am sorry I am so fat': A Narrative of 'Excess' in *Fat Girl: A True Story*	169
Bibliography	183

Primary Sources 183
Secondary Sources 183
Internet Resources 196

Acknowledgements

This book is based on my doctoral dissertation submitted to the School of English at Leeds University. I am grateful to a number of people whose crucial contribution to my research needs to be acknowledged. I am particularly indebted to Dr. Tracy Hargreaves and Dr. Fiona Becket for offering valuable insights into my work. I also thank the Fat Studies group (UK and USA) for promoting a stimulating and welcoming academic and social environment for invigorating discussions.

I am thankful to the Higher Education Council in Turkey and Ankara University for providing funds for my research. Special thanks go to the academic staff in the Departments of English Language and Literature, and American Culture and Literature at Ankara University, in particular to Prof. Dr. Ayşegül Yüksel, Prof. Dr. Sema Ege and Prof. Dr. Belgin Elbir. My grateful thanks go to Dr. F. Devrim Kılıçer for introducing me to Ibidem-Verlag.

I wish to thank my editor Mr. Koray Melikoğlu for his helpful comments and suggestions. Special thanks go to Ms. Jennifer Saftler for her kind permission to reproduce her painting as the cover image for this book.

I would like to express my thanks to Dr. Edel Porter, Dr. Catherine Bates, Ann Thompson and Marc Thompson for all their constructive suggestions. I am also thankful to Dr. Yeliz Biber for her friendship and company during many long sleepless nights. I want to specially thank Matthew Fenge whose kindness, loving support, encouragement, and faith in me has been the greatest gift.

Last but not least, I would like to thank my loving parents Emel and Halil Atayurt, and my sister Sedef Pişirensoy who have always encouraged me to follow my aspirations, and have given me every strength and support even across the miles. This work is especially dedicated to them.

Introduction

Difference of the Different: Challenges to the Homogenisation of 'Fatness' in Contemporary Western Culture

There has been a specific kind of 'visibility' of the female body since the late twentieth century owing to the dramatic advances in hi-tech visual communication. This 'visibility' constantly projected in advertisements, television reality shows and mainstream women's magazines[1] has increasingly standardised the notion of female beauty which is defined in terms of the attainment of a body that is lightly muscled, toned, and slender. The prioritisation of the lean physique has created a social environment of distress over food and discomfort with one's body size, which has a tendency to equate women's happiness, health and even success particularly with reference to size. The increasing bodily preoccupations with 'fat'[2], diet and slenderness, and the tendency to impose the idea of women's bodies 'as being in need of change, repair or improvement'[3] give rise to the underlying preoccupations of this thesis: How is the representation of the 'fat' female body constructed in women's fictional and non-fictional narratives? What kind of debates could possibly be instigated through an engagement with the representation of 'excessive' female embodiment? How does this construction transform, confront or speak to current perceptions of fatness that have been largely framed and stabilised by popular cultural concerns?

---

[1] Cover lines of some magazines continuously prescribe the ways to attain a slender body. For instance: '50 Shortcuts to a Sexier Body' (*Glamour*, January 2007), '6 Ways to Thin – Easy Diets that Really Work' (*Allure*, January 2007), 'Get a Bikini Body by Spring!' (*Shape*, January 2007).

[2] I shall be using inverted commas when employing the words 'fat', 'obese', 'excessive' because these words often represent a subjective viewpoint that tends to assign an individual to a marginalised position.

[3] O. Wayne Wooley, '...And Man Created "Woman"', in *Feminist Perspectives on Eating Disorders*, ed. by Patricia Fallon, Melanie A. Katzman, Susan C. Wooley (New York: The Guilford Press, 1994), pp. 17-53 (p. 19).

2   *Excess and Embodiment in Contemporary Women's Writing*

According to the first international survey of how women rate body image, commissioned by Dove, a large company in the health and beauty sector, in partnership with Nancy Etcoff and Susie Orbach, 'only one in five British females consider themselves attractive.'[4] Susie Orbach, who collaborated with Dove's 'real women' campaign,[5] says:

> Having worked for thirty years in the area of eating disorders, I began to think what visual culture was doing to us – the fact we see a minimum of 12,000 images a week; the way that for the generation of women who felt OK about their bodies it has destroyed that. But it really was a hunch until I read a study showing that in 1995, when TV was first brought into Fiji, a country that had no body-image eating problems, three years later 11.9% of the girls were throwing up over the toilet bowl. Visual culture is that powerful. So when Dove approached me, I felt we needed a way to diversify and challenge the digitally enhanced photos that are out there.[6]

As this example shows, the impact of the popular visual imagery is undeniably significant in terms of women's relationships to their bodies. The re-publication of two seminal works, Susie Orbach's *Fat is a Feminist Issue*[7] and Susan Bordo's *Unbearable Weight: Feminism, Western Culture and the Body*, 10 years after their latest publication is suggestive of their urge to re-address Western cultural obsession with

---

[4] Liz Hoggard, 'Why We're All Beautiful Now', *Observer*, 9 January 2005 <http://www.guardian.co.uk/media/2005/jan/09/advertising.comment> [accessed 15 November 2006] (para. 11 of 21).

[5] In 2004 Dove started a campaign featuring some plus size women against the weight-loss advertisement industry. The campaign was initially launched in the UK, a year later in the US and Canada. It has been reported to have increased Dove sales by 700 per cent.

[6] Hoggard, 'Why We're All Beautiful Now', (para. 14 of 21).

[7] It is significant that Orbach's former controversial title of her book *Fat is a Feminist Issue: The Anti-Diet Guide to Permanent Weight Loss* is shortened to *Fat is a Feminist Issue: The Anti-Diet Guide* in this edition. The omission of the words 'permanent weight loss' is suggestive of a shift in the writer's position, and a revised ambivalent attitude towards the superficial practices performed in the process of weight loss.

thinness, which has been rapidly increasing since the 1990s. Orbach's and Bordo's works speak to this cultural fixation, voicing in a mordant manner the desire to undo the prescribed body ideal constantly suggested by visual culture. While the pursuit of the perfect body shape is by no means a new phenomenon, the methods used to attain the image of body perfection are becoming more extreme, facilitated in part by new developments in technology and medical science. It is nowadays almost impossible not to read or hear about the new diets, advanced methods of weight-loss surgery[8] (such as gastric bypass surgery or stomach-stapling, laparoscopic bariatric surgery) that are performed in the name of attaining the perfect and supposedly healthy body – the body without 'fat'.

British culture's interest in obesity and its apparent panic over weight gain have been increasingly prevalent in the popular daily press. While there were only 78 newspaper articles on 'obesity'[9] in *The Guardian* between 1996 and 1999, this figure has risen to 3379 between the years 2000 and 2007, with 252 related entries on obesity only between January and June 2008 exploring the issue as a major health and aesthetic concern more than on a daily basis. There is also an increasing number of weight loss shows on British television which portray a cultural, even voyeuristic, interest in fatness as a sign of poor diet and poor health. 'You are What You Eat'[10], 'Fat Club'[11] and its spin-off series 'Celebrity Fit Club'[12], 'Biggest Loser UK'[13], 'Fat Men

---

[8] The bariatric industry produces many publications which appear in consumer and patient advocacy magazines, and even professional journals such as *Bariatrics Today*, *Obesity Surgery*, *Surgery for Obesity and Related Diseases*.

[9] It is interesting to note that the clinical term 'obesity' appears more frequently than the words 'fat' or 'overweight' in the popular British media. The exploitation of this word on a regular basis tends to magnify the association of 'obesity' with disease.

[10] Aired on Channel Four from 2004 to 2007, and presented by Dr. Gillian McKeith.

[11] Aired on ITV 1 in 2002.

[12] Aired on ITV 1 from 2002 to 2006, and hosted by Dale Winton.

[13] Aired on Living TV from 2005 to 2007, presented by Vicki Butler-Henderson.

Can't Hunt'[14] and its follow-on 'Can Fat Teens Hunt?'[15], 'Fat Chance'[16] are some of the shows that have promoted thinness and, ostensibly, demonstrated the amazing results that can be achieved through diet and exercise. Even though these programmes are seen to encourage healthy eating and fitness as a 'normalizing' strategy to help the 'victim', they also seem to dismiss the fact that 'the attainment of an "acceptable body" is extremely difficult for those who do not come by it "naturally" (whether aided by genetics, metabolism or high activity-level).'[17]

The popular culture, as Paul Campos states, 'exaggerates the health-risks associated with higher-than-average weight, while all sorts of related but far graver risks have been ignored'[18] as 'just being fat does not signify poor health.'[19] More importantly, these kinds of

---

[14] Aired on BBC 3 in 2007.
[15] Aired on BBC 3 from 2007 to 2008.
[16] Aired on ITV 1 in 2008, and presented by Pete Cohen and Jane DeVille-Almond.
[17] Susan Bordo, 'Reading the Slender Body', in *Body/Politics: Women and the Discourses of Science*, ed. by Mary Jacobus, Evelyn Fox Keller, Sally Shuttleworth (New York and London: Routledge, 1990), pp. 83-112 (p. 99).
[18] Paul Campos, *The Obesity Myth: Why America's Obsession with Weight is Hazardous to Your Health?* (New York: Penguin, 2004), p. xxv.
[19] The National Association to Advance Fat Acceptance (NAAFA), one of the most active fat liberation organisations in the United States since its foundation in 1969, asserts that 'the health risks once associated with weight may instead be attributable to yo-yo dieting. Because fatness is most often caused by heredity and dieting history and because 95-98% of all diets fail over three years, it is becoming apparent that remaining at a high, but stable weight and concentrating on personal fitness rather than thinness may be the healthiest way to deal with the propensity to be fat', cited in NAAFA, 'But Isn't it Unhealthy to Be Fat?' <http://www.naafa.org/documents/brochures/naafa-info.html#whatis> [accessed 5 November 2006] (para. 10 of 12). See also <http://www.foodmuseum.com/ex fatCulture.html> [accessed 1 September 2008]

In line with NAAFA, Size Acceptance Association UK adopts the notion of 'health at every size', and works to dismantle the tendency towards linking obesity to health problems while overlooking other potential factors: 'There are more than 100 independent risk factors for heart disease such as poor diet, lack of physical fitness, high stress levels, being poor and certain gene variations. But

shows, whether deliberately or not, contribute to the devaluation of the 'obese'. Such portrayals of eating disorders by the popular media, as Susan Bordo argues:

> encourage a 'side show' experience of the relationship of the ('normal') audience and those on view ('the freaks'). To the degree that the audience may nonetheless recognise themselves in the behaviour or reported experiences of those on stage, they confront themselves as 'pathological' or outside the norm.[20]

Popular media's painstaking attempt to bring 'fat' people under the spotlight seems to revive the nineteenth-century circus freak show tradition where 'fat' people are exposed to the public eye. However, in the nineteenth century, 'obesity' had not been viewed in terms of 'deviance', instead, it aroused attraction and fascination. 'Fat' in women had a sexual connotation being seen as 'erotically appealing'[21] and regarded as women's 'silken layer.'[22] Popular 'fat' ladies of the time, known as 'Dolly Dimples', 'Baby Ruth' or 'Jolly Irene'[23] had gained the attention and admiration of their viewers, and their 'superabundant' bodies had not been associated with 'lack of control', 'disease'. However, as opposed to the nineteenth century's response to 'obesity', contemporary Western culture views it as a hazardous, fearful state that should be treated or avoided altogether. The fear that 'obesity' arouses in fact unveils less a physiological than a social anxiety about excess and chaos. It might be argued that this anxiety is the projection of what culture most fears about itself, which can be attributed to the violation of social and cultural norms.

---

most studies linking obesity to heart disease lump them all in with being obese', in Jerome Burne, 'Obesity: Size Isn't Everything', 21 June 2005, cited in ISAA UK <http://www.size-acceptance.org/uk/> [accessed 22 April 2008] (para. 6 of 15).
[20] Bordo, 'Reading the Slender Body', p. 85.
[21] Leslie Fiedler, *Freaks: Myths and Images of the Secret Self* (Middlesex: Penguin, 1981 [1978]), p. 131.
[22] Naomi Wolf, *The Beauty Myth* (London: Vintage, 1990), p. 192.
[23] Fiedler, p. 129.

6   *Excess and Embodiment in Contemporary Women's Writing*

'The idea of society' as Mary Douglas defines, 'is a powerful image' which 'has form, has external boundaries, margins, internal structure' whose 'outlines contain power to reward conformity and repulse attack', and anyone who offends against this order has the potential to be regarded as an 'outcast' and embodiment of 'danger.'[24] Arguably, obesity, which is often described in terms of an epidemic that is almost out of control, is seen as a threat to society's order and its control mechanisms. However, according to Charlotte Cooper, 'when we define fatness as a "disease" we are acting within powerful social boundaries which control what we believe to be right and appropriate, or shameful and abnormal.'[25] 'Disease', as Cooper further argues, represents 'disorder, chaos, weakness and badness.'[26] Viewed in this context, the social response to this perceived threat can be in the form of fear and panic. 'Order implies restriction from all possible materials. So disorder by implication is unlimited, and is destructive to existing patterns as it symbolises both danger and power.'[27] It may well be argued that 'fatness' fits into this design of 'disorder', as it is considered as having the potential to disrupt the prevailing order. That is to say, fear of fat unveils an anxiety over the invalidation of the social, political and economic dynamics. This is a double-edged situation: on the one hand capitalism has created a consumerist culture that encourages people to consume in large quantities, which makes people susceptible to increase in size. On the other, 'fatness' is most often associated with a 'physical abnormality' caused by over-consumption, which has to be kept under control.

One way to combat weight gain and to establish an 'ascetic' control over the body is to make the body subject to a new regime of discipline through a vast variety of dietary practices. 'Diet and regulation

---

[24] Mary Douglas, *Purity and Danger: An Analysis of Concepts of Pollution and Taboo* (London and New York: Routledge, 2002 [1966]), p. 141.
[25] Charlotte Cooper, *Fat and Proud: The Politics of Size* (London: The Women's Press, 1998), p. 71.
[26] Ibid., p. 71.
[27] Douglas, *Purity and Danger*, p. 117.

of the body', as Bryan Turner points out, 'were related for many centuries to a religious discipline that aimed to control the soul.'[28] As Turner argues, 'within the ascetic tradition of the classical and Christian eras, the body was considered as a threatening and dangerous phenomenon, in that it was seen as a vehicle for the unruly, ungovernable and irrational patterns, emotions and desires.'[29] However, in contemporary Western society, 'asceticism is designed to produce an acceptable social self.'[30] According to Turner's argument, the attainment of 'an acceptable social self' is directly related to having a 'good' body image (one that is visually appealing to others), which is considered to be a major personal asset. However, the move from asceticism as a form of controlling appetite for disciplining the soul to controlling appetite to look desirable and socially acceptable has turned the body into an object of the manipulation of a consumerist society. The regulatory control of the body, which used to be a religious practice, has been replaced by the fashion and diet industries in contemporary Western societies that benefit from making people afraid to be fat. The massive diet industry finds it profitable to nurture and exploit the obsession with the thin ideal by manufacturing both chemical and herbal products that advance unhealthy practices in the name of rapid weight loss. However, it has well been established that when a person loses his/her excessive weight, s/he has a tendency to compensate for the appetite suppressed during the diet by again consuming in large amounts. As Hillel Schwartz has argued, 'the diet is the supreme form for manipulating desire', and 'it is through the constant frustration of desire that late Capitalism can prompt ever higher levels of consumption.'[31] Viewed in this respect, the promotion of diets and the portrayal of 'fatness' as a fearful condition thus serves as a strategy to establish

---

[28] Bryan S. Turner, *The Body and Society* (London, Thousand Oaks, New Delhi: Sage Publications, 1996), p. 23.
[29] Ibid., p. 11.
[30] Ibid., p. 23.
[31] Hillel Schwartz, *Never Satisfied: A Cultural History of Diets, Fantasies and Fat* (New York: Free Press, 1986), p. 328.

social control and legitimacy in a capitalist society. The media message of 'obesity prevention', therefore, can be seen as a manipulative social and cultural construct that may ultimately lead to social exclusion.

Within consumer culture, 'excessive' embodiment is often subjected to stigmatisation and discrimination. Overweight women are mostly disfavoured, and exposed to discrimination and bias in key areas of their life, including employment and health care. On 31st August 2006, for example, 'fertility experts announced that overweight women should not be allowed to have IVF on the NHS.'[32] In his defense of this measure, Richard Kennedy of the British Fertility Society (BFS) states that 'obese women are less likely to get pregnant and more likely to encounter health problems', however, the same sense of sensitivity to IVF treatment does not apply to smokers as according to the BFS proposals, 'smokers should not be barred from having IVF.'[33] Another example of size discrimination comes from countries such as China and South Korea which have placed restrictions on weight for prospective foreign adoptive parents.[34] The fact that twenty five-stone soprano Deborah Voigt was controversially denied the title role in *Ariadne auf Naxos* because she was considered 'too hefty'[35] and 'too large to wear a little black dress demanded by the director'[36] exemplifies yet another case of discrimination against 'fat' women. More re-

---

[32] Kira Cochrane, 'Too Fat for a Family?', in *Guardian*, 31 August 2006. <http://www.guardian.co.uk/society/2006/aug/31/health.medicineandhealth> [acessed 15 November 2006] (para. 1 of 15).

[33] 'Call for Fertility Ban for Obese' on BBC news, 30 August 2006. <http://news.bbc.co.uk/1/hi/health/5296200.stm> [accessed 17 October 2006] (para. 12 of 35).

[34] See Leslie Holt, 'China Toughens Adoption Standards' <http://www.icue.com/portal/site/iCue/flatview/?cuecard=35300 >[accessed 5 September 2009]

[35] Maev Kennedy, 'Only Sing When You're Slimming', in *Guardian*, 8 March 2004. <http://www.guardian.co.uk/uk/2004/mar/08/arts.artsnews> [accessed 12 September 2006] (para. 1 of 10).

[36] Charlotte Higgins, '"Too Fat" Opera Star Makes Slight Return', in *Guardian*, 04 April 2007. <http://www.guardian.co.uk/uk/2007/apr/05/classicalmusic.artnews> [accessed 20 October 2007] (para. 3 of 15).

cently, a British woman, because she was 'too fat',[37] was denied entry to New Zealand on the basis of her being a potential burden on the health care system. Perhaps, the most distinct example that showcases the emerging fat prejudice involves an overweight teenage girl who had to live with a cancerous tumour for two years because of the doctors' prejudiced attitude toward 'fat' that unhesitatingly led the doctors to relate the young girl's health problems directly to her weight resulting in their failure to 'diagnose her problem.'[38] Marilyn Wann, the co-director of the National Association to Advance Fat Acceptance (NAAFA), associates this increasing 'war against obesity' with a similar level of viciousness and discrimination practised in matters of race and gender. She says: 'We are in the middle of a witch hunt and we are the witches.'[39] Even though this analogy may seem exaggerated, it nonetheless draws attention to the current social stigma placed upon 'obesity' which has created a social environment that is extremely hostile toward weight gain and 'fat' people. In this social landscape fat is seen as 'repulsive, funny, ugly, unclean and, more importantly, something to lose.'[40]

The fear and dislike of fat, which tends to characterise Western society's cultural obsession with body size and obesity, inspired my critical interest in the representations of corpulent female bodies in the writings of Fay Weldon, Jeanette Winterson, Margaret Atwood, Claude Tardat, and Judith Moore. Obviously, these are not the only

---

[37] Simon Cable, 'British Woman Banned from Entering New Zealand', in *The Daily Mail*, 17 November 2007. <http://www.freerepublic.com/focus/f-news/1927165/posts> [accessed 19 November 2007] (para. 1 of 6).

[38] 'How did doctors miss my cancerous tumour?', in *Hull Daily Mail / East Riding Mail*, 15 January 2008. <http://www.thisisyourmail.co.uk/posts/your_patch/view/1805-how-did-doctors-miss-my-cancerous-tumour> [accessed 16 January 2008] (para. 1 of 1).

[39] Marilyn Wann cited in Paul Harris, '"Fat is Fabulous", insist Anti-Diet Protesters', in *Observer*, 8 August 2004. <http://www.guardian.co.uk/world/2004/aug/08/usa.health> [accessed 12 November 2006] (para.12 of 17).

[40] Kathleen LeBesco, *Revolting Bodies?* (Amherst and Boston: University of Massachusetts Press, 2004), p. 16.

writers whose works engage with bodily preoccupations and weight issues. Susan Sussman's *The Dieter* (1989), Jenefer Shute's *Life-Size* (1992), Helen Fielding's *Bridget Jones's Diary* (1996), Deborah Blumenthal's *Fat Chance* (2004), Liza Palmer's *Conversations with The Fat Girl* (2005), Candida Crew's *Eating Myself* (2006), Grace Bowman's *Shape of My Own* (2006) are some of the women's writings that explore women's problematic and unhappy relationship with food and their bodies in a materialistic society. However, in these works we read about women's dissatisfaction with their weight, and their collusion with attaining the thin ideal at the cost of their health (by becoming anorexic or bulimic) as we see in Shute's *Life-Size*, Bowman's *Shape of My Own* and Crew's *Eating Myself*. These fictional and autobiographical narratives explore the notion of bodily excess as an undesirable personal and social attribute affirming many of the problematic characteristics that Western culture tends to assign to female corpulence. By contrast, the selected texts in this study question the very social, cultural and psychological mechanisms operating underneath the antagonistic contextualisation of fatness. Thus, these works offer an engagement with the representation of 'fat' female body not merely as an aesthetic issue, but as a multi-faceted literary design to explore hidden implications and deeper layers of meaning that hold together various aspects of physical embodiment.

One of the factors that motivated this study is that the rhetoric of fatness in contemporary culture has situated fatness mainly within the contexts of health, aesthetics and morality transmitting the message that 'fatness is not only unhealthy, but also unsightly and immoral.'[41] As Eric Oliver has stated, 'to be overweight is to be, by definition, abnormal or different'.[42] Yet, it is interesting to see that despite the arguable difference ascribed to the 'fat' person, there is a tendency to homogenise the notion of fatness and situate it within narrow confines.

---

[41] J. Eric Oliver, *Fat Politics: The Real Story Behind America's Obesity Epidemic* (Oxford, New York: Oxford University Press, 2006), p. 2.
[42] Ibid., p. 15.

This process has tended towards the stigmatisation of 'fat' individuals. As a response to this process, we see the embodiment-fixated contemporary Western society preoccupied with fat-abhorring rhetorics and images which points towards '[the] general sense of the body's offensiveness spread[ing] out from the large body.'[43] The different representations of fatness in this study are not limited to these restrictive assumptions. Each text, as I will discuss later, offers a heterogeneous approach to reading 'excessive' female bodies where the representation of fatness becomes the measure of various states and positions, rather than a sole manifestation of a physical condition. In each text, the representation of female embodiment opens up a more nuanced debate for a reappraisal of the 'large' female body where the 'fat' female body not only becomes an integral aspect of the plotline, but also facilitates a multi-layered discussion that prompts intellectual challenges implicit in the social and cultural construction of weight.

At various points in the course of my analysis, I engage with Mikhail Bakhtin's theorisation of the grotesque and excess, as a useful theoretical framework within which we can examine the disruptive potential of the 'fat' body in dismantling the existing hegemonic idea(l)s of dominant cultural systems and restrictive norms. Through an analysis of my selected texts, I will argue the ways in which these texts metamorphose cultural obsessions with 'excessive' female embodiment into fictional and non-fictional narratives, and promote different responses to corporeality. Below are two quotations that exemplify these different attitudes:

> I had an *alter ego* who was huge and powerful, a woman whose only morality was her own and whose loyalties were fierce and few. She

---

[43] Michael Moon and Eve Kosofsky Sedgwick, 'Divinity: A Dossier, a Performance Piece, a Little Understood Emotion', in *Bodies Out of Bounds: Fatness and Transgression*, ed. by Jana Evans Braziel and Kathleen LeBesco (Berkeley, Los Angeles and London: University of California Press, 2001), pp. 292-328 (p. 294).

was my patron saint. [...] Whenever I called on her I felt my muscles swell and laughter fill up my throat.[44]

> The fat person lacks willpower, pride, 'self-esteem', and does not care about friends or family, because if he or she did care about friends and family, he or she would not wander the earth looking like a repulsive sow, rhinoceros, hippo, elephant, general wide-mawed flesh-flopping flabby monster.[45]

In Jeanette Winterson's novel, the glorification of the 'excessive' female body, embodied by the gargantuan Dog Woman, is transformed into the slender woman's alter-ego which furnishes her with an inner strength. Freud spoke of the ego as 'first and foremost a bodily ego', thus regarding the ego 'as a mental projection of the surface of the body.'[46] Nicky Diamond explains the process of the formation of the 'bodily ego' as follows:

> We are simultaneously dependent on a form of identification with fictional images, yet at the same moment set apart from the image we aspire to. [...] The idealization of 'ego'-ideals is important, for they are seen as always set apart, more perfect than we can ever be – occupying an impossible place.[47]

In contemporary Western society the 'thin' ideal often becomes the ego-ideal that many women aspire to attain. However, in Winterson's novel, the massive body of the Dog Woman is represented as the ego-ideal for the thin woman who regards the 'fat' woman's physical strength as an inspiration for the power to destabilise the dominant cultural and political codes. Winterson's construction of the Dog Woman's body as the ego-ideal for the modern woman challenges the stigmatisation of 'fat' people in the contemporary world as self-

---

[44] Jeanette Winterson, *Sexing the Cherry* (London: Vintage, 2001 [1989]), p. 125.
[45] Judith Moore, *Fat Girl: A True Story* (London: Profile Books, 2005 [2004]), pp. 1-2.
[46] Sigmund Freud, *New Introductory Lectures on Psychoanalysis* (London: Hogarth Press and the Institute of Psychoanalysis, 1974), p. 16.
[47] Nicky Diamond, 'Thin is the Feminist Issue', in *Feminist Review*, 19 (Spring 1985), 45-64 (p. 60).

indulgent, undisciplined, out of control, lazy, greedy and repellent, as depicted by Judith Moore in her memoir *Fat Girl: A True Story*. Winterson's text produces a highly imaginative and distinctive narrative strategy that enables a celebration of boundless possibilities where the embodiments of both the 'fat' and slender are rendered liberatory. However, the glorification of an 'obese' woman in Winterson's literary imagination may be too idealistic to correspond to the factual representation of 'fat' woman in contemporary society. Whilst fatness evokes the idea of strength and power for the young slender ecologist in Winterson's work, it embodies a traumatic experience for Judith Moore whose autobiographical narrative, based on the author's firsthand experience of being a 'fat' girl and woman, engages with the social and cultural stigma placed upon 'fat' people in contemporary Western society.

Drawing upon Judith Moore's agonising experience with her body that began in her childhood, it may well be argued that dislike and fear of fat is the outcome of a social and cultural conditioning which starts at a young age. According to a frequently cited study[48] in obesity research, children were shown a series of drawings of their peers – some 'fat', some with crutches or in a wheelchair, some with an amputated hand, some with a facial disfigurement. They were asked to rank them in terms of whom they would most like for a friend. School children ranked the 'fat' children last. A similar study[49] was carried out with adults in terms of preferred sexual/romantic relationships, and, again, obese people are ranked below amputees, people in wheelchairs, those who have previously made suicide attempts and those with a history of sexually transmitted diseases. The idea of ranking people in terms of their physical appearance is neither morally nor politically correct; however, the widespread uniformity found in these

---

[48] Stephen A. Richardson, Norman Goodman, Albert H. Hastorf and Sanford M. Dornbusch, 'Cultural Uniformity in Reaction to Physical Disabilities', in *American Sociological Review*, 26:2 (1961), 241-47 (p. 246).

[49] Eunice Y. Chen, Molly Brown, 'Obesity Stigma in Sexual Relationships', in *Obesity Research*, 13 (2005), 1393-97 (p. 1394).

studies raises interesting questions about the reasons behind negative stereotyping of obese individuals. The influence of the mass media in helping to regulate certain bodily ideals has been undeniably one of the most important factors in the results of this research. The media is often sympathetic to people who have impairments, whilst castigating 'fat' people, as fatness is thought to be a matter of voluntary control, even though empirical evidence suggests that 'body weight is determined by a complex interaction of biological and environmental factors'[50], and 'weight is a poor predictor of health.'[51] What is striking about these studies is that the first piece of research engages with the data that evidences antifat bias in the 1960s, while the other reveals the current fear and dislike of 'obesity'. It might be assumed that the stigma against obesity would have lessened in a period of more than forty years, as 'nearly two-thirds of us are said to be overweight or obese.'[52] Conversely, however, as the later research clearly indicates, the stigma is growing as the rate of obesity in contemporary Western societies is increasing.

According to the Obesity Report by the UK Health Select Committee, 'obesity has grown by almost 400% in the last 25 years.'[53] In support of the 'Obesity Report', the British national survey confirms the nation's increase in size, as the 2002 the first national survey in Britain since the 1950s demonstrates: 'men and women are not only

---

[50] Rebecca M. Puhl, Kelly D. Brownell, 'Psychosocial Origins of Obesity Stigma: Towards Changing a Powerful and Pervasive Bias', in *Obesity Reviews*, 4 (2003), 213-27 (p. 215).

[51] 'Obese Women Can Get Healthier without Resorting to Diets: States Study' (based on Dr. Erika Borkoles' research), *Reuters* Health (London), 5 December 2006. <http://www.health.am/weightloss/more/obese-women-can/> [accessed 6 December 2006] (para. 8 of 12).

[52] Campos, *The Obesity Myth*, p. xv.

[53] UK Health Select Committee, 'Obesity Report', in *Health Committee Publications*, 27 May 2004 <http://www.publications.parliament.uk/pa/cm200304/cmselect/cmhealth/23/2303.htm> [accessed 12 January 2007] (para. 1 of 15).

Introduction   15

getting bigger but also changing proportionally.'[54] The survey also shows that 'the average British woman has gained three kilos, 6.4 cm around the hips, and 16.5 cm around the waist compared to her 1950s' counterpart.'[55] This increase in weight gain is not only peculiar to British women. The national surveys provide that there has been a rapid rise in women's body weight over the last five years in other Western countries such as America, Canada and France. It is ironic that over the last twenty years, while Western women have become heavier, the contemporary ideal is still to be thin. What is the rationale implicit in this paradox? The dichotomy between fatness and the 'thin' ideal could be attributed to society's relation to consumption. In advanced consumer capitalism, 'an unstable, agonistic construction of personality is produced by the contradictory structure of economic life.'[56] Susan Bordo explains this contradiction in the following extract:

> On the one hand, as 'producer-selves', we must be capable of delaying, repressing desires for immediate gratification, on the other hand, as 'consumer-selves', we serve the system through a boundless capacity to capitulate to desire and indulge in impulse; we must become creatures who hunger for constant and immediate satisfaction. The regulation of desire becomes an ongoing problem as we find ourselves continually besieged by temptation, while socially condemned for overindulgence.[57]

The dichotomy between 'producer' and 'consumer' self finds a striking resonance in Fay Weldon's *The Life and Loves of a She-Devil*

---

[54] Hadley Freeman, 'Thinking Big as Women's Waists Expand', in *Guardian*, 26 August 2006. <http://www.guardian.co.uk/society/2006/aug/26/health.food> [accessed 12 January 2007] (para. 9 of 16).
[55] Ibid., para. 9.
[56] Robert Crawford, 'A Cultural Account of "Health" – Self-Control, Release and the Social Body', in *Issues in the Political Economy of Health Care*, ed. by John McKinlay (New York: Methuen, 1985), pp. 60-103, cited in Susan Bordo, 'Reading the Slender Body', p. 96.
[57] Bordo, 'Reading the Slender Body', pp. 96-97.

in which Weldon constructs a resourceful character who sets her mind to become a producer-self, yet who in the end gives in to the consumer impulses within her social climate by transforming into a romanticised image of femininity, one that she has formerly abhorred. The novel, thus, points to the difficulty of attaining a balance between 'producer' and 'consumer' aspects of the self for it is, in Weldon's literary imagination, an ideal too hard to implement.

The notion of the slender body as an indicator of a 'well-managed self'[58] is incessantly portrayed in the visual popular culture as the bodily ideal suggesting will-power, energy, and the 'ability to make something of oneself'[59]; whilst departure from this is often considered as evidence of some basic character defect and a situation of stigmatisation for these individuals can arise. Erving Goffman defines stigma as 'a significantly discrediting attribute possessed by a person with an undesired difference.'[60] Drawing upon Goffman's definition, it might be argued that stigmatisation is a socially constructed mechanism exercised to marginalise certain individuals with different attributes, resulting from the power of one social group over another. As Howard Becker points out:

> Social groups create deviance by making the rules whose infraction constitutes deviance, and by applying these rules to particular people and labelling them as outsiders. Deviance is not a quality of the act the person commits, but rather a consequence of the application by others of rules and sanctions to an offender.[61]

Labelling some people as deviant in terms of their non-conforming physicality is clearly less about the body image one has, than about the economy and manipulation of the consumerist culture

---

[58] Ibid., 97.
[59] Ibid., 94-95.
[60] Erving Goffman, *Stigma: Notes on the Management of a Spoiled Identity* (Englewood Cliffs, New Jersey: Prentice-Hall, 1963), p. 42.
[61] Howard S. Becker, *Outsiders* (New York: Free Press, 1963), p. 9.

that imposes acceptable norms, and encourages people to conform to them. Mike Featherstone argues:

> The perception of the body within consumer culture is dominated by the existence of a vast array of visual images. Indeed the inner logic of consumer culture depends upon the cultivation of an insatiable appetite to consume images. Day-to-day awareness of the current state of one's appearance is sharpened by comparison with one's own past photographic images as well as with the idealised images of the human body which the popular media proliferate.[62]

Popular media and commercial interests have often contributed to this process by setting new standards of appearance and bodily presentation, which 'associated slimness with worthiness as a person, and portrayed the 'fat' as glum and downcast: joke figures, survivals from a bygone age.'[63] According to a recent study which examined images in the media, 'overweight characters, especially females, appeared far less than their representation in the population, and were more likely than thin characters to be the objects of humour and less likely to be shown in romantic relationships.'[64] Beauty norms play an important role in the visual objectification of women. Being perceived as overweight may affect a woman's identity as there is a tendency to hold her responsible for her condition. Women, unfortunately, suffer more from stigma-laden meanings attached to their size than men. As Edwin Schur has argued, 'fat' men are often described as 'stocky', 'heavy-set', 'portly',[65] all of which suggest a cultural inclination to define male physical weight in parallel with social weight such as power, authority and prestige, whereas many 'fat' women are often viewed as

---

[62] Mike Featherstone, 'The Body in Consumer Culture' in *The Body: Social Process and Cultural Theory*, ed. by Mike Featherstone, Mike Hepworth and Bryon S. Turner (London, Newbury Park, New Delhi: Sage, 1991), pp. 170-196 (p. 178).
[63] Ibid., p. 183.
[64] Puhl and Brownell, 'Psychosocial Origins of Obesity Stigma', p. 214.
[65] Edwin M. Schur, *Labelling Women Deviant: Gender, Stigma, and Social Control* (Philadelphia: Temple University Press, 1983), p. 72.

'ugly, bad, and not valuable.'[66] Yet, this repressive cultural representation of female corpulence turns into a literary and subversive strategy in the work of a number of contemporary women writers such as Fay Weldon, Jeanette Winterson, Margaret Atwood, Claude Tardat, Judith Moore whose works –*The Life and Loves of a She-Devil* (1983), *Sexing the Cherry* (1989), *Lady Oracle* (1976), *Sweet Death* (1989) and *Fat Girl: A True Story* (2005) – represent intellectual challenges to the repressive meanings inscribed upon corpulent female bodies. This study engages with these writers' various representations of the 'fat' woman to explore the ways in which their narratives transform the cultural and personal obsessions surrounding 'excessive' embodiment, from a condition that is often defined in derogatory terms to an elaborate engagement with fatness through various literary strategies.

Second Wave Feminism and the backlash against feminism provide one political context in which to read Fay Weldon's construction of 'excessive' female body in *The Life and Loves of a She-Devil* in which Weldon's mordant narrative voice recognises, deflates and dismantles the social and symbolic implications attributed to women's bodies and lives.

In *The Life and Loves of a She-Devil*, the idea of fatness becomes the measure of a parodic engagement with the cultural production of femininity. The novel is about a gigantic and 'ugly' suburban wife's recreation of herself by going through a series of painful operations in order to attain what she considers to be the perfect image of female beauty. The novel's publication coincided with a period when an obsession with slimming had gradually begun to spread its roots with the help of the steady growth in visual communication[67], and conse-

---

[66] Laura S. Brown, 'Women, Weight and Power: Feminist Theoretical and Therapeutic Ideals', in *Women and Therapy*, 4:1 (1985), 61-71 (p. 65).
[67] For instance, the release of Jane Fonda's best-selling *Workout Book* (1982) and her exercise videos for fitness workouts gave the message that woman's attitude to life could change by transforming her body. The popular media in the 1980s used the 'looking good and feeling great' message as a saleable commodity. Popular newspapers like *The Sun* and *Mirror* passed on this message to a wider

quently, promotion of slenderness and the ways to attain it had started to reach out to a greater number of women in Western society. The novel's feminism derives from its satirical engagement with impossibly romanticised femininity as it is represented in women's romance literature. More importantly, the novel serves as a parody of cultural production of femininity by critiquing the popular culture's ability to make women, as Susie Orbach defines it, mere 'ideal sexual object[s]'.[68] Even though the two texts illustrate some discrepancies, as one promotes weight gain and the other weight loss, some points of intersection could be mapped out as they emerge through a particular political reading of the corpulent body within the context of feminist body politics.

Jeanette Winterson's *Sexing the Cherry* coincides with the rise of postmodernist fiction. Even though the novel's reception has generated a critical polarity regarding the problematic relationship between the novel's feminist appeal and the employment of postmodernist strategies, Winterson, in fact, adopts the postmodern concepts of plurality, diversity and relationality in her construction of various forms of embodiment. In doing so, her text not only offers a challenge to the cultural fat/thin dichotomy, but her unbiased approach to embodiment finds its reflection in her hyperbolic narrative bringing a celebratory insight to different forms of embodiment. For instance, the Dog Woman with her goddess-like physicality is an epitome of strength and power throughout the novel. The dancing princess Fortunata's lightness is constructed as yet another symbol of power. Here, the notion of lightness comes to denote not only an extreme sense of mobility, but also indicates a feminist resistance to oppression by patriarchal practices that tie women down into the roles of wife and mother. Win-

---

audience with frequent articles on slimming, exercise, health foods and appearance. In 1980s at least one dietary book was on the non-fiction best-sellers' list in England. For example Audrey Eyton's *The F-Plan Diet* (1987) has been one of the fastest selling British books of all time.

[68] Susie Orbach, *Fat is a Feminist Issue: The Anti-Diet Guide for Women*, (London: Arrow Books, 2006) p. 21.

terson's construction of the young ecologist can be considered as an amalgamation of the Dog Woman and Fortunata. The young scientist imagines a world where there is no gravity, which echoes Fortunata's aspirations. The ecologist also refers to a woman, reminiscent of the Dog Woman, who becomes her guiding spirit in her political activities. The positive enunciations of bodily diversity open up further possibilities for a more nuanced discussion of the representation of female embodiment.

Fictive confessional narrative as deployed in Margaret Atwood's *Lady Oracle* and Claude Tardat's *Sweet Death* offers another way of looking at the representation of corpulence in relation to trauma. As with Margaret Atwood's first novel *The Edible Woman* (1969), the issue of weight takes on a traumatic significance in *Lady Oracle*, which chronicles the novel's protagonist Joan's unhappiness as a child and young woman, her unloving relationship with her mother and her school friends because of her fatness. Written in the form of a journal, *Sweet Death* engages with an unnamed young woman's writing of her deliberate expansion in size to exact revenge upon her mother whom she situates as the source of her sufferings. Even though both texts display some structural similarities in terms of the representation of mother-daughter power relations that revolve around the disciplining of the body, these tensions stimulate nuanced responses to the trauma of excess (which is primarily induced by the mother) in the form of writing. In *Lady Oracle*, Joan as a writer of Gothic Romances uses this genre as a supposedly effective way of escaping her painful experiences of her 'fat' self, whilst in *Sweet Death*, the young woman's writing of her 'excessive' body into her journal is confrontational as it demonstrates the daughter's resistance to the mother who represents pressures to conform. Both daughter/authors' engagement with their traumatic memories through the medium of writing creates a highly inventive narrative style that not only offers a challenge to the idealisation of the mother as proposed in the theories of *l'écriture feminine*, but also invokes a concrete perspective to writing of the female embodiment

In Judith Moore's autobiography *Fat Girl: A True Story*, the author writes with first-hand experience of what it means to be a 'fat' girl and 'fat' woman in 1950s America, and mirrors the struggles of an overweight woman in contemporary society. Here, fat expresses an individual discomfort about being stranded outside the norm, which is transformed into self-loathing, humiliation and isolation caused by having a non-conforming body. The author's unpleasant experiences with her body read as a critique of contemporary American culture's articulation of excess. By writing the 'fat' female body in a cultural climate that encourages women to conceal their fat, Moore's autobiography exercises a subjectivity which connects the personal to the social. Her work reframes women's private experiences with their bodies on to a cultural and social agenda.

Interest in the cultural regulation of women's bodies and the politics of appearance has been the subject of concern for 'fat' activists[69]

---

[69] Lisa Schoenfielder and Barb Wieser, American radical fat activists, started The Fat Women's Liberation Movement in 1970s as an alternative to weight loss groups. They are also the founders of The Fat Underground, a faction of the National Association to Advance Fat Acceptance. Their work *Shadow on a Tightrope: Writings by Women on Fat Oppression*, published in 1983, represents the first ten years of the feminist fat liberation movement which has challenged the marginalisation of 'fat' women, and fought for their rights. Marcia Millman's *Such a Pretty Face* (1980) illustrates her extensive interviews and observational research in organizations for the 'overweight' that reveal the oppression of 'fat' women in America. Shelley Bovey's *The Forbidden Body: Why Being Fat is not a Sin* (1989) is another work that critiques the prejudiced perceptions directed against fatness. Bovey's text engages with the British culture's response to the emerging fat acceptance movements in the US. Marilyn Wann's book *Fat!So?: Because You Don't Have to Apologise for Your Size* (1998) examines the inequalities suffered by 'fat' people in health-care and health insurance. Charlotte Cooper's *Fat and Proud: The Politics of Size* (1998) explores the hatred and discrimination experienced by 'fat' women, whilst pointing out the strengths and weaknesses of the positions of the past books on fat. Sondra Solovay's *Tipping the Scales of Justice: Fighting Weight-Based Discrimination* (2000) reports the

such as Lisa Schoenfielder, Barb Wieser, Marcia Millman, Shelley Bovey, Marilyn Wann, Charlotte Cooper and Sondra Solovay whose works confront and critique cultural constraints against notions of fatness, and create paradigms for the development of fat acceptance within mass culture. Their works do not exist in a vacuum, however, as they have been heavily influenced by the writings of certain feminist critics such as Susie Orbach, Susan Bordo, Naomi Wolf and Kim Chernin who challenged the social, cultural and political positioning of the female body. For example, in *Fat is a Feminist Issue*, Susie Orbach argued that the ideal image of femininity has been subjected to new definitions, a situation which suggests the objectification of the female body:

> In the early 1960s, the only way to feel acceptable was to be skinny and flat chested with long straight hair. The first of these was achieved by near starvation, the second by binding one's breast with an ace bandage and the third by ironing one's hair. Then in the early 1970s, the look was curly hair and full breasts. Just as styles in clothes change seasonally, so women's bodies are expected to change to fit these fashions. Long and skinny one year, petite and demure the next, women are continually manipulated by images of proper womanhood, which are extremely powerful because they are presented as the only reality. To ignore them means to risk being an outcast.[70]

The one constant image in these representations, as Orbach has emphasised, is that 'a woman must be thin.'[71] Why is contemporary Western culture so fixated on female thinness when female corpulence was once associated with physical attractiveness, strength and fertility? 'Fat', as Nicky Diamond has argued, 'does not have a fixed referent',[72] as the construction of images and meanings, and their manifes-

---

horrors of discrimination that 'fat' people face in education, social life, employment and health-care, and makes suggestions about extending legal coverages against weight-based discrimination.

[70] Orbach, *Fat is a Feminist Issue*, p. 17.
[71] Ibid., p. 17.
[72] Nicky Diamond, 'Thin is a Feminist Issue', p. 49.

tations in male and female bodies vary in different historical, social and economic positions. For instance, as Naomi Wolf has pointed out, 'until seventy-five years ago in the male artistic tradition of the West, women's natural amplitude was their beauty; representations of the female nude reveled in women's lush fertility.'[73] Wolf has further suggested that from the fifteenth to the early nineteenth century 'female bodies with 'big, ripe bellies, plump faces and shoulders' were fashionable and considered sexually appealing in the West.'[74] However, in the late nineteenth century, whilst fatness was equated with social status, wealth and success for men, and eating in public symbolised economic power, for women, as Helena Michie argued, it symbolised 'unspeakable desires for sexuality and power',[75] and therefore was considered a taboo that had to be suppressed. The significance of food in relation to sexual appetites and desire for power has also been explored in Sarah Sceats's essay 'Eating the Evidence: Women, Power and Food', according to which 'food and eating are inseparable from both physical and psychic appetites and power relations' and 'writers use feeding, feasting, cooking and starving for more than simple mimetic effect.'[76] The selected works epitomise Sceats's argument since the act of feeding oneself becomes not only a culinary activity, but rather an empowering experience that functions as a way of defiance against the cultural tendency to impose control over women's appetites. This correlation between food and power, thus symbolises a resistance to what Orbach formulates as 'being marketed or seen as the ideal woman.'[77]

---

[73] Wolf, *The Beauty Myth*, p. 184.
[74] Ibid., p. 184.
[75] Helena Michie, *The Flesh Made Word: Female Figures and Women's Bodies* (Oxford: Oxford University Press, 1987), p. 13.
[76] Sarah Sceats, 'Eating the Evidence: Women, Power and Food', in *Image and Power*, ed. by Sarah Sceats and Gail Cunningham (London and New York: Longman, 1996), pp. 117-27 (p. 118).
[77] Orbach, *Fat is a Feminist Issue*, p. 18.

For Naomi Wolf, as for Orbach before her, 'female thinness is not an obsession about female beauty but about female obedience',[78] which she argues to be a form of control:

> We are in the midst of a violent backlash to feminism that uses images of female beauty as a potential weapon against women's advancement: the beauty myth. [...] As women released themselves from the feminine mystique of domesticity, the beauty myth took over its lost ground, expanding as it waned to carry on its work of social control.[79]

Drawing upon Wolf's insights, it might be argued that the 'fat' woman's body demonstrates that she has not submitted to culture's narrow permissions. This political position of the 'fat' woman confirms Orbach's theory of female corpulence which she described as a 'symbolic rejection of the limitations of women's role.'[80] Similarly, Kim Chernin's argument has a political resonance in her book *The Obsession: Reflections on the Tyranny of Slenderness* in which she critiques the cultural objectification of the female body and objects to the stigmatisation of 'fat' women as repulsive. For Chernin, the slim ideal and the imposition of various ways to attain this ideal is 'symptomatic of the cultural devaluing of women as it is an attempt to get rid of part of their body that make them women in the first place and the ideal is more similar to a pre-pubescent boy.'[81] Chernin claims that women who collude with the ideal feminine body image are making themselves 'smaller', and in doing so they 'become lightweight, lose gravity and be-little themselves'.[82] These critical texts suggest that if a woman controls the images made of her, she can be liberated from the boundaries of the socially-imposed models of femininity.

The category of the grotesque offers one way to challenge the oppressive cultural meanings attributed to bodily excess. Literally, the

---

[78] Wolf, p. 187.
[79] Ibid., p. 10.
[80] Orbach, *Fat is a Feminist Issue*, p. 22.
[81] Kim Chernin, *The Obsession: Reflections on the Tyranny of Slenderness* (New York: Harper & Row, 1981), p. 108.
[82] Ibid., p. 100.

Introduction 25

word 'grotesque' is characterised as 'odd, bizarre, fantastically extravagant, unnatural in shape and appearance characterized by distortion or unnatural combinations' (*OED*), yet the notion of the grotesque is a varied one and has been interpreted anew within various social, aesthetical, and literary contexts.[83] However, much critical work on the grotesque in literature has conceptualised it as a site of fear and disgust.[84] The category of the grotesque, which has been primarily established by male critics,[85] is reconfigured in the works of these writers, and it accommodates a more positive way of thinking about 'excessive' embodiment transforming it from a site of horror and repulsion.

---

[83] Eighteenth-century aestheticians used the grotesque in association with caricature, and overemphasised the ridiculous and bizarre nature of the grotesque. The grotesque in this century was mostly viewed as something essentially uncanny and unnatural, yet there was also a tendency to associate it with the comic and burlesque. The nineteenth century ascribed a social meaning to the grotesque as in this period it became associated with issues concerning social class and religion. Matthew Arnold related the grotesque to 'the hideous illusions of middle-class Protestantism' [in Matthew Arnold, *Culture and Anarchy* (Cambridge: Cambridge University Press, 1960), p. 38]. The grotesque in the late Victorian period echoes the earlier conceptual models of the category, and is articulated in terms of the diabolical and horrific. The grotesque in this period is viewed as 'an ambiguous presence, claiming for culture a metaphysical purity or authority, the experience of which is the registration of the perverse, absurd, incoherent and monstrous nature of life' [in *Victorian Culture and the Idea of the Grotesque*, ed. by Colin Trodd, Paul Barlow and David Amigoni (Hants: Ashgate, 1999), p. 17].

[84] For instance, Wolfgang Kayser situated the grotesque in the realm of fear, and interpreted it as 'an attempt to invoke and subdue the demonic aspects of the world'[84] in *The Grotesque in Art and Literature*, trans. by Ulrich Weisstein (Indiana: Indiana University Press, 1963), p. 188.

[85] Philip Thompson, *The Grotesque* (London: Methuen, 1972); Arthur Clayborough, *The Grotesque in English Literature* (Oxford: Clarendon Press, 1965); Mikhail Bakhtin, *Rabelais and His World*, trans. by Hélène Iswolsky (Bloomington: Indiana University Press, 1984 [1968]), Geoffrey Harpham, *On the Grotesque: Strategies of Contradiction in Art and Literature* (Princeton: Princeton University Press, 1982).

Of all the critics and writers of the grotesque, Bakhtin's idealistic account stands out in terms of his reclamation of the category from a 'basis of all abuses, uncrownings, teasing and impertinent gestures'[86] to a liberatory state of subversion that mind goes along with the body. For Bakhtin, the grotesque is as an expression of primordial energy which he conceptualised in relation to medieval carnival, where rigid hierarchies are distorted and challenged by triumphant laughter. The grotesque, for him, celebrates 'the gay freedom of thought and imagination' experienced in a world where 'the id is crowned and transformed into a "funny monster"',[87] and it functions to

> [c]onsecrate inventive freedom, to permit the combination of a variety of different elements and their rapprochement, to liberate from the prevailing point of view of the world, from conventions and established truths, from clichés, from all that is humdrum and universally accepted. This carnival spirit offers the chance to have a new outlook on the world, to realise the relative nature of all that exists, and to enter a completely new order of things.[88]

He defines this spirit of carnival as 'the true feast of time, the feast of becoming, change and renewal.'[89] As a victim of an oppressive totalitarian regime, Bakhtin celebrated the category as a strategy of subversion and liberation. Clark and Holquist state that Bakhtin responded deeply to the Renaissance period, for 'it was an age similar to his own in revolutionary consequences and in the acute sense it engendered of one world's death and another world's birth.'[90] It is not surprising that the publication of his seminal work *Rabelais and His World* coincided with the emerging liberatory movements in the 1960s which embraced the possibilities of social and cultural transformation – one of the corner stones of Bakhtin's grotesque-carnival form.

---

[86] Bakhtin, *Rabelais and His World*, p. 341.
[87] Ibid., p. 49.
[88] Ibid., p. 34.
[89] Ibid., p. 10.
[90] Katerina Klark and Michael Holquist, *Mikhail Bakhtin* (Cambridge, Massachusetts, London: Harvard University Press, 1984), p. 296.

Bakhtin suggests that the carnival is the grotesque event *par excellence*, a cathartic moment of discharging excessive emotions, a way of life and an expression of freedom. The carnival, as Dale Bauer suggests, 'is the realm of desire unmasked, taken out of the law of the culture, and involved in an economy of difference. While authoritative discourse demands conformity, the carnivalised discourse renders invalid any codes, conventions or laws which govern or reduce the individual to an object of control.'[91] The grotesque, by virtue of its links to carnival, 'may appear in anything, which is found to be in conflict with accepted standards.'[92] It disrupts rigid social structures, and limited attributes, and serves as a catalyst for possible change and a world of renewal, and ultimately strives for an inversion of systems. However, carnival permits only a short-term liberation as Bakhtin states, 'carnival celebrated temporary liberation from the prevailing truth and from the established order; it marked the suspension of all hierarchical rank, privileges, norms and prohibitions.'[93] Even though carnival is short-lived, it enables 'a break in the acknowledged order, an irruption of the inadmissible within the changeless everyday legality.'[94]

Clark and Holquist have suggested that for Bakhtin, the grotesque 'is the expression in literature of [this] carnival spirit. It incorporates what for him are the primary values: incompleteness, becoming, ambiguity, indefinability, non-canonicalism – indeed all that jolts us out of normal expectations and epistemological complacency.'[95] Bakhtin describes this grotesque expression as 'open', 'festive' and 'deeply positive'[96] which he affirms as the basic attribute of 'grotesque real-

---

[91] Dale Bauer, 'Gender in Bakhtin's Carnival', in *Feminisms: An Anthology of Literary Theory and Criticism*, ed. by Robyn R. Warhol and Diane Price Herndl (Houndmills, Basingtone, Hampshire: Macmillan, 1997), pp. 708-20 (p. 716).
[92] Arthur Clayborough, *The Grotesque in English Literature* (Oxford: Clarendon Press, 1965), p. 109.
[93] Bakhtin, p. 10.
[94] Jacqueline Howard, *Reading Gothic Fiction: A Bakhtinian Approach* (Oxford: Clarendon Press, 1994), p. 38.
[95] Clark and Holquist, p. 312.
[96] Bakhtin, p. 19.

ism'. He also perceives a dark side to the grotesque, which he defines as 'post-Romantic', invoking alienation, self-loathing, self-destruction, frustration and humiliation. Here, the body is not a matter for celebration but for destructive anguish.

In *Sexing the Cherry* the manifestation of the grotesque, invoked via the medium of Esther and the Dog Woman respectively, evokes the positive implication of Bakhtin's grotesque realism denoting the concepts of power and transgression. In Weldon's novel, the carnival-grotesque form could be seen to embody alternatives to challenge the social bodily constraints, whilst in Winterson's text, it challenges the upheld social order as it has been defined and imposed by hegemonic ideals of her culture.

However, Bakhtin's account of the grotesque as a transgressive construct has been viewed with suspicion by some critics. Mary Russo, for example, has found very little in Bakhtin's construction of the grotesque which is empowering for women, and has pointed to Bakhtin's 'fail[ure] to incorporate the social relations of gender in his semiotic model of the body politic.'[97] For Russo, the female body has already been positioned in terms of 'otherness', and placed in a certain relationship to normality and deviance. Therefore 'the body which is female and grotesque must be recovered from a place of double displacement.'[98] She has further argued that Bakhtin's carnival-grotesque falls short of accomplishing this recovery as his notion of the female grotesque remains in all areas 'repressed' and 'underdeveloped', because, for Bakhtin the grotesque body is 'a body always in the making, never completely finished, ever ready to create another body.'[99] She notes:

---

[97] Mary J. Russo, 'Female Grotesques: Carnival and Theory', in *Writing on the Body: Female Embodiment and Feminist Theory*, ed. by Katie Conboy, Nadia Medina and Sarah Stanbury (New York: Columbia University Press, 1997), pp. 318-36 (p. 325).
[98] Ibid., p. 326.
[99] Bakhtin, p. 285.

Introduction 29

There are special dangers for women and other excluded or marginalised groups within carnival, though even the double jeopardy may suggest an ambivalent redeployment of taboos around the female body as grotesque (the pregnant body, the aging body, the irregular body) and as unruly when set loose in the public sphere.[100]

Russo is sceptical about the grotesque as an empowering device to 'destabilise the idealisations of female beauty as the grotesque is often projected on the female body when it makes a spectacle of itself through pregnancy, age or other violations of feminine bodily containment.'[101] However, Bakhtin's study of the grotesque does not stand in complete opposition to feminist criticism. Firstly, this body should not be considered 'underdeveloped' as it is 'a subject in process'[102] that articulates a desire for social and cultural transformation. Secondly, a woman making a spectacle of herself, in fact, is not necessarily grotesque, and sometimes making a spectacle of oneself can be viewed as a displacement of social hierarchies by crossing the boundaries of a variety of social practices and aesthetic forms.

For Bakhtin, the Christian tradition showed women as 'the incarnation of sin, the temptation of the flesh', but the popular comic tradition was not hostile to women. He argues that in the category of the grotesque 'the image of woman is given on the level of ambivalent laughter, at once mocking, destructive, and joyfully reasserting. Can it be said that this tradition offers a negative, hostile attitude toward woman? Obviously not. The image is ambivalent.'[103] Bakhtin further notes that the comic tradition viewed women as representing 'the lower bodily stratum'[104] which focuses upon gaps, orifices and sym-

---

[100] Ibid., p. 320.
[101] Ibid., p. 327.
[102] Patricia Yaeger, 'Toward a Female Sublime', in *Gender and Theory: Dialogues on Feminist Criticism*, ed. by Linda Kauffman (Oxford: Basil Blackwell, 1990), pp. 191-213 (p. 211).
[103] Bakhtin, p. 241.
[104] Ibid., p. 240.

bolic filth, physical needs and pleasures, as opposed to the classical monumental body which conceals them. He states:

> She is the incarnation of this stratum that degrades and regenerates simultaneously. She is ambivalent. She debases, brings down to earth, lends a bodily substance to things, and destroys; but first of all, she is the principle that gives birth. She is the womb. Such is woman's image in the popular comic tradition.[105]

In Bakhtin's interpretation of the grotesque, woman becomes a part of this tradition as she is the principle that gives birth. According to his interpretation, the grotesque body is the body of generation, and the swellings which are associated with breasts and pregnant belly, clearly gender this body as 'the cavernous anatomical female body.'[106] Bakhtin's analysis, though reinforcing cultural assumptions about women's identification with the biological processes of their bodies has nonetheless emphasised the transgressive potential of the female grotesque. However, one failing that emerges from Bakhtin's construction of the female grotesque is that he tends to reduce it to the object of laughter, and therein underestimate the grotesque embodiment's potential to dismantle the dominant cultural codes.

The body, as Mary Douglas argues, is 'always treated as an image of society' where 'the bodily control is an expression of social control.'[107] It might be argued that in this context, the classical (beautiful) body, which is 'monumental, static, closed, and sleek, corresponding to the aspirations of bourgeois individualism' does not pose a threat to a society, whereas the grotesque body, which is 'the open, protruding, extended, secreting body, the body of becoming, process and change'[108], constitutes a rebellion against social boundaries and regulations. The grotesque body challenges the production of the 'docile

---

[105] Ibid., p. 240.
[106] Mary J. Russo, *The Female Grotesque: Risk, Excess and Modernity* (New York and London: Routledge, 1995), p. 1.
[107] Mary Douglas, *Natural Symbols: Explorations in Cosmology* (London: Barrie & Rockliffe, 1970), p. 71.
[108] Russo, *The Female Grotesque*, pp. 62-63.

body' – a term used by Michel Foucault in his *Discipline and Punish* (1977) to define bodies whose forces and energies are disciplined by external regulation and subjection. According to Foucault, the exercise of regulation and surveillance leads to the production of 'docile bodies', and he explains this process as a form of social control. 'Docile body' in this context represents the disciplined, obedient body that allows itself to be subject to external dictations and impositions. Foucault distinguishes between two modes of constructions of the body. The first one is the 'intelligible body' which sets the principles of the ideal, obedient body. The second is the 'useful body'/ 'docile body' which is the incarnation of the 'intelligible body', in other words, it is the 'trained, shaped body' that 'obeys and responds.'[109] The representation of the 'fat' female body, particularly in Tardat's *Sweet Death*, is conceptualised as a site of resistance to normative regulations of femininity. This refusal to conform to the cultural regulation of women's bodies finds its embodiment in the transformation of the grotesque body to a concealed modern body. That is to say, the festive mood of the carnival culture which is a communal 'feast of misrule' becomes private experience: consumption in abundance is still prioritised, but it has turned into a more solitary practice. This, in fact, signals that as the body becomes more closed to others, anxieties about the social body surface, because when the body is rendered perfectly visible, it is assumed to pose no threat. The visibility of the body in this context invokes the notion of panopticon which is based on Jeremy Bentham's utopian vision of prison and is further developed in Foucault's *Discipline and Punish* as an effective means of imposing control via surveillance. Although the panopticon was meant to invalidate the exercise of power, it reproduced the power and control dynamics in a seemingly more civilised way. Based on the idea of surveillance as a way of imposing control, it might be argued that when the body is less

---

[109] Michel Foucault, *Discipline and Punish: The Birth of Prison* (New York: Vintage, 1977), p. 139.

visible or concealed, this body increasingly turns into a stronger position threatening the social system and order.

The transformation of the carnival traditions into a concealed experience, here, resonates with Julia Kristeva's theory of abjection. The performance of excess in relation to eating in abundance and its manifestation in bodily fat has often been associated with contemptible positions such as dirt, repugnance and poor health. In this sense, 'excessive' consumption as an indicator of disease might arguably be considered 'abject' as the literal meaning of the word denotes a representation of that which is undesirable. However, for Kristeva the abject is related to a defiance of social pressures 'because it neither gives up nor assumes a prohibition, a rule or law; but turns these codes aside, misleads, corrupts; uses them, takes advantage of them.'[110] She argues that it is 'not lack of cleanliness or health that causes abjection but what disturbs identity, system, order. What does not respect borders, positions, rules.'[111] Kristeva's point is that foundations of Western civilisation are laid on suppression of the abject to reinforce conformity. Her theorisation of abjection is thereby meaningful for a consideration of corpulence as a subversive strategy. Thus, Kristeva's theory of abjection 'could be seen as a psychoanalytically inflected development of Bakhtin's grotesque',[112] and so we see abjection in this meaning as operating on a subconscious level, and manifesting a desire to violate borders, systems and rules. This ultimately resonates with the interpretation of the concealed modern female body which is suggestive of disobedience, and becomes a way of challenging the oppressive social control exercised on female bodies.

***

---

[110] Julia Kristeva, *Powers of Horror: An Essay on Abjection*, trans. by Leon S. Roudiez (New York: Columbia University Press, 1982), p. 15.
[111] Ibid., p. 4.
[112] Sue Vice, *Introducing Bakhtin* (Manchester and New York: Manchester University Pres, 1997), p. 163.

The construction of 'excessive' female embodiment as a subversive design is brought to the fore in Fay Weldon's *The Life and Loves of a She-Devil*, which I discuss in the first chapter. Here, I explore the nuanced implications carried by the construction of the 'excessive' female body in Weldon's work, as a response to the tendency to reduce fatness to a matter of health or beauty in Western culture in the 1980s. Although the novel ironically alludes to the 1980s backlash against feminism, I argue that it nonetheless fosters a feminist reading of the female body, one which casts a critical eye on the cultural ideals of female embodiment. In the course of my analysis, I examine the ways in which Weldon's construction of a 'fat' heroine represents aggressive attitudes toward valorised and oppressed female bodies within established disruptive forms, such as the grotesque-carnival and the mythical trickster figure[113] which enable a critical exploration of the social and cultural formulations inscribed upon women's lives and bodies represented in these novels.

The second chapter examines Jeanette Winterson's construction of various forms of female embodiment in *Sexing the Cherry* as illustrated by the fantastically huge Dog Woman, weightless Fortunata, the dancing princess, and the thin ecofeminist. Unlike Weldon's polarised exploration of female embodiment, Winterson's text offers heterogeneous representations of embodiment which operate outside the cultural fat/thin dichotomy, in that the text re-imagines female embodiment in exceptionally conflicting forms whilst permitting them agility, power and autonomy to resist the oppressive social, cultural and political regulations. Here, we see another incarnation of the trickster figure that is even more daring and stronger than its earlier representation in Weldon's novel. In this case, the trickster figure promulgates

---

[113] The word 'trickster' is often used to characterise someone who cheats or deceives. The mythical trickster figures (as evidenced mainly in Native American tales) represent duality, subversion and irony, features employed by the figure to disrupt existing social systems and widen their sphere of power. A detailed engagement with this figure will be conducted in the first and second chapters.

the idea of possibilities and hyperbole, notions which also define Winterson's poetics of representation.

The third chapter brings the representation of female corpulence from an ideal position to a traumatic experience influenced by mother-daughter power relations, as it is portrayed in Margaret Atwood's *Lady Oracle* and Claude Tardat's *Sweet Death*. In the course of my discussion, I engage with the theories of *l'écriture feminine* in terms of writing the female body, the appropriation of the 'excessive' embodiment in the mother-daughter dyad, and constructions of control, not as separate entities but as in relation with each other.

The study concludes with Judith Moore's autobiography *Fat Girl: A True Story*, which chronicles the writer's troubled experiences with her 'excessive' embodiment. Written in 2005, the work's importance stems from its mirroring of, and its contribution to, the current debates over obesity in contemporary American culture. In the course of my analysis I explore the limits of autobiography with reference to the extra-textual representation of the self, and look at the ways in which Moore's narrative offers a re-evaluation of the personal in relation to the social sphere whilst presenting a story that is unique. Based on the author's account of her experience with her 'excessive' body in a social landscape that often stigmatises and posits fatness as outside the norm, Moore's memoir presents an alternative narrative to the former fictional representations of obesity in this thesis where I discuss excess as metaphor for various forms of transgression.

The following chapters discuss the heterogeneity of female corpulence within a variety of its constructions which resist the cultural semiotics that tend to stabilise excess by using medical, biological or statistical data. Bakhtin's interpretation of the grotesque, the mythical trickster figure, feminist literary criticism and confessional narrative strategies facilitate nuanced ways of reading the 'excessive' female body that enable intellectual frames to explore and counterpoint the marginalisation of 'excessive' embodiment, whilst offering a multifaceted approach to the existing literature on fatness.

1 'A comic turn, turned serious': Reading the Female Embodiment in Romance, the Trickster and the Cyborg in *The Life and Loves of a She-Devil*

This chapter aims to explore the construction of 'excessive' and 'non-conforming' female body in Fay Weldon's *The Life and Loves of a She-Devil* (1984). My exploration here not only functions as a critical response to the often monolithic representations of 'fat' women in Western culture in the 1980s, and the tendencies to reduce fatness to a matter of health or aesthetics, as discussed in the introduction; but also identifies some of the issues that hold together various aspects of physical embodiment in relation to the social, cultural and individual. Although *The Life and Loves of a She-Devil* engages with the ideas and narratives that come out of the 1980s Third Wave Feminism marked as the backlash against feminism, the novel arguably offers a feminist reading of the female body. My aim here is to examine the ways in which Weldon's construction of a 'fat' heroine represents aggressive attitudes toward valorised and oppressed female bodies within established disruptive forms such as the mythical trickster. Rooted in transgression and subversion, the trickster can facilitate a critical exploration of the social and cultural codes represented in this novel. The figurative incarnation of the mythical trickster figure in *The Life and Loves of a She-Devil* offers one way to engage satirically with the repressive ideals of femininity and the normative Western regulations of female embodiment.

The metamorphosis of the private body into an object and exploration of the public is a prevalent theme in Weldon's *The Life and Loves of a She-Devil*[114]. Although Weldon's feminist salvo in her earlier novels is strategically replaced here by a backlash against femi-

---

[114] Fay Weldon, *The Life and Loves of a She-Devil* (London, Sydney, Auckland, Toronto: Hodder & Stoughton, 1983). All further references to the novel will be as *She-Devil*, and the page numbers will be given in brackets within the body of the text.

nism, the backlash becomes a measure of a parodic engagement with productions of femininity, particularly in romantic fiction.

The Life and Loves of a She-Devil has often been regarded as a 'feminist comedy.'[115] Yet, to view this work as a mere comedy would underestimate the serious issues that Weldon's allegorical novel enunciates. The novel chronicles a middle-aged suburban housewife's well-calculated revenge against her unfaithful husband and his demure, sexy mistress, Mary Fisher, the popular author of romantic fictions. *She-Devil* explores how Ruth defies her role as a housewife and wife, and remakes herself by undertaking painful plastic surgery in order to reconstruct herself from a six-foot-two, massive woman into the image of Mary Fisher, the epitome of glamour, fame and wealth. Underneath the novel's plotline, which foregrounds the idea of transformation, there lies a subversive narrative that satirically engages with cultural scripts that mythologise femininity in postmodern Western culture.

The novel's publication coincided with the 1980s backlash against feminism. This movement, mainly enforced by the media, 'worked to undermine women's social and economic statuses, and reclaimed women's role in the domestic sphere and encouraged domesticity as an alternative way to lead a happy life.'[116] Stories about 'stay-at-home' mothers and the 'dangers of women's career ambitions' were constantly paraded in the media with loaded phrases such as 'infertility epidemic among middle-class career woman'[117], 'the man shortage', 'the biological clock', 'the mummy track.'[118] Major feminist critics of the backlash such as Susan Faludi in her *Backlash* (1992), and Marilyn French in her *The War Against Women* (1992) saw it as a reversal of the achievements of the 1960s and 1970s Women's Liberation Movement. The recurrent idea which Faludi and

---

[115] See Regina Barreca, Flora Alexander, Lana Faulks.
[116] Susan Faludi, *Backlash: The Undeclared War Against Women* (London: Vintage, 1992), p. 60.
[117] Ibid., p. 49.
[118] Ibid., p. 101.

French strongly objected to was that women were doing society a disservice by placing their needs, desires and careers ahead of family life. Weldon, who has praised Faludi and French's works as 'powerful'[119], foregrounds and critiques the key issues of the backlash, in particular the idea of what Wolf explains as the 'beauty backlash'[120] in her text. In many ways Weldon's protagonist, Ruth both complies and conflicts with this backlash's motives. At the beginning of the novel, she is a competent mother, wife and housewife. Her mother-in-law is impressed with Ruth's domestic skills, observing 'How nicely she does everything' (16). However, the 'fat' and 'unattractive' Ruth cannot reconcile her 'angelic' – that is to say her 'loving and lovable soul' – with her physical appearance. She says:

> I [...] have one of those jutting jaws which tall, dark women often have, and eyes sunk rather far back into my face, and a hooked nose. My shoulders are broad and bony and my hips broad and fleshy, and the muscles in my legs are well developed. My arms, I swear, are too short for my body. My nature and my looks do not agree. (9)

Ruth's attitude toward her body represents that of the 1980s backlash, which, as Faludi argues, imposed the idea of beauty as a 'proof of a woman's internal purity, obedience and restraint.'[121] Ruth starts her narrative as a victim of normative femininity as it is produced by capitalist patriarchal culture which has conditioned her to assume that the self is defined by the body, and made her believe that the beautiful soul should be housed by a 'delicately formed' (6) body, like the body of Mary Fisher. As the plot progresses, she co-operates with the system that prioritises beauty and materiality which she has formerly found unjust. She willingly abandons her domestic roles to embark on a journey of transformation. At this point Ruth's liberation could be

---

[119] Robert Sullivan, 'Journalist of the Heart', in *Fay Weldon's Wicked Fictions*, ed. by Regina Barreca (Hanover and London: University Press of New England, 1994), pp. 153-62 (p. 155).
[120] Wolf, p. 283.
[121] Faludi, p. 241.

interpreted as a symbolic refusal of the backlash which imposes domesticity and the norms of acceptable femininity as the ideal. However, her wish to re-make herself into an image of conventional beauty reflects another aspect of the backlash, that is, the beauty myth. The 'feminine' traits the beauty industry has celebrated most, as Faludi points out, 'were grossly unnatural and achieved with increasingly harsh, unhealthy, punitive measures'[122] – 'one American doctor even promised to reduce women's height by sawing their leg bones.'[123] Ruth's collaboration with the beauty backlash has generated a critical polarity. Some critics[124] have found Ruth's bodily transformation rather oppressive as a 'reconfirmation of the concept of the female body as the object of necessary transformations into the ideal'[125]; while others found it 'liberating' and 'empowering'[126] viewing it as a gateway to Ruth's inner transformation, along with 'personal and eco-

---

[122] Ibid., p. 239.
[123] Ibid., p. 240.
[124] Such as Sara Martin, 'The Power of Monstrous Women: Fay Weldon's *The Life and Loves of a She-Devil* (1983), Angela Carter's *Nights at the Circus* (1984) and Jeannette Winterson's *Sexing the Cherry* (1989), in *Journal of Gender Studies*, 8:2 (1999), 193-210, Susan Jaret McKinstry, 'Fay Weldon's *Life and Loves of a She-Devil*: The Speaking Body', in *Fay Weldon's Wicked Fictions*, ed. by Regina Barreca (Hanover and London: University Press of New England, 1994), pp. 104-13, Alan Wide, '"Bold, but not too Bold": Fay Weldon and the Limits of Poststructuralist Criticism', in *Contemporary Literature*, 29:3 (1988), 403-19. Patricia Waugh, *Feminine Fictions: Revisiting the Postmodern* (London and New York: Routledge, 1989).
[125] McKinstry, p. 108
[126] For instance, Patricia Juliana Smith, 'Weldon's *The Life and Loves of a She-Devil*', in *The Explicator*, 51:4 (1993), 255-57, Honor McKitrick Wallace, 'Desire and the Female Protagonist: A Critique of Feminist Narrative Theory', in *Style*, 34:2 (2000), 176-87, Pamela Katz, 'They Should Have Called it "She-Angel"', in *Fay Weldon's Wicked Fictions*, ed. by Regina Barreca (Hanover and London: University Press of New England, 1994), pp. 114-19, Kathy Davis, *Reshaping the Female Body: The Dilemma of Cosmetic Surgery* (New York and London: Routledge, 1995).

nomic gain' this position provides 'for herself and for the women around her.'[127]

The critical controversy about the novel can be attributed to Weldon's ambiguous views about women's relationship with their bodies. In her first novel *The Fat Woman's Joke*, which portays a woman who deliberately becomes a compulsive eater, Weldon had challenged and trivialised the 'thin/sexy/demure' feminine image by making the fat woman smart, powerful and intelligent, thereby parodying cultural notions about what woman should or should not be like. However, in her more recent writings she has contradicted her former position. In her article, 'Is Thin Better?', she says, 'fat is depression. Fat is wanting minor pleasure now instead of major pleasure later.'[128] Weldon's latest non-fictional work, *What Makes Women Happy?* (2006), is yet another text that suggests her resigned acceptance of a status quo that promotes weight loss. In the 'Food' section, she advises women to be thin so as to have a happy life. She writes that 'it is not good to be fat. [...] Slim wins the alpha male, fat gets the leftovers',[129] 'so be thin.'[130] As Finuala Dowling suggests, Weldon 'is overtly commercial in her fictional enterprise, and in journalistic efforts and interviews, she reveals herself as flippant, imprecise and inconsistent.'[131] A similar kind of controversy marks her ongoing ambivalence towards feminism as well. Interviewed by John Haffenden in 1982 Weldon stated that she wrote 'literature with intent to reform'[132], and she assumed feminism to be a practical way of fulfilling this intention. She associated good writing with writing with a feminist affinities:

---

[127] Smith, p. 256.
[128] Fay Weldon, 'Is Thin Better?', in *FEMINA: Fashion and Beauty File*, April 1995, pp. 66-67.
[129] Fay Weldon, *What Makes Women Happy* (London: Fourth Estate, 2006), p. 72.
[130] Ibid., p. 77.
[131] Finuala Dowling, *Fay Weldon's Fiction* (London: Associated University Presses, 1998), p. 14.
[132] John Haffenden, *Novelists in Interview* (London: Methuen, 1985), p. 308.

> I am a feminist and I write novels, and because I believe feminism to be a true view of the world what I write is bound to come out to be feminist. You could advance the view that all good writing is bound to be feminist.[133]

Yet three years later, in an interview with Valerie Grove for ICE Video, Weldon took a rather different position. When Grove asked her if she called herself a feminist writer, she replied: 'depends on the company'. She responded in a similar way in a 1986 *Contemporary Authors* interview.

> 'Feminist' was not a label I would ever disown, because it would seem as if I were disowning it for all the wrong reasons. Many feminists wouldn't consider me a feminist at all. Many non-feminists would think I was. I flicker in and out of the mainstream.[134]

Weldon's contradictory position vis à vis feminism make her fictions 'provocative' and 'ambiguous.'[135] In 'Rewriting the Feminine Script: Fay Weldon's Wicked Laughter', Ann Marie Hebert states:

> Weldon refuses containment within patriarchal law, but she also steadfastly refuses an easy or artificial feminist solution. That no one is innocent, man or woman, complicates her searing critique of the current construction of heterosexual gender relations and makes her novels unsettling to conservatives and feminists alike.[136]

Weldon on the one hand critiques the normative regulations of femininity, which encourage women to internalise and embody all the values of domesticity; on the other, her attitude sometimes represents conformity with cultural mainstream trends. It might well be argued

---

[133] Ibid., p. 318.

[134] Barbara Harte, *200 Contemporary Authors: Bio-bibliographies of Selected Leading Writers of Today with Critical and Personal Sidelights*, ed. by Linda Metzger and Deborah A. Straub (Detroit: Mich Gale Research Company, 1986), p. 424.

[135] Martin, p. 199.

[136] Ann Marie Hebert, 'Rewriting the Feminine Script: Fay Weldon's Wicked Laughter', in *Critical Matrix: The Princeton Journal of Women, Gender and Culture*, 7:1 (1993), 22-40 (p. 28).

that the influence of culture plays an important role in Weldon's writing career. For instance, in her earlier novels the influence of the Women's Liberation Movement provides a political context for her writing, whereas *She-Devil* comes out of a period which saw the backlash against feminism. In accordance with the social and cultural trends of her time, Weldon situates her female protagonists in conflicting discourses where they defy domesticity and/or live up to the male notion of female beauty and femininity. *She-Devil* employs some of these contradictions. In a talk given at Morley College, Weldon commented on the paradox of the novel:

> This is a slightly frivolous novel, though the first half sets out a feminist position. My anti-heroine burns her house down to cheat him of insurance, gives her horrible children away, then frames her husband to get him imprisoned. She does things which one half of you will applaud, the other not. Next she gets herself turned into a sex object, and lives happily ever after.[137]

This chapter takes issue with Weldon's description of her novel as 'slightly frivolous'; to be fair, despite the fact that Weldon later on compensates for her earlier assumption in an essay, 'On the Reading of Frivolous Fiction', published eight years after *She-Devil*, in which she says that 'the frivolous can be fantastic.'[138] *She-Devil* is not a 'frivolous' novel, it is a novel that, in Avril Horner and Sue Zlosnik's words, 'spin[s] a darkly comic tale of literary and literally constructed "woman."'[139] My reading of the novel situates it as a feminist text in spite of the considerable critical focus on the anti-feminist agenda of

---

[137] Fay Weldon cited in Olga Kenyon, *Women Novelists Today: A Survey of English Writing in the Seventies and Eighties* (Sussex: Harvester Press, 1988), p. 127.

[138] Fay Weldon, 'On the Reading of Frivolous Fiction' (1991), in *Fay Weldon's Wicked Fictions*, ed. Regina Barreca (Hanover and London: University Press of New England, 1994), pp. 227-28 (p. 228).

[139] Avril Horner and Sue Zlosnik, 'Agriculture, Body Sculpture, Gothic Culture: Gothic Parody in Gibbons, Atwood and Weldon', in *Gothic Studies*, 4:2 (2002), 167-77 (p. 173).

the novel brought about by Ruth's collusion with the 'beauty backlash'. However, the cultural and sociological motives that have led Ruth to operate in this fashion have not been thoroughly addressed. The novel comes out of a period when obsession with slimming had gradually begun to spread its roots with the help of the steady growth in popular media.[140] Consequently, the promotion of slenderness and the ways to attain it had started to reach a greater number of women in Western society. The 1960s protests[141] against the commodification of the female body were replaced by a constant fixation with ways to look desirable and attractive in the commercial culture of the 1980s, which 'enslaved women by ludicrous beauty standards.'[142] As Wolf has pointed out, the focus on the appearance of women's bodies has increased at the same time that women have claimed economic and intellectual power for themselves. As a response to the rapidly emerging independent woman, Western culture has created 'body anxiety': a new way to regulate women's lives. Wolf focuses in particular upon images of women in magazines and television, and the ways in which

---

[140] The popular media in the 1980s constantly emphasised slimming, exercise, health foods and appearance. According to the book lists, in the 1980s at least one dietary book every year was on the non-fiction best-sellers' list both in England and America. For example, Judy Mazel's *The Beverly Hills Diet* (1981), Jane Fonda's *Workout Book* (1982), Victoria Principal's *The Body Principal: The Exercise Program for Life* (1983), Jean Nidetch's *Weight Watchers Quick Start Program Cookbook* (1984), Stuart M. Berger's *Dr. Berger's Immune Power Diet* (1985), Martin Katahn's *The Rotation Diet* (1986), Audrey Eyton's *The F-Plan Diet* (1987), which has been one of the fastest selling British books, Elizabeth Taylor's *Elizabeth Takes Off* (1988), Jean Nidetch's *Weight Watchers Quick Success Program Book* (1989). These books insist on the message that woman's attitude to life could change by transforming her body.

[141] The protests started with a demonstration against the Miss America contest in Atlantic City in 1968. Similar protests followed in many other countries from Miss New Zealand to the Miss World Contest held in London in 1970. Demonstrators' actions included a 'Freedom Trash Can', which encouraged women to get rid of the 'objects of female torture' such as high heels, bras and girdles as a means to revoke a system that measured female value by appearance.

[142] Susan Brownmiller, *Femininity* (London: Hamish Hamilton, 1984) pp. 24-25.

1 'A comic turn, turned serious' 43

the slimming and beauty industry encourage women to undergo cosmetic surgeries[143] for the sake of meeting cultural norms of beauty. As Chernin states: 'a culture based on the suppression of women will be inclined [...] to turn away from whatever is powerful in women. The image in fashion magazines reflects this turning away from female power.'[144] As opposed to the escalating publicity of the 'beauty backlash', there was also a resistance. The launch of an American TV sitcom, *Roseanne* (aired on ABC in the US, and Channel 4 in the UK between 1988-1997), for instance, represented a breakthrough as it was one of the first shows to cast an overweight, dominant and smart woman in the lead role. Yet, the media declared the title character 'the most hated woman in America'[145], labelling her 'a nasty, filthy, ugly, Jell-O-Bodied tasteless monster.'[146] Interestingly, the star of *Roseanne*, Roseanne Barr, also played the central character in Susan Seidelman's *She-Devil* (1989), a screen adaptation of *The Life and Loves of a She-Devil*.

Seidelman's choice of Roseanne Barr to play the part of Ruth generates contradictory insights. First of all, Barr's appearance in the film tends to relate the construction of Ruth to an 'unlikeable' character, as the viewer may possibly associate the character with Roseanne of the TV series – a hyperbolical representation of an overdomineering wife and mother. Second, the film's Ruth is not a faithful physical representation of Ruth as constructed by Weldon. Her Ruth is a massive woman in comparison to Roseanne Barr's physical features. More importantly, the film does not strongly represent Weldon's satirical voice that interrogates the culturally imposed prescriptive norms of femininity, and the consequences of colluding with these bodily ideals. The film ends with Ruth recovering her former position as a wife and mother, whilst forgiving and accepting her husband's infidelity.

---

[143] According to the UK Cosmetic Surgery Statistics, cosmetic operations have doubled in frequency since 1981.
[144] Chernin, *The Obsession*, p. 108.
[145] Faludi, p. 178.
[146] Ibid., p. 179.

The film misses out Weldon's critical salvo, and it reproduces the notions 'domesticity', 'passivity' and 'obedience' which have been aggressively challenged in the novel. The film, in effect, collaborates with the backlash with its emphasis on a socially acceptable femininity with non-threatening codes. Seidelman's adaptation of the novel for screen is yet another example of a manipulative visual culture which implements the backlash and encourages the ideological restrictions within which women are contained.

The collusion of women's popular romance literature with the media-led pervasive beauty regimes forms another part of the backlash against the tenets of Second Wave Feminism. Romance fiction 'served to keep women in their place'[147], imposing the image of the complacent, heterosexual and home-and-family oriented woman. Despite the arguable patriarchal aspirations of this genre, romances have a worldwide reading public of women from different cultures and lifestyles. As Rosalind Coward points out, 'the extraordinary rigidity of the formula of the Mills and Boon romantic novels, where the heroine invariably finds material success through sexual submission and marriage, does not prevent their publishers having a larger sales than Pan and Penguin.'[148] In addition to the popularity of romantic fictions (despite their prescriptive plots which are 'based on [the heroine's] sexual, racial and class submission'[149]), this genre has also produced a sort of collective consciousness through its construction of idealised images of femininity which promote the 'thin', 'demure' female form imposing the idea that the slender woman is 'happier, more successful,

---

[147] Tania Modleski, *Loving with a Vengeance: Mass-Produced Fantasies for Women* (New York, London: Routledge, 1990 [1982]), p. 37.

[148] Rosalind Coward, 'Are Women's Novels Feminist Novels?', in *The New Feminist Criticism: Essays on Women, Literature and Theory*, ed. by Elaine Showalter (London: Virago, 1986 [1985]), pp. 225-39 (p. 230).

[149] Helen Taylor, 'Romantic Readers', in *From My Guy to Sci-Fi*, ed. by Helen Carr (London, Winchester, Sydney, Wellington: Pandora, 1989), pp. 58-78 (p. 60).

more well-adjusted, and generally better liked.'[150] Romantic fiction implies a particular idea of 'love' as the supreme good in the life of a woman, and this kind of love is dependent on physical attractiveness which 'reinforce[s] the valorisation of female beauty.'[151] There are, however, some recently published exceptional romance fictions in which the heroines are constructed as 'fat' to challenge the fixation with slenderness that mainstream romance fictions promote. For instance, Pat Ballard (known as 'the queen of Rubenesque Romances') is famous for her plus-size heroines, yet even in her novels[152] we see her protagonists constructed in conformity with beauty standards: they are erotically appealing and feminine in their 'acceptably' large and voluptuous bodies. It may be argued that in *She-Devil*, Weldon satirically engages with the collaboration of women's romance literature with the backlash against feminism, in terms of this genre's tendency to rescript an impossibly romanticised femininity, a representation that risks objectifying women. She writes:

> These books open a little square window on the world and set the puppets parading outside for you to observe. They bear little resemblance to human beings, to anyone you ever met or are likely to meet. These characters exist for purposes of plot, and the books they appear in do not threaten the reader in any way, they do not suggest he or she should reflect, let alone change. [...] To believe a Mills & Boon novel reflects real life is to live in perpetual disappointment.[153]

---

[150] Kathy Davis, *Reshaping the Female Body: The Dilemma of Cosmetic Surgery* (New York and London: Routledge, 1995), p. 42.
[151] Pilar Hidalgo, 'The Female Body Politic: From Victimization to Empowerment', in *English Studies in Transition*, ed. by Robert Clark and Piero Boitani (London and New York: Routledge, 1993), pp. 289-305 (p. 296).
[152] For example, in *Wanted: One Groom* (2000), *His Brother's Child* (2001), *A Worthy Heir* (2002), *Nobody's Perfect* (2004), Ballard situates various plus-size heroines within the traditional romance story, where her heroines celebrate the idea of being loved as they are.
[153] Fay Weldon, *Letters to Alice: On First Reading Jane Austen* (London: Coronet, 1985 [1984]), pp. 12-13.

It is significant to note that Weldon's writing of this novel is firmly situated within the landscape of the 1980s backlash, and her satirical style can be viewed as a response to this climate. However, to critique women's popular romantic fictions merely on the grounds of their formulaic plot-lines and restrictive, one-dimensional notions of femininity may run the risk of dismissing an important aspect of this genre which Margaret Atwood brings to the fore in her novel *Lady Oracle* (1976). Here (as I shall be discussing in greater detail in Chapter Three) Atwood adopts a different critical approach to the genre of romantic fiction where she engages with, and seeks to explore, the psychological motives that lie behind romantic fictions' popular appeal. Despite Atwood's subtle and stylised use of the genre in *Lady Oracle*, it has been argued that the novel 'exploits the inherited mass-culture fictions which, in transmitting a conservative literary and cultural message, help perpetuate women's consent to femininity.'[154] However, in *Lady Oracle*, there is a shift of emphasis from the genre's reinforcement of cultural representations of ideal femininity to an engagement with the genre on a psychological platform which argues against this reading of the text via the medium of Atwood's protagonist Joan, who uses this genre as a possible escape mechanism. 'Escape literature', as Joan affirms, 'should be an escape for the writer as well as the reader.'[155] As a young girl Joan retreats into the fantasy world of romances as a way to escape her unhappiness. The genre gives a certain sense of euphoria to Joan, as her imaginary identification with romantic heroines brings a temporary relief to the humiliations she has experienced as a 'fat' girl. As a writer of romances in her adulthood, she strongly believes that the genre nurtures the 'pure quintessential need for escape'[156], and produces a therapeutic effect on her readers who 'had babies too early, who wanted princes and castles and

---

[154] J. Brooks Bouson, *Brutal Choreographies: Oppositional Strategies and Narrative Design in the Novels of Margaret Atwood* (Amherst: The University of Massachusetts Press, 1993), p. 63.
[155] Margaret Atwood, *Lady Oracle* (London: Virago, 1976), p. 155.
[156] Ibid., p. 34.

ended up with cramped apartments and grudging husbands.'[157] In this sense, her writing invokes a sense of fulfilment for her readers who delve into a temporary escape from their discontentment through the medium of fantasies Joan creates for them. However, she is nonetheless aware that they also 'exploit the masses, corrupt by distracting, and perpetuate degrading stereotypes of women as helpless and persecuted.'[158] According to Eleonora Rao, this controversial position of the genre, as plainly expressed by Joan, can be attributed to the prevalent disinclination 'to distinguish the possible pleasing effect of the text on the reader from the ideology of it', and to a tendency not to read it as 'merely a form of escapism.'[159]

As a reader, Weldon's Ruth initially takes refuge in women's popular romantic fictions with a similar motive to escape from her circumstances. She reads romances even including those written by Mary Fisher with a desire to be a part of that illusionary world where 'little staunch heroines raise tearful eyes to handsome men, and by giving them, gain them' (24). However, unlike Joan's response to Romances, for Ruth, these novels bring less a short-lived satisfaction, but more the painful realisation of herself in comparison to the romantic heroines.

> I am jealous of every little, pretty woman who ever lived and looked up since the world began. I am, in fact, quite eaten up by jealousy, and a fine, lively, hungry emotion it is. [...] I want, I crave, I die to be part of that other erotic world, of choice and desire and lust. [...] What I want is power over the hearts and pockets of men. It is all the power we can have, down here in Eden Grove, in paradise, and even that is denied me. (24)

Despite the contradictory employments of the different forms of this genre presented in Weldon's and Atwood's novels, as one cri-

---

[157] Ibid., p. 95.
[158] Ibid., p. 34.
[159] Eleonora Rao, *Strategies for Identity: The Fiction of Margaret Atwood* (New York: Peter Lang, 1993), p. 36.

tiques and the other reclaims the genre, both texts in fact have a conscious attempt to work within the tradition of a Romance, as they both adopt the stylistic and structural devices of the genre. *Lady Oracle* for instance, mimics the Gothic Romance in terms of form and content. The popular definitions of the Gothic Romance dwell upon two main features of the genre mainly encapsulated by the notions of fear and romance. For Tania Modleski the element of fear dominates the category of popular romantic fiction in which the heroine 'often suspects her lover or her husband of trying to drive her insane, or trying to murder her or both.'[160] However, for Anne Williams, the romance element precedes the fear factor, as the genre affirms a happy ending that reintegrates the female protagonist into a wider community through marriage, which symbolises the heroine's 'wedding to culture.'[161] It is reasonable to say that *Lady Oracle* represents both interpretations of the genre to a certain extent. Atwood constructs Joan as a woman who physically spends her life on the run out of her fear that her former 'fat' self would be found out. However, she is not under the potential threat of a supposed male figure but a female figure, which I will further explore in my detailed analysis of the text. Regarding the second interpretation, Joan's 'wedding to culture' in fact refers to her desire to live up to the normative regulations of femininity, which she abandons at the end of the novel.

Stylistically, *Lady Oracle*, particularly the extracts from Joan's Gothic Romances, initially imitates the language of the genre of romance that has erotic overtones regarding the description of Joan's heroines (i.e. 'the bodice of her scarlet dress was cut low, displaying the swell of her white breasts'[162]). Similarly, in *The Life and Loves of a She-Devil* Weldon employs a strategy of constructing cliché-ridden, short and simple sentences resulting in a tone that has been reviewed

---

[160] Modleski, p. 60.
[161] Anne Williams, *Art of Darkness: A Poetics of Gothic* (Chicago: Chicago University Press, 1995), p. 103.
[162] Atwood, *Lady Oracle*, p. 31.

as 'slippery, flippancy of the soft-sell.'[163] This linguistic verisimilitude is in fact deliberately established not only to satirise the simplicity of popular romance fictions, but also to undermine their depiction of a world that measures women's success and happiness in relation to their attainment of love and money.

In popular romance fictions most often 'the heroine starts off as a self-sufficient and independent woman, and at the end usually melts in a lifetime of dependency.'[164] This pattern is prevalent in Weldon's novel where the construction of the romantic heroine and the reader's affiliation with that representative ideal are articulated by Mary Fisher and Ruth in contradictory and reversible positions. The polarisation of these female characters enables us to explore the potential of romances in increasing possible feelings of insecurity, envy and inadequacy experienced by their readers. In many ways, Mary Fisher initially leads the life of a romance heroine, and she even talks like one: 'All I have is you, Bobbo' (49). She 'writes about the nature of love, and sees no reason why everyone should not be happy' (49). Just like the protagonists of mainstream romantic fictions, she is a 'small and pretty' (8) woman who has always had a man to love her. She has her economic freedom, her novels 'sell by the hundred thousand in glittery pink and gold covers' (24). She lives 'in a High Tower, on the edge of the sea' (5), a perfect setting in which to write her novels. However, when Mary's ideal state of life is disrupted by Ruth's children and once she confronts emotional difficulties, her life is thwarted by the 'tides of practical detail', which 'overwhelm the shifting sands of love' (99). At this point, Mary's visions of romance begin to collapse, like her ivory-towered, illusionary world, a place where she wishes never to have lived. Her complacency is shattered, and she

---

[163] Barbara Marshall, 'Notes', in *The Life and Loves of a She-Devil* (London, Sydney, Auckland, Toronto: Hodder and Stoughton, 1989 [1983]), pp. 183-209 (p. 201).
[164] Jeanne Dubino, 'The Cinderella Complex: Romance Fiction, Patriarchy and Capitalism', in *The Journal of Popular Culture*, 27:3 (1993), 103-18 (p.110).

gradually loses her ability to write romances to formula, as she does not inhabit that fantasy world any more.

As opposed to Weldon's construction of Mary, who primarily represents a romantic heroine with 'power over the hearts and pockets of men' (24), yet later turns into an anti-romantic one when she starts to lose her 'power', Ruth starts her journey from a disadvantaged position. While Mary is 'petite, pretty, and delicate', Ruth is 'gigantic and unattractive'. Mary is soft, Ruth is hard, 'rough-hewn in granite' (95). Mary is demure, whilst Ruth is clumsy: '[her] weight swayed from one massive leg to another and shook the house each time it fell. Houses in Eden Vale were designed not just for littler people, but for altogether lighter ones' (23).

Due to her physical appearance, Ruth is the antithesis of the traditional romantic heroine. She inhabits instead the position of a stereotyped romantic fiction reader, who believes in the dream of romance. Even though she later disapproves of romantic fictions, which she thinks 'tell lies to the world' (5), she initially reads them, including those written by Mary Fisher. Mary's novels fit well into the consumerist, materialistic life in Eden Grove – a suburban development 'planned as paradise' (8) – where Ruth and Bobbo live. In this superficial environment Ruth is a dissatisfied Eve. The emptiness and artificiality of this fake paradise are evident not only in the deceit that characterises Ruth's marriage but also in the social interaction among the neighbours, as Ruth says: 'My neighbours and I give dinner parties for one another. We discuss things, rather than ideas; we exchange information, not theories; we keep ourselves steady by thinking about the particular. The general is frightening' (8). This is an empty, depthless environment, one that values surface appearances, and prioritises investments and purchases. There are many references to money issues throughout the novel. Bobbo is an accountant, and Mary Fisher is one of his clients. The novel in fact opens with Ruth revealing Mary's riches in detail. Even though the novel does not give the exact location as to where the incidents take place, Eden Grove might be thought to represent any suburbia in a capitalist, consumerist culture. Drawing upon the popularity of Mary's novels in Eden Grove, it could be argued that Weldon appropriates this materialistic suburban life with a similar drive to point out that both Eden Grove and Mary Fisher's novels come out of and serve a consumerist society. Viewed from another angle, the steady rise of the romance fiction industry[165] since the 1970s Women's Liberation Movement is also indicative of a possible collaboration of the romance writing with a patriarchal society that tends to promote women's subservience, and the norm and ideal of white middle-class heterosexual union. In this sense Bobbo and Mary make a perfect union, symbolising the bond between a capitalist and patriarchal society. While Ruth inhabits this oppressive world at the beginning of the novel, she is soon disillusioned after a family gathering which ends in disaster, and Bobbo finally articulates his contempt for her. He accuses her of being 'a third-rate person, a bad mother, a worse wife and a dreadful cook' (42); he cannot love 'what is essentially unlovable' (40), as he thinks Ruth is 'not a woman at all', and calls her a 'she-devil' (42). It is at that very moment that Ruth decides to become a 'she-devil'. In one of her interviews, Weldon points out culture's tendency to associate 'a married woman with children' as 'a good woman'[166], and likewise in her novel Ruth's transformation into the 'she-devil' occurs when she begins to do away with her role as the suburban monogamous homemaker and mother. Ruth says: 'Peel away the wife, the mother, find the woman, and there the she-devil is' (44). Here, the 'she-devil' image represents a satirical

---

[165] From a sale of 6 million in 1965, Harlequins sold 218 million in 1982. Figures are drawn from John Markert's 'Romance Publishing and the Production of Culture', in *Poetics*, 14:1 (April 1985), and *The Progress of Romance: The Politics of Popular Romance Fiction*, ed. by Jean Radford (London: Routledge, 1986).

[166] Erin Alicandro, 'Fay Weldon on Writing and Feminism', University of Connecticut, *Creative Writing Program*, Spring 2006. <http://longriver.uconn.edu/cw/cw_newsletter2006.pdf> [accessed 3 April 2007] (page 1 of 6, para. 8).

inversion of Virginia Woolf's 'angel in the house'[167] stereotype, and symbolises the suppressed other of a romanticised version of femininity. Becoming a 'she-devil' means that Ruth abandons the principles listed in the 'Litany of the Good Wife' which is based on the emotional and physical exploitation of the wife:

> I must be grateful for the roof over my head and the food on my table, and spend my days by showing it, by cleaning and cooking and jumping up and down from my chair.
> I must build up my husband's sexual confidence, I must not express any sexual interest in other men, in private or in public; I must ignore his way of diminishing me, by publicly praising women younger, prettier and more successful than me, and sleeping with them in private, if he can. (25)

Ruth's first major act of rebellion happens when she burns down the house in Eden Grove. In her act of destruction, it is notable that Ruth starts with the kitchen, which signals the first steps she takes toward her new identity outside the 'feminine mystique'. Her setting of her house on fire, further, puts her in good literary company with some Gothic romantic heroines such as Bertha Mason in Charlotte Brontë's *Jane Eyre* and Mrs Danvers in Daphne du Maurier's *Rebecca*. However, unlike her predecessors, Ruth is in a stronger position as she lives on to take revenge upon an oppressive cultural landscape that has situated women as passive and obedient. At the beginning she is represented in conformity with the ideological restrictions imposed upon women's lives. She says: 'I thought I was a good wife tried temporarily and understandably beyond endurance, but no. He says I am a she-devil. [...] I really assume he is right' (43). At this point, Ruth's collusion with her husband's assumption that she is a 'she-devil' might be considered as her submission to yet another form

---

[167] In her essay, 'Professions for Women' (1932) published in *The Death of the Moth and Other Essays*, Virginia Woolf defined and critiqued the 'angel in the house' image in relation to an internalised pressure imposed upon women that denied them the possibility of gaining an identity independent of men, home and family.

of a repressive stereotypical image. However, Ruth's newly-gained identity signals her emancipation from oppressive feminine roles, and marks the beginning of her quest for self-transformation, as she says: 'This is exhilarating! There is no shame, no guilt, no dreary striving to be good' (43). Her transformation from an over-worked and under-appreciated housewife into a 'she-devil' suggests her desire to experience a new kind of freedom outside patriarchal authority, where she could exercise her own rules. Her departure from Eden Grove evokes and disrupts the myth of the fall from heaven. Ruth is willing to depart from the Garden where she has experienced humiliation, degradation and injustice, and it marks the beginning of her quest for self-transformation. She starts looking for ways to make her own paradise where she can be all-powerful, and her urge to gain ultimate power initiates her transformation into the she-devil, as she says:

> I went into the garden and turned the soil with a fork, and power moved into my toes and up my stubborn calves and rested in my she-devil loins: an urge and an irritation. It said there must now be an end to waiting: the time for action had come. (50)

Becoming a 'she-devil', she frees herself from the demands of being a wife and mother. She gives up her children, her feelings, her identity, and above all her ability to love, as she says: 'any lingering spark of compunction, any trace of those qualities traditionally associated with women – such as sweetness, forgiveness, forbearance, and gentleness – were at that moment quite obliterated' (116). Refusing to be defined within culturally imposed repressive terms, she sets outs on a journey to rescript an idea of femininity as powerful.

In the process of her transformation into a 'she-devil', Ruth displays some affinities with the mythical trickster figure, a hybrid, transgressive construct that functions outside society's accepted norms and values. This furnishes her with autonomy and power to overturn existing social structures to serve her own means. As opposed to the flat, stable and normative representations of women as promoted in fairy tales and romance fictions, the articulation of the trickster in this novel embodies a manipulative strategy – an 'aggressive liberation'[168] to challenge 'all that is stultifying, stratified, bland, or prescriptive.'[169] Reading Ruth as a trickster figure enables a critical scrutiny of the oppressive prescriptive models imposed by culture, and an exploration of the fundamental contradiction between the individual and society, between freedom and constraint. The trickster, as Radin points out, is 'the spirit of disorder and 'the enemy of boundaries.'[170] 'Prompted by his appetites', as Andrew Wiget argues, 'the trickster fixes his mind on a single goal, but the means required to achieve this goal will effect a radical transformation of his personal identity or society's norms.'[171] The trickster signals the need to break from structure and view possibility with new eyes that defy reason. Mary Douglas also views the trickster figure as 'having a social function of dispelling the belief that any given social order is absolute and objective.'[172] However, the traditional trickster figure has often been gendered as male[173], whereas Ruth's position as a female trickster re-constructs the traditional image as even more daring and powerful than a male trickster, as she says: 'There is only, in the end, what you want. And I can take what I want. I am a she-devil!' (43). She distinctly attributes her power to her womanhood. She consciously 'aligns herself with Satan's power,

---

[168] Gerald Vizenor, 'Trickster Discourse', in *American Indian Quarterly*, 14 (Summer 1990), 277-87 (p. 285).

[169] Jeanne Rossier Smith, *Writing Tricksters: Mythic Gambols in American Ethnic Literature* (Berkeley and Los Angeles: University of California Press, 1997), p. xiii.

[170] Paul Radin, *The Trickster: A Study in American Indian Mythology* (London: Routledge & K. Paul, 1956) p. 185.

[171] Andrew Wiget, 'His Life in His Tail', in *Redefining American Literary History*, ed. by. A. LaVonne Ruoff and Jerry W. Ward, Jr. (New York: The Modern Language Association of America, 1990), pp. 83-96 (p. 88).

[172] Douglas, 'The Social Control of Cognition: Some Factors in Joke Perception', in *Man*, 3 (1968), 361-76 (365).

[173] In many of the traditional trickster tales it is often the male trickster who assumes the role of a hero or saviour. See 'Coyote Creates the World', 'Coyote Steals Fire', 'Coyote Kills the Terrible Monster', in *American Indian Trickster Tales*, ed. by Richard Erdoes and Alfonso Ortiz (New York: Viking, 1998).

knowing that as a woman, she may succeed where her predecessor has failed'[174]: 'She laughed and said she was taking arms against God Himself. Lucifer had tried and failed, but he was male. She thought she might do better, being female' (82). The trickster constantly transforms his identity whilst disrupting social norms. Ruth's trickster-like qualities epitomise the most characteristic dichotomies such as order/chaos, creation/destruction, altruism/ego-centrism, which allows her free movement and interplay among the various forms she assumes and those she challenges.

Her alliance with the Devil is her first aggressive act against the idea of an omnipresent and just God who she thinks failed in creating her by making her look extraordinary. Not having been treated very well by God, Ruth thinks she has every reason to try something else: 'His ways are far too mysterious for me to put up with any more' (114). In her challenge with God, Ruth recreates herself by taking even the act of creation away from God: 'I will mould a new image for myself out of the earth of my creation. I will defy my Maker, and remake myself' (159). Her insatiable desire for an 'autogenic condition', as Alan Wide argues, 'makes her the shaper of her own form, fate, and being, a triumphant Satan, God to her own Adam (or Eve), and of course Frankenstein and his monster at once.'[175] However, to define Ruth as a 'monstrous' being, or in Sara Martin's words, as a 'moral monster'[176] would be unjust to the critical implications of the text which challenges a culture that is preoccupied with 'good looks', and renders non-conforming bodies invisible. Ruth's motives in recreating herself underpin her desire to revenge herself upon the hostile and shallow environment that marginalised and positioned her as an 'excessive' other. The idea of re-making herself ironically demonstrates the awful power of the ideals of physical beauty. Susie Or-

---

[174] Julie Nash, 'Energy and Brashness', in *Fay Weldon's Wicked Fictions*, ed. by Regina Barreca (Hanover and London: University Press of New England, 1994), pp. 93-103 (p. 95).
[175] Wide, p. 413.
[176] Martin, p. 201.

bach's sarcastic statement, 'to be unattractive is not to be a woman'[177], in fact illustrates Ruth's social landscape that privileges the looks.

Earlier in the novel she says: 'how do ugly women survive, those whom the world pities? The dogs, as they call us. I'll tell you; they live as I do, outfacing truth, hardening the skin against perpetual humiliation, until it is as tough and cold as a crocodile's' (10-11). Based on what she has read about the ideal feminine images represented in romances, Ruth thinks that only with a beautiful, firm and small body like that of the heroines in these fictions can one have access to love. She initially accepts that as a woman her physical match is 'an odd, epileptic, half-witted man' (56). Then her discomfort with her grotesquely disproportionate body, and her hidden anger towards accepted patterns of society, which situated her as an outcast functioning outside the desired norms, start to emerge. She accuses Mary Fisher of writing novels which collude with normative models of beauty: 'I can, in the end forgive Mary Fisher for many things. [...] But I don't forgive her novels' (180). Thinking that because of her 'ugly and discordant body' (11) she has lost the love of her husband, she sets out to change her shape. Ruth embraces the idea of a physical transformation as a gateway to gain 'power, money, revenge, and the ability to be loved without returning it' (43), things that have been denied her in a society which prioritises the looks. Even her experience with a 'separatist feminist' commune called 'the Wimmin', which asserts the futility of physical appearance, Ruth argues the opposite, as she observes that even within the commune 'the best looking would suffer least while the worst looking most' (204).

Knowing the unlikelihood of changing her culture in which women have been determined by their bodies, Ruth decides to confiscate her own body: 'Since I cannot change the world, I will change myself' (56). Yet, in order to achieve her goal, she is aware of the price she has to pay. In the process of her transformation she assumes a series of traditional female roles such as servant in a nursing home, a

---

[177] Orbach, *Fat is a Feminist Issue*, p. 158.

nurse in a mental hospital, and a housekeeper/mistress to a sexually sadistic judge. With each role, like the devil or the trickster figure, she takes on a succession of false identities for the various personae she adopts as a she-devil, becoming in turn Vesta Rose, Polly Patch, Molly Wishant, Millie Mason, Marlene Hunter and finally Mary Fisher: roles that enable her to engage with the law, with religion, with success, with violence, and with repression. In all these roles she subverts stereotypical representations of femininity that associate it with submissiveness, powerlessness, helplessness, dependence, and locates them as the source of her power. She moves effortlessly from one menial position to another. As a nursing home orderly, she gains access to Mary Fisher's mother; as a housekeeper for a judge, she makes her husband's sentence even harsher, as a domestic help for a priest, she leads him out of a life of celibacy, and sends him off to seduce Mary Fisher. Her malicious actions disrupt order at one level while reestablishing it at another. Her violation of the laws, prohibitions, and restrictions that determine the structure and order of ordinary life, becomes a parodic engagement with the vulnerability of these institutions exercised by male hegemony in the novel. She can easily influence the sadistic judge upon her husband's prison sentence and manipulate the priest to serve her means. She overwhelms the doctors and cosmetic surgeons she hires to remake herself in the image she chooses.

Her motives, however, are not entirely self-centred. She uses Bobbo's money to run an employment agency which benefits hundreds of women who use its service. Her identity as Vesta Rose becomes an inversion of the mythological goddess of the hearth, home and family. Her employment agency of the same name benefits many women and liberates them from being enslaved to 'the feminine mystique'. The small steps she takes on her way result in many improved lives, particularly women's: 'Perhaps what Jesus did in his day for men, so I do now, for women' (164). Ruth's own miserable experience as a housewife increases her consciousness about the plight of other women with whom she can easily sympathise. In the course of her vengeance she even helps Mary Fisher, who formerly looked down on mothers and housewives and considered herself outside the category of 'maternal type' (71). Mary Fisher starts to take responsibility for Ruth's children. Furthermore, Ruth ironically helps her to confront real life and stop living the lie which she depicted previously in her romantic fictions. The fact that Ruth can be successful, useful and even heroic, and that many people love her despite her big body does not yet stop her from her pursuit of attaining perfect femininity. Ironically, Ruth has been a highly desired and an influential figure even before her physical transformation: whether it is a sales representative whose conjunctive eye she heals with her ring; a nurse with whom she has an affair and for whom she establishes a profitable business; a judge or a priest. For Pamela Katz, Ruth's transformation embodies a 'spiritual journey from helplessness to power, from victim to the avenger.'[178] However, Ruth uses her power and strength to turn herself into 'an impossible male fantasy made flesh' (224). By transforming herself into the image she desires, she challenges Ovid's King Pygmalion myth, for the woman whom Pygmalion creates is the projection of his own desire: she is submissive, silent and responsive. Yet, contrary to the passive female image exercised by this myth, Ruth is eager to have her body reshaped to become an instrument of her assertiveness and willpower. Ruth has her jaw re-formed, teeth filed down, arms shortened, face remodelled and torso reshaped. She even has her legs trimmed half a foot. Ruth's wish to undergo a hyperbolic process of technological reconstruction with the purpose of 'revising herself physically into the image of the perfect woman'[179] makes Ruth

> become a discourse of absence as her body shrinks in every dimension – height, jaw, teeth, limbs – and her story seems to represent the symptoms of femaleness. [...] That reduction of self to body, the re-

---
[178] Katz, p. 123.
[179] McKinstry, p. 110.

duction of body to image fulfils the perceived desire of the culture for female beauty.[180]

Even though Ruth allows her body to be reduced, her hyperbolic transformation in fact reads as a critique of an oppressive society that allows the highest fulfilment to those who conform to its norms. In this respect, her metamorphosis into a 'discourse of absence' means her metamorphosis into an image that has been imposed upon women since childhood, and becomes a satirical medium to criticise the cultural construction of these repressive images represented in myths, fairy tales and popular romance fictions. Her story revisits Hans Christian Andersen's story of the little mermaid. In her retelling of the story, the mermaid

> wanted legs instead of a tail, so that she could be properly loved by her Prince. She was given legs, and by inference the gap where they join at the top, and after that every step she took was like stepping on knives. (148)

Ruth's likeness to the little mermaid critiques the suffering that women undergo in order to achieve perfect femininity as produced by the fantasy of the male gaze. Looking exactly like Mary Fisher, but even more beautiful, Ruth, as Patricia Waugh argues, 'has exchanged one form of submission for another.'[181] For Sara Martin, Ruth's wish to change her 'fleshy envelope' could be linked to her desire to 'attract many men.'[182] However, the idea that underlines her transformation should not be reduced solely to the notion of being desirable. On the one hand, Ruth, who has started her journey as anti-romantic heroine, metamorphoses into a 'formula' romance heroine and her final union with the man she loves and her new life at the High Tower emphasise the notion of desire. On the other hand, we realise that Mary's phallic abode symbolises Ruth's desire which is not for Bobbo, but for Mary's body, which is 'ordinary' (218). As Kathy Davis argues, 'in

---
[180] Ibid., pp. 110, 112.
[181] Waugh, p. 194.
[182] Martin, p. 198.

order to become ordinary, a woman may find that an extraordinary step may be, paradoxically, the only course of action.'[183] Ruth's remaking herself is her challenge to a cultural view that rendered her large body unnatural and unfeminine. Her transformation enables her to turn into a figure of power in her fight against a society which made her an outcast. However, this leads to a bittersweet victory.

Weldon's construction of Ruth juxtaposes critically the representation of femininity in cultural scripts with the technology used in the production of ideal images of femininity in postmodern Western culture since the 1980s. The enforcement of modern technological processes onto her body makes Ruth 'more than human, hence the term transhuman'[184] – a phenomenon which Orbach uses to describe the body that is 'supremely dematerialised and ironically disembodied.'[185] Ruth's reconstruction of her body via new technology, thus, affiliates her with the 'cyborg' image. The concept of the cyborg represents, as Haraway has stated, 'an apocalyptic *telos* of the West's resistance to seductions to organic wholeness.'[186] The cyborg, which could be defined as a half-organic, half-technological figure, functions as a paradigm for, 'transgressed boundaries, potent fusions, and dangerous possibilities.'[187] The boundaries that the cyborg trespasses can be attributed to those between nature and culture. In her 'Cyborg Manifesto', Haraway has argued the potential liberatory aspect of the cyborg imagery for women, which serves as a means of 'building and destroying machines, identities, categories, relationships.'[188] In Ruth's case the image arguably represents this double-edged position. On the one hand, it is liberatory as it enables Ruth to undermine and trans-

---

[183] Kathy Davis, 'Remaking the She-Devil: A Critical Look at Feminist Approaches to Beauty', in *Hypatia*, 6:2 (1991), 21-43 (p. 38).
[184] Susie Orbach, *Bodies* (London: Profile Boks, 2009), p. 107.
[185] Ibid., p. 108.
[186] Donna Haraway, *Simians, Cyborgs and Women: The Reinvention of Nature* (London: Free Association Boks, 1991), pp. 150-51.
[187] Ibid., p. 154.
[188] Ibid., p. 181.

gress her natural boundaries in the act of recreating herself. On the other, it is containing as it reinforces the idea of a technological recreation of the female body into the image of a perfect femininity, which is suggestive of Ruth's entrapment in cultural boundaries. On another level, Ruth's fixed identity in the image of a female cyborg shatters her previous affiliation with the trickster figure whose position is defined in its very flexibility and mutability. It is the very ending of the novel in which Ruth says, 'I'm a lady of six foot two, who had tucks taken in her legs. A comic turn, turned serious' (240), she points at the bitter consequence of conforming to a social, cultural and technologically imposed female body ideal. Despite Ruth's assertion that 'life is very pleasant' (240), the final chapter serves as her 'apologia in which she reveals her own self-deception in her smug superiority.'[189] Ruth's confession in the end when she says of Mary Fisher, 'She is a woman: she made the landscape better' (230), reinstates her position as a cultural and technological edifice of femininity, and reads as a critique of what it looks like if cultural bodily ideals are taken to their hyperbolic extreme, and made literal.

As I have discussed, Ruth's affiliation with the controversial figure of the cyborg in *She-Devil* brought about sharp contrasts to the promotion of the female body normalised by cultural and social practices, whilst producing a critical narrative on the beauty norms held by these practices. In the next chapter, in which I am going to engage with Jeanette Winterson's critically acclaimed novel *Sexing the Cherry*, the cultural bodily ideal is further dismantled in the image of a huge woman whose power becomes inspirational for a modern slender woman in her fight against the politics of her society. However, unlike Weldon's text which engages with the twentieth-century debates over fatness, and which, arguably, reproduces the cultural fat/thin dichotomy, Winterson's novel liberates both the 'fat' and the 'thin' body from these confines, and lays the emphasis on the notions of interconnectedness and unity.

---

[189] Smith, p. 256.

2 'I still think it was poetic': The Poetics and Politics of Hyperbole in *Sexing the Cherry*

Jeanette Winterson's *Sexing the Cherry* explores a particular notion of embodiment, one that differs from that of Weldon, in that she engages with the idea of embodiment in a multifarious fashion. In this text, the embodiment is not represented solely as a physical form but also as a literary trope as a means to explore the poetics of representation, thus offering a narrative that emphasises alternative possibilities. As Winterson has stated in her foreword to the 1996 edition of her novel *The Passion* (1987): 'I wanted to write a separate world, not as an escape, as a mirror, a secret looking glass that would sharpen and multiply the possibilities of the actual world.'[190] It is Winterson's subtle construction of a highly imagined alternate reality which for her 'allows for an expansion of perspectives'[191] and 'offers up many possibilities, many points of view.'[192] This aspect of her writing prevails in her later novel, *Sexing the Cherry*, where Winterson's celebration of boundless possibilities becomes evident not only in her construction of the characters in her novel, but also in her framing of the text in different time periods. The novel oscillates mainly between the seventeenth and twentieth centuries with an apparent digression in the middle where Winterson produces a feminist revision of the Grimm Brothers' story of 'The Twelve Dancing Princesses'. This interweaving of history (the English Civil War, the execution of King Charles I, and the Restoration of Monarchy) with story is explored from the points of view of five characters: the Dog Woman and her adopted son Jordan, Fortunata and the unnamed ecologist and the sailor Nicolas Jordan, fusing the female and male voices in a blend of the factual and

---

[190] See Jeanette Winterson, *The Passion* (London: Vintage, 1996 [1987]).
[191] Raphaëlle Rérolle, 'Interview with Jeanette Winterson', *Le Monde* (English), April 2002. <http://www.jeanettewinterson.com> [accessed 04 July 2005], (para. 2 of 5).
[192] Jeanette Winterson interviewed by Helen Barr, 'Face to Face: A Conversation between Jeanette Winterson and Helen Barr', in *English Review*, 2:1 (1991), 30-33 (p. 31).

the fabulous. The outcome of this is a narrative that engages with multiple perceptions and misconceptions; imagination and reality; clarity and obscurity – notions which are represented through a set of journeys that are both physical and metaphysical.

Winterson in this novel uses the medium of journeys as a way of telling stories, some of which belong to the historical as we see in the 'real' voyages of Tradescant (John Tradescant, the English botanist who introduced exotic fruits to England in the seventeenth century), and some are metaphorical, and operate in the realm of imagination. These metaphorical journeys are primarily represented by Jordan who oscillates between light and darkness, between vision and its obscurity as we see in his opening comments of his narrative:

> The fog came towards me. […] I began to walk with my hands stretched out in front of me, as do those troubled in sleep, and in this way, for the first time, I traced the lineaments of my own face opposite me.[193]

In this early memory Jordan walks like a sleepwalker, and in that liminal state traces the lineaments of his own face as though he is divided from himself, which in a sense he is. As Jordan tells us from the outset of his narrative, 'every journey conceals another journey within its lines: the path not taken and the forgotten angle' (9). He restates this idea of concealed complexities within a journey later: 'every mapped-out journey contains another journey hidden in its lines' (23); 'I gave chase in a ship, but others make the journey without moving at all. […] In a single day the mind can make a millpond of the oceans' (80). As Jordan states, it is these journeys that he wishes to record – 'not the ones [he] made, but the ones [he] might have made, or perhaps did make in some other place or time' (10). He elaborates on this idea through an analogy:

---

[193] Jeanette Winterson, *Sexing the Cherry* (London: Virago, 2001 [1989]), p. 9. Further references to the novel will be given in brackets.

For the Greeks, the hidden life demanded invisible ink. They wrote an ordinary letter and in between the lines set out another letter, written in milk. The document looked innocent enough until one who knew better sprinkled coal-dust over it. What the letter had been no longer mattered; but what mattered was the life flaring up undetected. [...] Gradually I began to find evidence of the other life and gradually it appeared before me. (10)

It is these multiple possibilities that the text explores and the narrative shapes we choose to give to events to turn them into meaningful stories. For instance, Jordan's quest for the weightless, dancing princess Fortunata may not be a search for an embodied figure, not a quest narrative for the other but a quest for self-discovery, as Jordan curiously asking, 'Was I searching for a dancer whose name I did not know or was I searching for the dancing part of myself?' (40) suggests. This search is also a motif re-engaged in different places in the text, for instance, 'Where are you?' (10) is a question that Jordan asks at the very beginning of his narrative. In this text we see that the notion of place is metaphysical as much as it is physical. This interplay between the physical and metaphysical also recurs in Winterson's use of the concept of 'weight': depending on how her protagonists negotiate it, read it, see it, or escape it; 'weight' acquires varied meanings both metaphorically and somatically. For instance, in the section where Jordan narrates about the city of words, he says, 'to escape from the weight of the world, I leave my body where it is, in conversation, or at dinner, and walk through a series of winding streets to a house standing back from the road' (17). Here, the concept of weightlessness is a metaphor for Jordan's ability to operate simultaneously on two separate planes – socially in the 'real' world, and in the realm of imagination. In Jordan's imaginary journey to the 'city of words', we see the idea of weightlessness represented in the words that pervade this imagined world. Winterson indirectly refers to words as 'the heaviest of things' (18) that in this world, once uttered, become 'the lightest of properties' (18) as they become physically present and float freely around, filling the air in perpetuity. In another example we once again see a metaphorical connotation of the idea of 'weight' where Jordan refers to 'the school of heaviness' as an institute that 'tie[s] down love, desire and passion' (38-39). *Sexing the Cherry* has been described as 'a comprehensive celebration of weightlessness'[194]; and in both these examples, we can see free expression as being related to weightlessness. The material implications of weight are brought to the fore through Winterson's representations of her female protagonists of contrasting embodiments. Winterson's writing assumes a fluidity in relation to her protagonists' embodiments, neither consistently adopting a fat-positive or fat-negative stance. In her representation of these two very different characters, Winterson is able to mount a thorough exploration of transgression as they both transcend and transform this metaphorical notion of 'weight' via the extreme natures (excessively heavy/weightlessness) of their embodiment. With these two antithetical but complimentary constructions of female embodiment Winterson allows the 'fat' and the 'thin' to sit side by side harmoniously, exploring their liberatory potential, and bringing them to synthesis in the character of the anonymous young ecology activist. In this way Winterson represents a celebratory bodily diversity that is not confined to an oppressive cultural 'fat/thin' dichotomy as the novel contests this 'either/or' positioning of the female form.

Sexing the Cherry allows Winterson a textual space to exaggerate and engage playfully with 'the unlikely', 'the miraculous' and with 'family life carried to the grotesque.'[195] The gargantuan Dog Woman and the weightless Fortunata are figures who exercise supernatural control over their bodies, which enables them not only to perform miraculous or gravity-defying acts, but also to use their body as a resistance to conform to the various normative social, cultural and political regulations depicted in the novel. For instance, the Dog Woman's huge bodily strength becomes her weapon in her fight with the repres-

---

[194] Lorna Sage, 'Weightlessness and a Banana', in *Observer*, 10 September 1989, p. 51.

[195] Cited in Jeanette Winterson's website. <http://www.jeanettewinterson.com/pages/content/index.asp?PageID=14> [accessed 15 August 2007]

sive, hypocritical ideologies embraced by Puritans. Fortunata's narrative is centered around the story of her liberation from her oppressive father's rules. Winterson, here, uses dance as a metaphor with its associations of free expression and flexibility to represent Fortunata's achievement of a liberated state, both mentally and physically. Her 'floating' body constitutes a challenge to the cultural myths and fairy tales that restrain and punish female bodily desires. The ecofeminist's internalisation of both the Dog Woman and Fortunata gives her the spiritual strength in her fight against the politics of capitalism. The novel's male voice, (Nicholas) Jordan, questions conventional views of time, space and body through his outward and inward journeys. The alternating narration between the male and female characters brings to mind Bakhtin's dialogic interrelation. According to Bakhtin, a novel should be viewed as a heterogeneous entity, a medley of many styles and voices, and 'be inherently "dialogic" or, in an alternative formulation, "polyphonic" – an orchestration of diverse discourses culled both from writing and oral speech.'[196] Winterson's text thus illustrates Bakhtin's account of 'polyphonic' narration by creating multiple points of view, and bringing together various styles of discourse into play where history and fantasy operate within the same frame.

This fusion between historical fact and fiction has led to a critical consensus which has situated the novel as an example of 'historiographic metafiction', a term coined by Linda Hutcheon for the paradigm case of postmodern fiction to define novels that 'are both intensely self-reflexive and yet paradoxically lay claim to historical events and personages.'[197] For Catherine Belsey, Winterson's work exemplifies Hutcheon's conceptualisation of historiographic metafiction, by 'call[ing] into question the relationship between past and present, event and text, by rendering critical the "obvious" distinction be-

---

[196] David Lodge, *After Bakhtin: Essays on Fiction and Criticism* (London and New York: Routledge, 1990), p. 76.
[197] Linda Hutcheon, *A Poetics of Postmodernism: History, Theory, Fiction* (New York: Routledge, 1988), p. 5.

tween fact and fiction.'[198] Such fiction 'problematises both the nature of the referent and its relation to the real and historical world by its paradoxical combination of metafictional self-reflexivity with historical subject matter.'[199]

The critical reception of the novel as a form of historiographic metafiction led some critics to over-emphasise the postmodernist strategies employed in the text which arguably risked situating it within limiting confines and labels (a position which Winterson strongly refutes). For instance, Michael Gorra reviewed Winterson's text as trotting out 'the clichés of postmodernism.'[200] Sonya Andermahr has characterised Winterson's writing as 'synonymous with postmodern aesthetic techniques', further stating that Winterson's books 'display how-to guides to the postmodern text.'[201] Similarly, Lucie Armitt has focused on the postmodern aspects of Winterson's writing, particularly *Sexing the Cherry*, and pointed out that 'despite its seventeenth-century thematic concerns', *Sexing the Cherry* is 'an exemplary late-twentieth-century postmodern narrative compromising clashing spatio-temporal planes, multiple narrative perspectives and competing, even contradictory, versions of history.'[202] Lyn Pykett is another critic who has considered *Sexing the Cherry* as a postmodernist text which 'foreground[s] the subjectivity and cultural relativism of space and time.'[203] In line with Pykett, Bente Gade has also engaged

---

[198] Catherine Belsey, 'Postmodern Love: Questioning the Metaphysics of Desire', in *New Literary History*, 25 (1994), 683-705 (p. 688).

[199] Hutcheon, p. 19.

[200] Michael Gorra, 'Gender Games in Restoration London', in *New York Times Book Review*, 29 April 1990, p. 24.

[201] Sonya Andermahr, 'Cyberspace and the Body', in *British Fiction of the 1990s*, ed. by Nick Bentley (London and New York: Routledge, 2005), pp. 108-22 (p. 108).

[202] Lucie Armitt, 'The Grotesque Utopias of Jeanette Winterson and Monique Wittig', in *Writing and Fantasy*, ed. by Ceri Cullivan and Barbara White (London and New York: Longman, 1999), pp. 185-97 (p. 188).

[203] Lyn Pykett, 'A New Way with Words? Jeanette Winterson's Post-Modernism', in *Postmodern Studies 25 ('I'm telling you stories': Jeanette Winterson and the*

with the novel's tendency to destabilise conventional notions of 'time and matter' to 'reinstate them as cultural conventions.'[204] An explicit example of this undermining of general perceptions of time and matter can be found in the epigraph to the novel:

> The Hopi, an Indian tribe, have a language as sophisticated as ours, but no tenses for past, present and future. The division does not exist. What does this say about time?
>
> Matter, that thing the most solid and the well-known, which you are holding in your hands and which makes up your body, is now known to be mostly empty space. Empty space and points of light. What does this say about the reality of the world? (8)

Support for those controversial notions is offered halfway through the novel in the sections entitled 'Hallucinations and Diseases of the Mind' and 'Lies', in which Winterson negates the conventional view of time and space:

> *Lies* 1: There is only one present and nothing to remember.
> *Lies* 2: Time is a straight line.
> *Lies* 3: The difference between the past and the future is that one has happened while the other has not.
> *Lies* 4: We can only be in one place at a time.
> *Lies* 5: Any proposition that contains the word 'finite' (the world, the universe, experience, ourselves…)
> *Lies* 6: Reality as something which can be agreed upon.
> *Lies* 7: Reality as truth. (83)

Winterson adopts a sceptical attitude towards fundamental concepts by challenging their validity through a distinct narrative style which interweaves history and story, fusing female and male voices in a blend of the factual and the fabulous. In this respect *Sexing the*

Politics of Reading), eds Helena Grice and Tim Woods (Amsterdam, Atlanta-GA: Rodopi, 1998), pp. 53-61 (p. 54).

[204] Bente Gade, 'Multiple Selves and Grafted Agents: A Postmodern Reading of *Sexing the Cherry*', in *Sponsored by Demons: The Art of Jeanette Winterson*, ed. by Helene Bengston (Denmark: Scholars' Press, 1999), pp. 27-39 (pp. 27, 31).

Cherry can be seen to exemplify some postmodern literary strategies, but to consider her work solely within the grounds of postmodern poetics would not do justice to the other pioneering elements in her text. The role of imagination, for instance, is particularly significant for Winterson, as she writes in *Art Objects*:

> I have twice used the device of history [*The Passion* and *Sexing the Cherry*], not because I am interested in Costume Drama Realism, or Magic Realism or any other Realism but because I wanted to create an imaginative reality sufficiently at odds with our daily reality to startle us out of it.[205]

In her earlier novel, *The Passion*, we see Winterson's use of history fused with fantasy. Set in the early nineteenth century, the novel looks at the period of the rise and decline of Napoleon Bonaparte. Winterson explores this historical period from the points of view of Henri, a young French peasant, chicken chef to Napoleon to whom he is passionately devoted, and Villanelle, the novel's cross-dressed, bisexual Venetian girl, born with webbed feet, a feature peculiar to the males in the Venetian fishing community. These two alternating narrations are set against each other with Henri offering a credible depiction of the historical period, whilst in Villanelle's narration we see a more fantastical style which is driven by fairy-tale overtones, in particular her phantasmagorical account of shape-shifting, fluid Venice, where 'streets appear and disappear overnight, new waterways force themselves over dry land.'[206] Villanelle's depiction of the city's labyrinthine structure invokes the idea of a city within a city, and this can be seen as analogous to Winterson's literary strategy in which her writing emerges as a series of stories.

In a similar way to *The Passion*, in which myths, tales of the supernatural, and the picaresque build a fantastical world on the foundation of the factual and historical, the focus on 'imaginative reality'

---

[205] Jeanette Winterson. *Art Objects: Essays on Ecstasy and Effrontery* (London: Jonathan Cape, 1995), p. 188.
[206] Winterson, *The Passion*, p. 97.

turns out to be an important aspect in the narrative style in *Sexing the Cherry*, as Winterson writes:

> It is certainly true that a criterion for true art, as opposed to its cunning counterfeit, is its ability to take us where the artist has been, to this different other place where we are free from the problems of gravity. [...] We are no longer bound by matter, matter has become what it is: empty space and light. (91)

Winterson's claim is that true art, like her project, should succeed in freeing readers 'from the problems of gravity'. Her strong emphasis on this very notion of materiality in her novel, which is illustrated via her characters' experiences with their bodies, offers a glimpse into a world significantly different from our own 'daily reality' where the notion of 'size' ceases to be a denigrated issue. For instance, according to contemporary Western beauty norms, the Dog Woman's huge embodiment might be associated with the literal meaning of the 'grotesque'. When the Dog Woman's 'grotesque' embodiment is contrasted with Fortunata's weightless 'floating body', it seems at first glance that Winterson is deliberately constructing embodiments that illustrate both ends of the weight spectrum. However, the Dog Woman is both huge and paradoxically weightless, and a more nuanced reading is called for where room is made for these non-rigid embodiments to exist on a long continuum rather than defining them as extremes set against one another. Viewed in this context, it might be argued that Winterson's text offers an exploration of female embodiment as an alternative to its rigid representations as displayed in mainstream Western culture. 'Resignification of discourse', as Judith Butler has argued in *Bodies that Matter*, 'echoes prior actions, and accumulates the force of authority through the repetition or citation of a prior, authoritative set of practices.'[207] In her study, Butler has explored the reiteration of 'discourse' in relation to the term 'queer' which 'has become linked to

---

[207] Judith Butler, *Bodies that Matter: On the Discursive Limits of 'Sex'* (New York and London: Routledge, 1993), p. 227.

accusation, pathologisation, insult' through its 'past interpellations.'[208] Yet, for Butler, resignification may not be conclusive as it always has the potential to create new discourses to change and challenge the validity of pre-stated assumptions. Written four years prior to Butler's publication of her seminal book, it is interesting to see that Winterson's *Sexing the Cherry* foreshadows Butler's emphasis on the 'resignification of discourse' in that the text not only offers a nuanced poetics of representation which is inherently literary, but also a politics of representation which transforms repressive and stereotypical constructions of various female embodiments into the realm of power.

However, many feminist critical responses to the novel have been dismissive of Winterson's liberatory constructions of diverse embodiments and her positive body politics, as they merely have laid the focus on the Dog Woman's physicality, engaging with her embodiment either as 'grotesque' or 'monstrous', or exploring Winterson's feminist revision of the Grimms Brothers' traditional tale 'The Shoes that Were Danced to Pieces.'[209] Jan Rosemergy for instance focused on 'the theme of women's empowerment'[210] employed in the novel with a specific reference to Winterson's construction of her Twelve Dancing Princesses who challenge the narrow confines of normative regulations of femininity. Marilyn R. Farwell has explored Winterson's Dog Woman, examining her as 'a construct that refutes the dominant images of woman as body – as beauty, as object of desire, as totally controlled desire.'[211] Elizabeth Langland has developed a similar reading of the Dog Woman and stated that she is 'the most radi-

---

[208] Ibid., p. 226.

[209] In the original version the theme that runs through the story is that if you break the rules of the father, if you disobey, you will be punished. In Winterson's subversive revision, the twelve dancing princesses find happiness after they get rid of their husbands in their unique ways.

[210] Jan Rosemergy, 'Navigating the Interior Journey: The Fiction of Jeanette Winterson', in *British Women Writing Fiction*, ed. by Abby H. Werlock (Tuscaloosa and London: The University of Alabama Press, 2000), pp. 248-70 (p. 258).

[211] Marilyn R. Farwell, *Heterosexual Plots and Lesbian Narratives* (New York: New York University Press, 1996), p. 170.

cally unconventional physical presence in the novel'[212] that 'destabilises gender norms and exposes their cultural construction.'[213] For Paulina Palmer, Winterson's 'complex treatment of the Dog Woman transforms her from an image of monstrosity to a signifier of female heroism.'[214] Sara Martin, with a similar focus, reads the Dog Woman's grotesque monstrosity from 'an ideological point of view'[215] to destabilise hegemonic constructions of femininity. For Laurena Russell, the monstrous representation of the Dog Woman 'creates a narrative "queering field", effectively challenging normative configurations of female heterosexuality.'[216] In her reading of the Dog Woman, De Zordo defines the monstrosity of this character as 'mythical', and associates her effect on others with 'fear.'[217] For Jane Haslett, Winterson's Dog Woman 'is an absolute escape from the image of the proper feminine body, overcontrolled by the notion of femininity.'[218] Haslett's essay is perhaps the most recent critical writing that offers a re-exploration of the Dog Woman in a dialogue with norms of contemporary Western beauty; her argument nonetheless does not seem to provide a thorough engagement with Winterson's heterogeneous constructions of female embodiment in her novel. It can be seen that much of the criticism on the Dog Woman tends to study her as a site of transgression representing a resistance against the domination

---

[212] Elizabeth Langland, 'Sexing the Text: Narrative Drag as Feminist Poetics and Politics in Jeanette Winterson's *Sexing the Cherry*', in *Narrative*, 5:1 (1997) 99-107 (p. 101).
[213] Ibid., p. 102.
[214] Paulina Palmer, 'Foreign Bodies: The Grotesque Body in the Fiction of Jeanette Winterson', in *Gramma*, 11 (2003), 81-93 (pp. 87-88).
[215] Martin, p. 208.
[216] Laurena Russell, 'Dog-Women and She Devils: The Queering Field of Monstrous Women', in *International Journal of Sexuality and Gender Studies*, 5:2 (2000), 177-93 (p. 178).
[217] Ornella de Zordo, 'Larger than Life: Women Writing the Excessive Female Body', in *Textus*, 13 (2000), 427-48 (pp. 428, 444).
[218] Jane Haslett, 'Winterson's Fabulous Bodies', in *Jeanette Winterson: A Contemporary Critical Guide*, ed. by Sonya Andermahr (London, New York: Continuum, 2007), pp. 41-55 (p. 42).

and oppression of the female. In her interview with Jackie Kay, Winterson explains her motives for constructing the Dog Woman as she does:

> With the Dog Woman in *Sexing the Cherry*, I wanted to create a woman that was not in any way a female stereotype, who wasn't clean, particularly loveable or desirable or attractive or any of these things, and yet proved to be enormously sympathetic and vulnerable. So that again you couldn't hate her. The Dog Woman's violence is very personal. Although she murders hundreds of people in the course of the novel, she never hits out at anybody that hasn't hurt her. She murders people whom she sees are hypocritical and are effectively damaging her life. Her violence isn't senseless.[219]

Winterson challenges the stereotypical representations of femininity which tend to simplify and reduce women to certain characteristics by constructing a character who categorically refutes them. In line with Butler, who pointed out the necessity of finding ways to avoid construction of women on 'a single or abiding ground'[220], Winterson seeks to create liberating role models for women, as she has pointed out in an interview: 'it is important that women should have role models, should have positive heroines.'[221] Here, Winterson's notion of 'positive' heroines is suggestive of women whose ambiguous and unidentifiable features situate them outside a common identity for women. In this respect, it might be argued that not only Winterson's Dog Woman but also her other female protagonists in the novel, Fortunata and the ecologist, fulfil Winterson's aspiration of constructing 'positive heroines' in their own nuanced ways.

The Dog Woman, a dog breeder, is a figure of hyperbole: everything about her is over-determined, exaggerated, 'grotesque', or perhaps 'abject'; she is like 'a caricature that has reached fantastic di-

---

[219] Jackie Kay, 'Unnatural Passions': Interview with Jeanette Winterson', in *Spare Rib*, 209 (1990), 26-29 (p. 27).

[220] Judith Butler, *Gender Trouble* (New York and London: Routledge, 1999), p. 8.

[221] Helen Barr, 'Face to Face: A Conversation between Jeanette Winterson and Helen Barr', in *The English Review*, 2:1 (1991), pp. 30-33 (p. 31).

mensions.'[222] Her 'gross' physicality has affinities with Bakhtin's interpretation of the grotesque body, which juxtaposes incompatible and paradoxical elements to create a sense of shock. For instance, the Dog Woman for all her size and weight can become invisible at will or 'melt into the night as easily as a thin thing that sings in the choir at church' (14). Owing to her strength she can do incredible things: she can fit eleven oranges into her mouth and can make an elephant fly 'the way a terrier does a rat' (88). Echoing Bakhtin's account of the grotesque body, the Dog Woman's body 'transgresses its own limits.'[223] It is a body in which the 'mouth' becomes the most important part in relation to 'sucking, devouring, and swallowing.'[224] The Dog Woman herself constantly implies her grotesqueness by describing her body as a 'hill of dung' (11) and 'mountain of flesh' (14). As she says:

> How hideous am I?
> My nose is flat, my eyebrows are heavy. I have only a few teeth and those are a poor show, being black and broken. I had smallpox when I was a girl and the caves in my face are home enough for fleas. (24)

The Dog Woman's description of her appearance as hideous might initially be considered as an indication of her concern over her physical appearance outside of dominant aesthetic standards. However, here the word 'hideous' rather suggests her difference from others, which she subsequently cherishes and redeems by saying, 'but I have fine blue eyes that see in the dark' (24). Here, the Dog Woman counters the hyperbole of her physicality by turning how she is perceived into how she is the perceiver, with her eyes that see in the dark. It is interesting to see that this section where she describes her grotesqueness is set against her love for Jordan: 'how could I lose Jordan, so dear to me and my only comfort?'(28). Against this maternal devotion and unconditional love, she asks her question again, 'how hideous

---

[222] Bakhtin, p. 306.
[223] Ibid., p. 26.
[224] Ibid., p. 317.

am I?' (26), and we see once more how her 'monstrosity' is countered by her ability to love and care.

The above examples suggest that the Dog Woman is a paradoxical figure: she is both violent and tender, grotesque and invisible, as she says, 'I who must turn sideways through any door, can melt into the night as easily as a thin thing' (14). If her flesh is 'mountain', her voice is 'as slender as a reed' (14). Establishing a relative attitude towards her embodiment, the Dog Woman questions the notion of 'size': 'What it says of my size I cannot tell, for an elephant looks big, but how am I to know what it weighs? A balloon looks big and weighs nothing' (25). This relative perception ascribed to the Dog Woman's weight encapsulates Winterson's assertion that 'we are no longer bound by matter, matter has become what it is: empty space and light'. As in the case of the Dog Woman, if matter is heavy, it is also weightless; she says: 'in the dark and in the water, I weigh nothing at all' (40) and 'like the angels I can be invisible when there is work to be done' (89). Winterson's construction of the Dog Woman questions the social perception of weight, pointing out its relativity, and highlighting our possibly deceptive judgements. The Dog Woman could well be considered 'morbidly obese' in a fat-abhorrent society, but the imaginative landscape that Winterson casts her in compels us to think again and to re-perceive what her physicality – here constructed through hyperbole rather than 'diagnosed' as 'morbidly obese' – might now signify or entail. For her foster son Jordan, she stands as an almighty, dominant, ideal being that exists in myths and fairy tales, a figure precisely to be imagined:

> I imagine her on the bank, in a bottle. The bottle is cobalt blue with a wax stopper wrapped over a piece of rag. A woman coming by hears noises from the bottle, and taking her knife she cuts open the seal and my mother comes thickening out like a genie from a jar, growing bigger and bigger and finally solidifying into her own proportions. She grants the woman three wishes and throws the bottle out to sea, and now she has forgotten all that and sits with her dogs watching the tide. (79-80)

Here, Jordan thinks about the Dog Woman as a figure whose promise and possibility was released. Sitting with her dogs, and watching the tide she becomes a reflective figure represented here in a narrative almost without content. Jordan expresses a sense of inferiority in the Dog Woman's presence: 'she is always huge and I am always tiny. I'm sitting on her hand, the way she holds her puppies. [...] She is like a mathematical equation, always there and impossible to disprove' (79). The Dog Woman resides in Jordan's unconscious as his ego-ideal. As he puts it:

> I want to be like my rip-roaring mother who cares nothing for how she looks, only for what she does. She has never been in love, no, and never wanted to be either. She is self-sufficient and without self-doubt. (101)

By bringing together images of physical power and superhuman qualities, Winterson associates the Dog Woman with mythical heroines. As Susana Onega suggests, the very name of the Dog Woman 'brings to mind the Dog Men, the highly sexed creatures from a distant land who mated with a race of voluptuous Amazonian women, a recurrent patriarchal myth in the mythology of the West, India and China.'[225] For Onega, Winterson parodically inverts the male myth by creating a female equivalent of the Dog Man. Thus, the Dog Woman's immense strength and fury is reminiscent of a mythical Goddess. According to Jung, the goddess archetype belongs to the category of the mother, an image which encapsulates 'maternal solicitude, sympathy and authority.'[226] However, differing from the Jungian archetype of the goddess, whose power is most often connected to her reproductive capacity, the Dog Woman is not a biological mother. Her power is

---

[225] Susana Onega, 'Jeanette Winterson's Politics of Uncertainty', in *Gender Ideology: Essays on Theory, Fiction and Film*, ed. by Chantal Cornut-Gentille D'Arcy, José Ángel García Landa (Amsterdam, Atlanta, GA: Rodopi, 1994), pp. 297-313 (p. 304).

[226] C.G. Jung, *The Archetypes of the Collective Unconscious*, trans. by R.F.C. Hull (Princeton: Princeton University Press, 1990 [1959], p. 82).

not, therefore, restricted to a view of femininity as reproductive, and her physical and moral strength become a part of her political mission to punish the hypocrisy of the Puritans.

The Dog Woman's unruly nature is in fact suggestive of the subversive trickster figure – the 'deceiver-trick-player, shape-shifter, situation-invertor, messenger/imitator of the gods, sacred/lewd bricoleur.'[227] The trickster, as I discussed in the previous chapter, is often defined in terms of 'paradox, marginalit, peripherality, liminality, and inversion.'[228] For Jung, the trickster represents 'an archetypal psychic structure of extreme antiquity. In his clearest manifestations he is a faithful reflection of an absolutely undifferentiated human consciousness, corresponding to a psyche that has hardly left the animal level.'[229] Jung associates the inconsistent and irreconcilable nature of the trickster figure with the alchemical figure of Mercurius, and interprets the trickster as a release of repressed thoughts and values, a subversion of the established binaries such as good and evil, sacred and profane. 'In Freudian terms the trickster constantly oscillates back and forth between self-gratification and cultural heroism.'[230] That is to say, the trickster corresponds to the clash between individual desires and social boundaries. For Radin, the trickster serves primarily 'to add disorder to order and make a whole, to render possible, within the fixed bounds of what is permitted, an experience of what is not per-

---

[227] William J. Hynes, 'Mapping the Characteristics of Mythic Tricksters: A Heuristic Guide', in *Mythical Trickster Figures: Contours, Contexts and Criticisms*, ed. by William J. Hynes and William G. Doty (Tuscaloosa and London: The University of Alabama Press, 1993), pp. 33-46 (p. 34).

[228] William G. Doty and William J. Hynes, 'Historical Overview of Theoretical Issues: The Problem of the Trickster', in *Mythical Trickster Figures: Contours, Contexts and Criticisms*, ed. by William J. Hynes and William G. Doty (Tuscaloosa and London: The University of Alabama Press, 1993), pp. 13-32 (p. 25).

[229] Jung, p. 260.

[230] William J. Hynes, 'Inconclusive Conclusions: Tricksters-Metaplayers and Revealers', in *Mythical Trickster Figures: Contours, Contexts and Criticisms*, ed. by William J. Hynes and Willliam G. Doty (Tuscaloosa and London: The University of Alabama Press, 1993), pp. 202-218 (p. 209).

mitted.'[231] Following the Jungian interpretation of the trickster, Radin redefines the duality inherent in the archetypal figure and provides a basic personality profile that is still cited:

> Trickster is at one and the same time creator and destroyer, giver and negator, he who dupes others and who is always duped himself. He wills nothing consciously. At all times he is constrained to behave as he does from impulses over which he has no control. He knows neither good nor evil yet he is responsible for both. He possesses no values, moral or social, is at the mercy of his passions, and appetites yet through his actions all values come into being.[232]

Radin's definition reconfirms the trickster as a liberatory figure whose duality is a major trait. Similarly, Lewis Hyde points out the trickster's artistic function as a boundary crosser who acts as a 'creative idiot, therefore the wise fool.'[233] In his essay 'Trickster Discourse', Gerald Vizenor contemplates the freedom expressed by the trickster, which he explains in relation to the unconscious:

> The trickster is chance and freedom in a comic sign. [...] The trickster, as a semiotic sign is imagined in the narrative voices, a communal rein to the unconscious, which is comic liberation; however, the trickster is outside comic structure. [...] The trickster is agonistic imagination and aggressive liberation, a "doing" in narrative points of view, and outside the imposed structures.[234]

Here, the relation of the trickster to the primitive urges of the human psyche is expressed in similar terms to the Bakhtinian carnival of the feast of misrule that renders invalid any codes, conventions or laws that govern or reduce the individual to an object of control. The trickster challenges any system of beliefs, and suggests a world of

---

[231] Paul Radin, *The Trickster: A Study in American Indian Mythology* (London: Routledge & K. Paul, 1956), p. 185.
[232] Ibid., p. ix.
[233] Hyde cited in *The Trickster Lives: Culture and Myth in American Fiction*, ed. by Jeanne Campbell Reesman (Athens and London: The University of Georgia Press, 2001), p. xx.
[234] Vizenor, 'Trickster Discourse', p. 285.

change as well as a world of possibilities in that it leads us to consider the possibility of altering the restraints that govern our behaviour. With its ambiguous and transgressive nature, the trickster produces an alternative way to break the binaries.

However the trickster, who is usually believed to be male, is highly sexed and his tales are phallogocentric.[235] In their entry 'The Native American Trickster' in the *Dictionary of Native American Literature*, Barbara Babcock-Abrahams and Jay Cox summarise: 'That trickster is generally male and characterized by exaggerated phallicism may be the result of male bias in the collection and interpretation of trickster tales compounded by the Anglo bias of identifying Indian women with stability.'[236] For Lewis Hyde 'the standard tricksters are male, some of whom on rare occasions became briefly female, usually for deceitful purposes.'[237]

Jung's followers had come to see the archetypes as 'unchanging and unchangeable', or as the material contents of the collective unconscious. However by giving a material and specific identity to the trickster, Winterson re-inscribes the archetype in a way that is fluid, allowing the trickster free movement and interplay among the various forms it assumes such as 'the story-teller, transformer, a master of borders and exchange.'[238] Here, we have a trickster figure that is much more powerful and fierce than the previous configuration of the same figure in Weldon's literary imagination. In *Feminist Archetypal Theory* Estella Lauter and Carol Schreiner Rupprecht point out that

---

[235] Particularly Coyote – a dominant figure in Native American tales – plays tricks on women, and his tales (for instance 'Coyote's Amorous Adventures') portray female tricksters as less smart and less mobile than their male counterparts.

[236] Barbara Babcock-Abrahams and Jay Cox, 'The Native Trickster', in *Dictionary of Native American Trickster*, ed. by Andrew Wiget (New York: Garland Publishing, 1994), pp. 99-105 (p. 100).

[237] Lewis Hyde, *Trickster Makes This World: Mischief, Myth and Art* (New York: Farrar, Straus and Giroux, 1998), p. 336.

[238] Smith, *Writing Tricksters*, p. xiii.

in the case of feminist theory, if we regard the archetype not as an image whose content is frozen but [...] as a tendency to form and reform images in relation to certain kinds of repeated experience, then the concept could serve to clarify distinctly female concerns that have persisted throughout human history.[239]

By 'forming and re-forming' the construct, Winterson creates her own variation of the trickster figure who is free from any kind of social restrictions and who has a desire to destroy anything connected with the system of rules by her individualistic and autonomous pursuit of satisfaction and autonomy. Unlike Radin's description of the trickster as a figure who 'possesses no values, moral or social' and has 'no control over his impulses', Winterson constructs the Dog Woman as fully conscious of her endeavours, and as a woman who strongly holds on to her own values, moral and social, which often situate her against the regulations of her society. Winterson creates a dynamic, fluid and contradictory space for the Dog Woman where the Dog Woman, as in Mcleish's words, a 'simpleton, a holy fool'[240], fits into the trickster's function with regard to her position as 'the wise fool, the crossdresser, the speaker of sacred profanities'[241], as she believes that the world is 'entirely flat' (23). Her naivety functions as a form of resistance and becomes a way of questioning the political order and gender hierarchies that impose oppressive stereotypical images on women, such as the monstrous-feminine and *femme fatale*. When the Dog Woman is in the brothel, she exposes her genitalia to one of the clients who, horrified at the sight, says: 'I cannot take that orange in my mouth. It will not fit. Neither can I run my tongue over it. You're too big, madam' (107).

---

[239] Estella Lauter and Carol Schreier Rupprecht, 'Introduction', in *Feminist Archetypal Theory: Interdisciplinary Re-Visions of Jungian Thought*, ed. by Estella Lauter and Carol Schreier Rupprecht (Knoxville, Tenn.: University of Tennessee Press, 1985), pp. 1-22 (pp. 13-14).

[240] Kenneth Mcleish, 'Larger than Life', *The Times* (London), 10 September 1989.

[241] Jeanne Campbell Reesman, *The Trickster Lives: Culture and Myth in American Fiction* (Athens and London: The University of Georgia Press, 2001), p. xx.

Bakhtin identifies the grotesque body mostly with 'the lower stratum' in that 'the belly, buttocks and genital organs'[242] become important features in the formation of laughter. In Bakhtin's account, the grotesque body is that of re-generation and the swellings associated with breasts and pregnancy, which clearly gender it as 'the cavernous anatomical female body.'[243] Yet, it is also often associated with a Freudian sense of the uncanny, thereby relating female sexuality to something fearful and terrifying. As Barbara Creed points out, 'the feminine is constructed as a monstrous sign within a patriarchal discourse which reveals a great deal about male desires and fears.'[244]

Winterson's representation of the Dog Woman offers a satirical engagement with these misogynistic conceptualizations of the female body. The Dog Woman manipulates this image of the monstrous feminine in hyperbolic terms when she parades the castration fear. The Dog Woman, for instance, bites off the penis of a man who has persuaded her to perform oral sex, naively claiming that she hurt him because she believed a man's genitals could grow again after an accident. Later, when she is better informed, she comes to the conclusion that '[it] seems a great mistake on the part of nature, since men are so careless with their members and will put them anywhere without thinking' (106).

The Dog Woman's adventures with male genitalia are evident throughout the text and her engagement with male sexuality echoes the overt sexuality found in Native American trickster tales. In a male-oriented society, the male trickster has advantages which permit him mobility, autonomy and the power to deconstruct existing political, social and economic structures. Female tricksters, on the other hand, are usually denied that level of mobility. However, the representation of the female trickster in Winterson's text re-forms this traditional

---

[242] Bakhtin, pp. 20-21.
[243] Russo, *The Female Grotesque*, p. 1.
[244] Barbara Creed, 'Horror and the Monstrous-Feminine – An Imaginary Abjection', in *Screen*, 27:1 (1996), pp. 44-70 (p. 70).

trickster image, as she becomes a liberatory figure undermining the power systems operating in her society. Her embodiment and her trickster-like qualities combine to make her a powerful, unruly and strong figure that constitutes a threat to the norms of her society. She kills her own father, who wanted to sell her to a man to make her a subject of an exhibition. This act of patricide subverts the gendered power structure and symbolises, ultimately, the death of the 'law of the father'. The Dog Woman is, therefore, a woman who makes her own rules, and that is one of the reasons why she hates the Puritans:

> The Puritans, who wanted a rule of saints on earth, and no king but Jesus, forgot that we are born into flesh and in flesh must remain. Their women bind their breasts and cook plain food without salt, and the men are so afraid of their member uprising that they keep it strapped between their legs with bandages. (67)

For Puritans the body was considered a vehicle for the unruly, ungovernable and irrational patterns, emotions and desires. This view clearly contradicts the Dog Woman's sense of order, conformity and morals. She says: 'I am a sinner, not in the body, but in mind' (35), which emphasises her position not simply as represented via her body, but also through her mind, which challenges socially and religiously imposed restrictions. She is unable to accept the Puritans' sexually repressive, rigid life-style: 'I heard from Preacher Scroggs' wife that he makes love to her through a hole in the sheet [...] for fear of lust' (27). However, later in the novel, we see Preacher Scroggs in a brothel committing adultery. This incident illustrates why The Dog Woman has such an intense dislike of the Puritans. Though she is loyal to the King, her dislike of the Puritans stems mainly from her association of their asceticism with corruption and hypocrisy: 'I would rather live with sins of excess than sins of denial' (67).

Within the ascetic tradition, corpulence was considered inappropriate as it signalled the soul's weakness to resist temptations. As Bryan Turner has argued, 'according to the ascetic attitude towards the body, flesh stood in the same sphere as sub-human animality [...]

and was given therefore a darker meaning as the metaphor of mankind fallen from grace.'[245] This notion of the body 'required the discipline of diet, meditation and religious practice.'[246] As a fictional inhabitant of this social and religious climate, the Dog Woman resists the ascetic notion of the body as 'evil'. Her excessive body cannot be attributed to a 'lack of willpower and self-discipline' or a weakness in character and thereby defies the derogatory attributions of the Puritanical view of the 'excessive' body, as well as the regulatory control of her own body in the name of a religious practice, for example, by reacting against cleanliness: 'I hate to wash, for it exposes the skin to contamination. I follow the habit of King James, who only ever washed his fingertips and yet was pure in heart enough to give us the Bible in good English' (35).

As a heroic figure, the Dog Woman supports the Royalists, not the Puritans, and she kills King Charles' executioners ruthlessly. Yet she is both heroic and base combining her physical strength with the behaviour of the trickster who uses duplicitous and subversive tactics to exploit the existing political and sex-gendered system. Though Winterson seems to favour a poetics of representation over a politics of representation, in her construction of the Dog Woman we see both the poetics and politics of re-inscription operating simultaneously. We see the Dog Woman as an essentially literary figure, a poetic trope or a metaphor for hyperbole in one of the stories of the Twelve Dancing Princesses borrowed from the original tale, 'The Shoes that Were Danced to Pieces', where one of the dancing princesses describes her husband in quite hyperbolic terms: 'his eyes were brown marshes, his lashes were like willow trees. [...] I still think it was poetic' (50).

The rewriting of fairy tales in this fashion allows Winterson to unsettle the rigid and recurrent patterns existent in tales of the super-

---

[245] Bryan S. Turner, *The Body and Society*, p. 12.
[246] Ibid., p. 12.

natural, and so serves her purpose to 'tell the story again.'²⁴⁷ For Winterson, 'in the re-telling comes a new emphasis or bias.'²⁴⁸ As she points out:

> I've always liked to work with existing texts. I like to do cover versions of stories that we know very well. [...] It's a way of rewriting what we know, but in the rewriting we find new angles, new possibilities, and the rewriting itself demands an injection of fresh material into what already exists, so the story changes.²⁴⁹

Winterson, thus, presents a completely new version of the story with a new emphasis in which 'the magical literal alterations are replaced with a satirical literal concreteness.'²⁵⁰ In the Grimm Brothers' traditional story twelve princesses secretly fly off every night to dance with twelve princes. Their father, the King, suspects that the princesses are in their bedroom sleeping sound, although their shoes are worn out. He hires men to find out where the princesses go at night, and whoever finds out will be rewarded with his choice of princess. Failure will result in decapitation. Though many suitors try, only the unknown soldier finds out where the princesses go at night, and he marries the oldest one. The princes are bewitched for as many days they had danced with the twelve princesses. As Nancy Walker suggests, 'all fairy tales arise from particular cultural contexts' and 'embody a message that reflects the ideologies of the cultures that produce

---

²⁴⁷ Jeanette Winterson, *Weight* (Edinburgh, New York, Melbourne: Canongate, 2006 [2005]), p. xviii.
²⁴⁸ Ibid., p. xviii.
²⁴⁹ 'From Innocence to Experience', Louise Tucker's Interview with Jeanette Winterson, in *Lighthousekeeping* (London, New York, Toronto and Sydney: Harper Perennial, 2005), pp. 2-14 (p. 2).
²⁵⁰ Emilie Walezak, 'They lived happily ever after, or did they? The Rewriting of Grimms' *The Twelve Dancing Princesses* in Jeanette Winterson's *Sexing the Cherry*' (Conference paper at '"Rewriting/Reprising" – La reprise en littérature', Lyon, France, 13-14 October 2006). <http://conferences.univ-lyon2.fr/index.php/reprise/paper/view/58/108|> [accessed 5 August 2009] (para. 6 of 13).

them'.[251] In this story the message revolves around the theme of disciplining disobedient women. In Winterson's version, the twelve princesses were all unhappily married to princes and found happiness in anything but their husbands, who have all been done away with in uniquely violent ways. Each princess, except Fortunata, tells her story about the way she got rid of her husband. Actually only the marriage of two women, which lasted for eighteen years, is represented as the most satisfactory, affectionate and loving relationship among other unions. Although Winterson's revisions of stories have been reviewed as 'pretexts for her vengeful hostility to men and marriage, and her compensatory vision of women as the stronger, more sane, and even physically dominating sex'[252], her objective in reconstructing fairy tales and myths yet serves a different purpose. As Winterson points out,

> storytelling teaches us to be unafraid of our imaginative power and I think it teaches us to be unafraid of the exuberance and the unruly, untamed nature of life, of our lives. So in a world which is obsessed with taming, obsessed with making sense of things – which often means reducing those things – stories are a way of making sense differently, of enlarging upon what we are and not being afraid of the unruly elements within it.[253]

Through this imaginative power of storytelling, Winterson constructs a female embodiment that performs an extreme sense of mobility to the extent of being 'a point of light' (72), a figure whose weightless body becomes a metaphor of free expression and transcendence. Her dancing body, as Walezak states, 'is a tight trope for the poetic body of the text.'[254] What Walezak suggests here is an allegorical construct that enunciates the idea of cherishing artistic freedom that sur-

---

[251] Nancy A. Walker, *The Disobedient Writer: Women and Narrative Tradition* (Austin: University of Texas Press, 1995), p. 49.
[252] Rosellen Brown, 'Fertile Imagination', in *Women's Review of Books*, 7 (1990), pp. 9-10 (p. 10).
[253] Winterson, 'From Innocence to Experience', p. 5.
[254] Walezak, para. 11 of 13.

passes repressive boundaries, that is to say freeing the mind and body from physical and aesthetic constraints. Earlier in the novel, we see Jordan talking about the 'school of heaviness' (38) which he interprets as an instruction to put one off from following his/her pursuits and desires. Set against the school of heaviness, Fortunata's school of lightness teaches her pupils how to defy gravity, that is to say, free the spirit and the body from any imposed limitations. The allusion to the mythological story about Goddess Artemis to 'Fortunata's story' (131) serves to reinstate Fortunata's empowered position over the abuse of the female body. The similarity between these characters derives from their physical strength. The physical strength of Artemis finds its embodiment in Fortunata's practice of lightness through which she frees both the body and the mind from restrictive constraints. This pursuit of freedom also places her in the imagination of the young ecologist who envisages a world where there is 'no gravity' and 'no holding force' (124).

Just as the physical strength of Artemis is relocated in the weightless body of Fortunata, so the gigantic body of the Dog Woman comes to rest in the imagination of a twentieth century female activist who, like the Dog Woman, has no name or companion. This character also sees herself as marginal: 'When I'm dreaming I want a home and a lover and some children, but it won't work. Who'd want to live with a monster?'(127). This echoes the Dog Woman's assertion: 'I am too huge for love. No one, male or female, has ever dared to approach me. They are afraid to scale mountains' (34), 'they were abashed at my magnanimousness' (66). The modern counterpart of the Dog Woman is as resilient as her forebear and similarly expresses a longing for transformation. Travelling through her childhood memories she wants to assign a meaning to her hidden desires:

> I wasn't fat because I was greedy; I hardly ate at all. I was fat because I wanted to be bigger than all the things that were bigger than me. All the things that had power over me. It was a battle I intended to win.

It seems obvious, doesn't it, that someone who is ignored and overlooked will expand to the point where they have to be noticed, even if the noticing is fear and disgust. (124)

Here, getting bigger becomes a means of satisfying her demand for power and control. Like the Dog Woman, literally a giant, the ecofeminist realises that she has to be fat so that she will be strong enough to fight against a capitalist society that destroys the world. After she internalises the Dog Woman's strength, she loses weight but maintains this 'alter ego', 'the other one, lurking inside' who 'fits, even though she is so big' (128). She imagines a figure much like the Dog Woman:

I had an *alter ego* who was huge and powerful, a woman whose morality was her own and whose loyalties were fierce and few. She was my patron saint, the one I called on when I felt myself dwindling away through cracks in the floor or slowly fading in the street. Whenever I called on her I felt my muscles swell and laughter fill up my throat. Of course it was only a fantasy, at least at the beginning... (125)

The activist draws potency from the Dog Woman as her 'patron saint' (125) and absorbs that huge body into her inner strength. The fat woman within becomes the source of this young woman's power: 'I'm a woman going mad. I am a woman hallucinating. I imagine I am huge, raw, a giant' (121). Here, the activist's ego strives to retain the Dog Woman's fantastic body as her ideal of perfection. In contemporary society it is often the 'thin' ideal which becomes the ego-ideal that many women aspire to attain. However, in Winterson's novel, the massive body of the Dog Woman is represented as the ego-ideal for the thin woman, who regards sheer physical strength as an inspiration for the power to challenge 'men in suits [...] discussing how to deal with the problem of the Third World' (122).

Viewed from a different perspective, this internalised, almost archetypal, image of the Dog Woman in the young ecofeminist's imagination can also be linked to Jung's contextualization of the archetypes in relation to the collective unconscious. According to Jung, whilst personal motives reside in the individual unconscious, impersonal motives are to be found in the collective unconscious, which consists of pre-existent archetypes. Jung's thesis is that 'in addition to our immediate consciousness there exists a second psychic system of a collective, universal and impersonal nature, which is identical in all individuals. This collective unconscious does not develop individually but is inherited.'[255] The existence of the Dog Woman in the young activist's imagination arguably illustrates this 'pre-existent' form that functions as a 'collective shadow figure.'[256] The Dog Woman's huge shadow occupies the mind and spirit of the young activist. In her unconscious, the image of the Dog Woman gains a spiritual and collective dimension and becomes the embodiment of the fertile earth, the ancient Goddess of nature and spirituality.

Riane Eisler discusses the relevance of spiritual traditions to a solution of the ecological crisis:

> Prehistoric societies worshipped the Goddess of nature, our great Mother. They were societies which had what we today call an ecological consciousness: the awareness that the Earth must be treated with reverence and respect. And this reverence for life-sustained powers of the Earth was rooted in a social structure where women and 'feminine' values such as caring and compassion are not subordinate to men and the so-called masculine values of conquest and domination.[257]

Eisler's idealization of pre-historic Goddess worship transforms into a contemporary rebirth of Goddess spirituality exercised by the young ecofeminist in *Sexing the Cherry*. This character glorifies the Dog Woman from whom she gains the inner strength to protest against environmental pollution. Her aspirations are analogous to the

---

[255] Jung, p. 43.
[256] Ibid., p. 270.
[257] Riane Eisler, 'The Gaia Tradition and the Partnership of Future: an Ecofeminist Manifesto', in *Reweaving the World: The Emergence of Ecofeminism*, ed. by I. Diamond and G.F. Orenstein (San Francisco: Sierra Club Books, 1990), pp. 23-34 (pp. 23-24).

black, metallic giantess in Ted Hughes' story for children, *The Iron Woman* (1993), in terms of the radical, violent methods used to teach patriarchal man to behave properly.

The ecologist is motivated by similar utopian desires that encourage the transformation of society. She imagines a society in which people act collectively for the good of human kind: 'Then they start on the food surpluses, packing it with their own hands, distributing it in a great human chain of what used to be power and is now co-operation' (123). She emphasises social change and envisions creating the world anew:

> We change the world, and on the seventh day we have a party at the wine lake and make pancakes with the butter mountain and the peoples of the hearth keep coming in waves and being fed and being clean and being well. And when the rivers sparkle, it's not with mercury... (123)

In her version of Genesis, power is replaced by co-operation. However, she is aware of the fact that in order to realise her dream, she should take action, and by means of her 'one-woman campaign' (123) she sets out to change society's treatment of the environment. Just like the Dog Woman, who is outraged by the 'stinking' (11) Thames and London which she perceives as a corrupted place, 'full of filth and pestilence' (141), her reincarnation sees the mercury polluted river as a symbol of the 'hypocritical stinking world' (124) which she longs to change. The Dog Woman's narrative in the seventeenth century ends with the Great Fire of 1666 which she has triggered by 'pouring a vat of oil on to the flames' (143). She says: 'God's revenge is still upon us. We are corrupt and our city is corrupted. [...] This city should be burned down' (141). The fire marks the end of the order of the Puritans. Similarly, the unnamed protestor, disgusted by corporate and governmental abuses of power and nature, is inspired to burn down the mercury factory.

In the merging of the Dog Woman of the past with the ecofeminist of the present, *Sexing the Cherry* focuses on the relationship between power and gender. This convergence also brings past and present together, enabling them to exist on the same time line. Hence the Dog Woman's story in the seventeenth century overlaps with the unnamed ecofeminist's childhood memories, as she recalls when she used to get fatter by the day.

> At that time we lived in a council flat on Upper Thames Street in London, by the river.
>
> I looked at my forearms resting on the wall. They were massive, like thighs.
>
> Now I wake up in the night shouting 'Who? Who?' like an owl. Why does that day return and return as I sit by a rotting river with only the fire for company? (128, 129)

These childhood memories resonate with that of a woman quite similar to the Dog Woman in the part entitled *Time 2* in 'Hallucinations and Diseases of the Mind':

> They are cat-calling the girl as she comes out of school. She hates them, she wants to kill them. They tell her she smells, that she's too fat, too tall. She walks home along the river bank to a council flat in Upper Thames Street. […] She can see her hut. She laughs, and the wind blows through the gaps in her teeth. Jordan will be waiting for her. (82)

Although these overlapping memories make the text operate on a similar plot structure, they also serve to translate the mythical into the political. While the Dog Woman's narrative revolves around her exercise of power, her gender-based remarks conversely indicate that she has not been completely liberated from gendered identities and power structures. For instance, while she is waiting for her foster son Jordan's arrival, she says: 'I busied myself as a good woman should, cleaning the hut and brushing down the dogs' (135). Her narrative evokes, as Langland suggests, 'gender norms of tenderness, charity or maternality.'[258]

---

[258] Langland, p. 102.

The Dog Woman's twentieth century counterpart internalises these 'feminine values' and locates them at the centre of her ecological conscience. She wages war against a capitalistic patriarchal society which she holds responsible for extinguishing natural sources. She pictures a scenario in which she invades the World Bank boardroom and the Pentagon, putting 'men in suits' (122) into a huge bag and taking them to 'the butter mountains and wine lakes and grain silos and deserts and cracked earth and starving children and armed dealers in guarded palaces' (123). She will train them in 'feminism and ecology' (123), because as an ecofeminist she relates the oppression of women to the degradation of nature. Here, we see a representation of woman that contrasts with the ascribed notion of nurturing, and where environmental degradation emerges as a form of negative embodiment. The 'grotesque' body of the Dog Woman can be linked to this if one considers her embodiment as a metaphor for the decaying (environmentally degraded) earth.

This linking of 'fat' in its over-consumptive guise to the environmental problems facing the earth (to a large extent driven by over-consumption) is highlighted by the ecofeminist, as she envisions 'all the fat ones to go on a diet' (123). Fat is given a negative meaning in this context and is shown as something to lose, but here the criticism is mainly directed at *male* corpulence. Throughout the novel there are several instances[259] where male corpulence is associated with repulsion, inverting the proposition in the 'rule book' that 'men deem themselves weighty and women light' (32). For the young ecofeminist, female corpulence has a spiritual resonance which she associates with an almighty, powerful Goddess image, whilst corpulence in men is related to over-consumption and capitalist practices. This gendered outlook on fatness, where fatness is associated with greed for men, and with power for women, can be observed within two social perspectives. First, associating fatness with over-consumption in the last

---

[259] For instance, one of Winterson's twelve dancing princesses kills her husband because 'he is very, very fat' (55).

part of the novel, Winterson scales this issue up as a metaphor for an over-consumptive society. From the point of view of the ecologist, we see the representation of fatness as a political issue associated with a destructive impulse for consumption exercised by capitalist economies. Second, fatness in men has often been associated with status, wealth and prosperity. By making the corpulent Dog Woman an ego-ideal for the modern woman, Winterson offers a challenge to the denigration of 'fat' women. Her construction of the ecologist as a slender woman might appear to be in conflict with Winterson's politics of representation. However, the ecologist slims down naturally without the aid of diets, whilst internalising her former 'fat' self, which ultimately points to the novel's emphasis on the material as metaphorical.

Sexing the Cherry alludes to the process of botanical grafting, which helps recreate various species of plants to increase their strength and resistance. Just as botanical grafting produces the stronger cherry, the synthesis of the Dog Woman and Fortunata in the character of the young ecologist at the end of the novel envisions stronger and more empowered selves, outside of repressive dualities: 'a new kind of grafted human being [...] in a radically free and joyfully carnivalesque order.'[260] Accordingly, in this carnivalesque order, bodily hierarchies cease to exist: 'fat' and 'thin' sit together harmoniously, creating a sense of diversity and interconnectedness. Winterson's various phantasmagorical representations of the female body demonstrate this liberating sense of an embodiment through a constant interplay between the poetics and politics of representation. However, as I argue in the next chapter, the 'fat' body transforms into a cultural impossibility, and embodies a site of repression in Margaret Atwood and Claude Tardat's fictive confessional narratives where excess becomes a core of trauma which is situated at the centre of mother-daughter relationships.

---

[260] Onega, pp. 308-09.

3 Mothers, Daughters and Excess in *Lady Oracle* and *Sweet Death*

In the previous chapter, the representation of 'embodiment' was shown to be less explicitly about a form of physical embodiment, and more about a particular kind of expression regarding narrative shape and language where notions of self/other, story/history, weight/ weightlessness are closely woven into each other. Winterson's underlying emphasis on the need for interconnectedness and unity produced a highly imaginative representation of embodiment that is inherently literary. Margaret Atwood's *Lady Oracle* (1976) and Claude Tardat's *Sweet Death* (1989) offer a more somatic engagement with female embodiment; both texts explore the implications of separation and segregation triggered by bodily differences which result in tensions and power struggles between mothers and daughters. This chapter examines the negative and potentially traumatic consequences of having an 'excessive' embodiment in an environment in which slenderness is held up as the ideal within the mother-daughter dyad where the slender mother imposes normative expectations about femininity on her 'fat' daughter.

Both *Lady Oracle* and *Sweet Death* explore a daughter's troubled relationship with her mother to offer insight into the culturally scripted sense of embodiment that women inherit from their mothers; in both texts, we see this relationship from the point of view of the daughter. As the mother-daughter relationship unfolds, we observe the daughter's 'obese' body becoming a stimulus for creative endeavour: in *Lady Oracle*, Joan's former 'obesity' operates as a subconscious driving force that motivates her writing, whereas in *Sweet Death*, the protagonist's meticulous diarisation of her deliberately excessive consumption is a conscious attempt to exact revenge upon her mother. Contained within both texts is a challenge to the normative requirements of the female body and the idealisation of the mother as proposed in the theories of *l'écriture féminine* and particularly found in the writings of Hélène Cixous. Cixous's emphasis on celebrating and retrieving the bodily in writing is well known: 'woman, writing herself, will go back to this body that has been worse than confiscated, a body replaced with a disturbing stranger, sick or dead, who so often is a bad influence, the cause and place of inhibitions.'[261] Cixous directs her criticism against the objectification of women in a type of writing that 'has been run by a libidinal and cultural – hence political, typically masculine – economy.'[262] For her, writing the body enables the woman writer to liberate herself from this economy that has written stories for her. To emancipate women's subjectivity, Cixous draws on the significance of the mother, and situates the maternal into the source of feminine writing. For Cixous, as Bray argues, 'the mother is a metaphor for those subversive exiled energies which threaten the coherence of phallocentric thought.'[263] That is to say, 'the rhythms and articulations of the mother's body have a continuing effect, and the inscription of these rhythms is important in preventing the codes of the patriarchal symbolic from becoming rigidified and all-powerful.'[264] Cixous expands her concept of feminine writing by claiming its proximity to the mother's voice which 'sings from a time before law, before the Symbolic took one's breath away and re-appropriated it into language.'[265] This view of writing the female body, inspired by the mother's body (that evokes feminine bodily rhythms), as a stimulus to authenticate a rhythmic and nonsensical language as against the phallogocentric writing is motivated by a textual subversion of the Symbolic. For Cixous, this feminine writing celebrates the pre-Symbolic – the stage prior to the entry to the lan-

---

[261] Hélène Cixous and Catherine Clément, *The Newly Born Woman*, ed. by Hélène Cixous and Catherine Clemént, trans. by Betsy Wing (Manchester: Manchester University Press, 1986), p. 97.

[262] Hélène Cixous, 'The Laugh of the Medusa', in *New French Feminisms*, ed. by Elaine Marks and Isabelle de Courtivron (Brighton: Harvester, 1980), pp. 245-64, p. 249.

[263] Abigail Bray, *Hélène Cixous: Writing and Sexual Difference* (Basinstoke, Palgrave, 2004), p. 74.

[264] Susan Sellers, *Hélène Cixous: Authorship, Autobiography and Love* (Cambridge: Polity Press, 1996), p. 7.

[265] Cixous and Clément, *The Newly Born Woman*, p. 93.

guage – and thus, aims to establish a 'site of difference' from the phallogocentric conceptualisation of women.

Cixous aspires to replicate this elevated notion of the female body into writing, and thus promises to challenge phallogocentric representations of the female body. However, her utopian conceptualisation of the female body has the effect of homogenising women's bodily experiences. Arguably, her discourse assumes that all women have the same body, are subject to the same psychical processes and that writing this body will enable a powerful and provocative narrative that reclaims the female body from its stereotyped and acculturated constructions in the symbolic. However, Cixous is dismissive of the possible 'feminine' narratives that may come out from real, materialistic and subjective experiences of the female body in its diverse forms and shapes, where this body may come to be not a site of celebration, but a site of humiliation and repulsion for the subject. In this respect, Cixous's elevated notion of the female body offers little about its somatic experience but, as Bray argues, proposes an image of the body, 'which is divorced from the complex historical and social contexts in which women live their bodies.'[266]

Lady Oracle and *Sweet Death* explore these potential conflicts between the subjectively experienced body and the culturally situated body, that is to say the body shaped and influenced by the culture in which it is placed. It might be argued that these novels imaginatively engage with the female body in terms that conflict with Cixous's conceptualisation of writing the female body. Firstly, the representation of the mother in these works can be identified with 'presence' which disputes the association of the mother with powerlessness, 'lack' and absence in the patriarchal order. Furthermore, the mother with her 'presence' also presents a challenge to classic representations of the mother as the passive, altruistic, selfless woman. However, operating in the realm of power, the mother arguably becomes a 'phallic mother' by

---

[266] Bray, p. 31.

mimicking a masculine role imposing male ideals of femininity onto the daughter.

Here, the notion of the phallic mother denotes neither a mythical image of a devouring, monstrous female nor a Freudian sense of a threat of castration. The idea of the 'phallic mother' in these texts in fact refers to the mother's position as an enforcer of the Symbolic Law of the Father which replaces the maternal authority that represents, in Kristeva's words, 'a universe without shame.'[267] As Kristeva argues, the period of the 'mapping of the self's clean and proper body'[268] is characterised by the exercise of 'authority without guilt'[269], in other words, by the maternal authority, whilst the Symbolic world embodied by the Law of the Father represents the territory of embarrassment, shame and guilt. Kristeva 'identifies the Symbolic with syntax or grammar, and the ability to take a position, whereas she links the maternal authority to the semiotic element of language – that is the sounds and rhythms primarily associated with the maternal body.'[270] According to her, the Symbolic exacts the abjection of the mother so as to initiate the entry to language and to perform social codes and regulations. However, in her theorisation of the semiotic, Kristeva argues that 'abjection of the mother has been misplaced onto women', in that the mother has been reduced to the 'maternal container.'[271] 'Because the cultural representations of women have often been linked to the maternal function', Kristeva, in Oliver's words, 'suggests that everyone must separate from their mother by abjecting her.'[272] In *Lady Oracle* and *Sweet Death*, we see the daughters' constant attempts to 'abject' the mother, but the 'abjection' here diverges from Kristeva's position, as the motive beneath the abjection of the mother in these

---

[267] Kristeva, *Powers of Horror*, p. 72.
[268] Ibid., p. 72.
[269] Ibid., p. 74.
[270] Kelly Oliver, 'Julia Kristeva's Feminist Revolutions', in *Hypatia*, 8:3 (Summer 1993), 94-114 (p. 95).
[271] Ibid., p. 104.
[272] Ibid., p. 104.

works arises differently. In both novels the daughters 'abject' the mother not because of her 'maternal function', but because of her appropriation of the role of the Law of the Father. In adopting this role, the mother's 'voice' masquerades as the voice of masculine authority creating a need for the daughter to voice her anger towards the mother. This in effect stimulates the daughter's creative response, i.e. expressing her animosity via the vehicle of writing. In this respect, Atwood and Tardat's narratives re-emphasise the mother as the 'source of writing'[273] through their construction of daughters who are in complicity with Virginia Woolf's observation that 'a woman writing thinks back through her mothers.'[274] Indeed, the mother represented in *Lady Oracle* and *Sweet Death* is the 'source of writing' but not in the sense that Cixous described, since the mother in these texts is far from Cixous's ideal model of the mother as a 'love object' who 'makes everything all right, who nourishes.'[275] As Cixous writes, 'a woman is never far from "mother". [...] There is always within her at least a little of that good mother's milk. She writes in white ink.'[276] The daughters in these texts assert their autonomy as writing subjects, and in so doing give the mother, in turn, their own 'milk'. In this sense, the ink they use is not just the mother's milk returned but the blood of a new and a more liberated writing self which enables them to demystify and challenge the ideal position ascribed to the mother. An interesting aspect of this is that we see the writer assuming a form of resistance in the mother-daughter power dynamic by having conscious control over her motives as she writes and thus being able to undermine the mother's authority. In this way, we see the writing of the daughter's 'obese' body in these texts at the centre of mother-daughter power relations where the 'excessive' body constitutes a tex-

---

[273] Verena Andermatt Conley, *Hélène Cixous: Writing the Feminine* (Lincoln and London: University of Nebraska Press, 1984), p. 83.
[274] Virginia Woolf, *A Room of One's Own* (London: Penguin, 2000 [1929]), p. 96.
[275] Cixous, 'The Laugh of the Medusa', p. 252.
[276] Ibid., p. 251.

tual battleground that enables the daughter to express resistance to and resentment of the slender and elegant mother.

More importantly, by writing the 'obese' embodiment, these confessional narratives also creatively and critically facilitate a reconsideration of 'obesity' in relation to a particular subjectivity: it is the daughter's painful and traumatic experiences with her 'excessive' embodiment that moulds her future self. Even though there is a time span of more than a decade between the publication of these works, as one was written in 1970s Canada, the other in late 1980s France, they are arguably motivated by a similar critical focus on contemporary Western cultural notions of femininity and beauty. Both texts explore the ways in which externally imposed ideals shape and construct a woman's identity, and the ways in which the daughter copes with this pressure via forms of 'escape'.

The notion of 'escape' as a response to the daughter's painful experiences as a result of her embodiment could be assumed to be a key idea that is employed in both novels. In *Lady Oracle* escapism enables Joan to avoid confrontation with traumatic memories of being 'overweight'. For the anonymous young woman in Tardat's *Sweet Death*, death becomes the ultimate form of 'escape'. Even though in *Lady Oracle* there is a desire to escape the past, and in *Sweet Death* the future, we see in both novels the improbability of escaping the cultural implications written on the body, as they become heavily embedded in one's existence, shaping one's personal and social reality.

3.1 'The outline of my former body still surrounded me like a mist': Traumatic Resonances of 'Excess' in *Lady Oracle*

In an interview with Elizabeth Meese, Atwood stated: 'I think that people very much experience themselves through their bodies and through concepts of the body which [...] they pick up from their culture and apply to their own bodies. This is my concern in *Lady Ora-*

cle.'[277] Atwood's comment on the novel emphasises its theme, of how a woman experiences herself through her body. In her novel, Atwood brings the issue of weight to the fore through her construction of Joan whose narrative reveals the burdens of being fat in a society that tends to denigrate and stigmatise it. But, more importantly, Atwood's text explores how embodiment is understood within cultural and literary representations of the female body, and she shows that these representations are at the core of a woman's ontology, literally shaping who she is, and thus creating a form of collective consciousness about what a woman should be like.

The novel utilises several intertextual references to folkloric representations of contained images of ideal femininity to demonstrate Joan's entrapment in a culture enthralled to these images. References to Hans Christian Andersen's 'Little Mermaid' and the screen adaptation of Andersen's 'The Red Shoes', and to Alfred Lord Tennyson's poem 'The Lady of Shalott' as well as the pre-Raphaelite paintings[278] inspired by the Lady in the poem, intensify the novel's interrogation of prescribed images of femininity that advocate mutilation, female passivity, selflessness and sacrifice to attain the love of a man. These, as Eleonora Rao suggests, establish 'the theme of sexual politics'[279] in the novel. Atwood's satirical engagement with these representations and their potential influence on the formation of one's self are made

---

[277] Elizabeth Meese, 'The Empress Has No Clothes', in *Margaret Atwood: Conversations*, ed. by Earl G. Ingersoll (London: Virago, 1982), pp. 177-91 (p. 187).

[278] The imagery Atwood uses in depicting Joan's mock suicide bears a resemblance to John William Waterhouse's version of 'The Lady of Shalott' (1888) which shows the lady casting off in a boat for Lancelot, implying her expected tragic end. The idea of escapism prevalent in the poem is a vivid theme in the painting as well. However, while Tennyson's Lady of Shalott sacrifices her life for the love of a man, Joan murders her 'fat' self that she sees as a blemish to her latter feminine image.

[279] Eleonora Rao, 'Margaret Atwood's *Lady Oracle*: Writing Against Notions of Unity', in *Margaret Atwood: Writing and Subjectivity: New Critical Essays*, ed. by Colin Nicholson (Houndmills, Basingstoke, Hampshire, London: Macmillan, 1994), pp. 133-53 (p. 144).

explicit through her construction of Joan whose identity is 'dispersed in a multitude of projected personae ranging from film stars to heroines of fairy tales.'[280] Atwood's use of intertextual references indicates how 'cinema and fairy tales construct female subjectivity and female desire and how they function for the female spectator.'[281] Joan grows up reading these cultural and literary stereotypes of women which considerably shape her notion of the norms of femininity. What she has seen in the fairy tales and the movies is that a woman has to sacrifice her aspirations for acceptance. Andersen's *Little Mermaid*, for instance, has to sacrifice her voice – the ability of self-expression – to have legs and feet, and to attain the love of the Prince. The girl in *The Red Shoes* is punished for her disobedience, and indulgence in dancing. Powell and Pressburger's feature film *The Red Shoes*[282] (1948) is an adaptation of the fairy tale, now given a romantic plot. Moira Shearer plays a ballerina who has to make a choice between her career and marriage, and who faces death in the end because she cannot choose. Although Joan is fascinated by the film's beautiful actress Moira Shearer, who plays the lead role of Vicky, she does not want to experience Vicky's dilemma, as she wants to have 'both at once.'[283] However, Joan's self-inflicted entrapment in double identities, both physical and psychical, marks her adult profile. Atwood's construction of Joan as a woman who is imprisoned in two contradictory positions, the unruly, subversive 'fat' girl and the 'feminine', submissive

---

[280] Ibid., p. 144.

[281] Ibid., p. 144.

[282] Even though the film is based on Andersen's story, its discrepancies with the actual story are noteworthy. Andersen's story emphasises the idea of rewarding 'virtue', and punishing 'vice'. The story ends with the little girl Karen's redemption from the burden of the red shoes at the expense of losing her feet, and her re-acceptance by society. However, the film gives a tragic account of a young woman, Vicky, whose life is torn between her career as a ballet dancer and her lover, a conflict which ultimately causes her death. Whilst the story pinpoints the importance of female obedience, the film focuses on a woman's divided self.

[283] Margaret Atwood, *Lady Oracle* (London: Virago, 1997 [1976]), p. 82. Subsequent references to the novel will be given in brackets.

woman, can be seen as a projection of Atwood's own stance in feminism. In her essay 'On Being a Woman Writer: Paradoxes and Dilemmas'(1976) Atwood voiced her concern about the development of what she terms 'one-dimensional' feminist criticism, a term she defines as 'a way of approaching literature produced by women that would award points according to conformity or non-conformity to an ideological position.'[284] As Atwood further states: 'There is a lot of social pressure on a woman to be perfect, and also a lot of resentment of her should she approach this goal in any but the most rigidly prescribed fashion. [...] Women, both as characters and as people, must be allowed their imperfections.'[285] Atwood's own words suffice to show her intentions on this point: 'If I create a female character, I would like to be able to show her having the emotions all human beings have without having her pronounced a monster, a slur, or a bad example.'[286] Atwood achieves this by constructing Joan as a multi-faceted woman who 'makes decisions, performs actions, causes as well as endures events, has some creative power'[287], and who contains feelings of hate, lust, anger and fear. In so doing, Atwood gives her protagonist a witty voice that disrupts the ideological confines of womanhood and femininity.

This aspect of Atwood's construction of Joan has received much critical attention, the thrust of which has tended to seek to view the novel in terms of a deliberate attempt to parody representations of women in folkloric culture, and thereby demystify them. Emily Jensen has interpreted the novel as a 'parable' that 'conveys a serious message about the problems confronted by a woman who believes that she can both have a successful, rewarding career and "the love of a good

---

[284] Margaret Atwood, *Second Words: Selected Critical Prose* (Toronto: Anansi, 1982), p. 192.
[285] Ibid., p. 227.
[286] Ibid., p. 227.
[287] Ibid., p. 223.

man.'"[288] Similarly, Sharon Rose Wilson has engaged with the text's allusions to fairy tales reading it as a 'parody of the either/or choices for women.'[289] A corresponding response to the novel comes from Linda Hutcheon, who has stated that *'Lady Oracle* both mirrors and contains that which it consistently parodies: the forms of popular art.'[290] Amongst these forms of popular art, perhaps Gothic Romance is the one that *Lady Oracle* mimics most.

However, to appropriate Atwood's construction of *Lady Oracle* in the form of a Gothic Romance as a mere parodic design may risk simplifying the novel's subtle engagement with this genre which operates on various levels. First, extracts from Joan's Gothic novels featuring the entrapped position of her heroines build a subtext which parallels Joan's own imprisonment in her socially acceptable role and image, and her other personae as a 'fat' girl. Second, her experience with automatic writing in the production of her 'Lady Oracle' poems expands this subtext, and functions as a way of unfolding Joan's troubled relationship with her mother who is situated at the centre of her unpleasant experience with her embodiment. In this way, the Gothic resonance of Joan's life, which is also reflected in her writing, is more than a parody of the genre, as it functions as an intricate literary design becoming a medium to unearth Joan's internalised fears and repressions related to her former 'obese' embodiment.

Joan's position as a writer of romances permits her to create an alternative imagined space which initially enables her to escape her unpleasant experiences with her corporeality, and rewrite her traumatic past. [Earlier in the novel, Joan remembers her Aunt Lou saying that 'you can't change the past' (10), but for Joan it 'was the only thing she wanted to do' (10).] However, as I will argue, Joan's escapism

---

[288] Emily Jensen, 'Margaret Atwood's *Lady Oracle*: A Modern Parable', in *Essays on Canadian Writing*, 33 (Fall 1986), pp. 29-49 (p. 29).
[289] Sharon Rose Wilson, *Margaret Atwood's Fairy-Tale Sexual Politics* (Jackson, MS, University Press of Mississippi, 1993), p. 122.
[290] Linda Hutcheon, *The Canadian Postmodern: A Study of Contemporary English-Canadian Fiction* (Oxford and Toronto: Oxford University Press, 1988), p. 146.

proves an ineffective remedy, and paradoxically revives her painful memories which she desperately longs to forget. As she takes refuge in Romance, we find her repressed and traumatised other unintentionally leaking out and influencing the construction of her characters. In this respect, the textual subtlety generated by the genre of romance within the novel serves as a strategic device for an exploration of subconscious motives in Atwood's protagonist's embodied self/selves. Whilst Atwood's use of romance could be read superficially as a parodic device, here it serves a deeper purpose providing space to explore the psychological implications of Joan's former 'obesity' and her troubled relations with her mother.

3.1.1 'Obesity', Trauma, and its Manifestations within the Mother-Daughter Dyad

Despite the fact that *Lady Oracle* engages with how 'excessive' female embodiment is received and experienced in a fat-phobic culture, the novel was initially reviewed as 'urbane comedy', which perhaps under-emphasises Atwood's explicit critique of obesity's stigma and its traumatic effects for the subject. In her review of the book Katha Pollitt questions if 'being fat really is the stuff of which successful blackmail is made.'[291] Pollitt's stance reveals a lack of empathy with Joan's situation; her argument seems to dismiss the potential long-term psychological trauma of being 'obese' in a fat-abhorrent society as represented in *Lady Oracle*. In fact, Atwood successfully prepares a realistic groundwork through the psychological construction of her protagonist whereby the reader is not left feeling that the concept of 'blackmail' in this case is improbable. Indeed, more than half of the book is dedicated to exploring Joan's traumatic experiences with her embodiment which date back to her childhood and early adolescence; and it is this dedication to detail that undermines Politt's critique and

---

[291] Katha Pollitt, 'New Fiction', in *The New York Times*, 26 September 1976. <http://partners.nytimes.com/books/00/09/03/specials/atwood-oracle.html> [accessed 21 December 2007] (para. 2 of 5).

allows this concept to stand up to scrutiny. It is with this thorough depiction of Joan's inner world that the reader anticipates and indeed is able to accept that 'being fat' for Joan turns into a realm of fear and trauma that shapes her persona.

Trauma, from the Greek meaning 'wound', was originally a specific medical term used to refer to 'a physical or physiological wound' and later acquired a new additional meaning to designate 'a spiritual, psychic, or mental injury', what Ian Hacking has called 'a wound to the soul.'[292] Freud in his early studies in the 1890s (*Studies on Hysteria* [1895]) identified trauma with a sexual content relating it to childhood experiences that become intelligible after puberty. In his later studies (*Moses and Monotheism* [1939]), however, this notion of trauma in relation to sexuality acquired a social content exploring the concept in terms of a range of social experiences that are emotionally painful, distressing, or even shocking, and which often result in profound suffering for the subject after a temporal delay. The study of trauma in social contexts has often emphasised certain kinds of extreme suffering and the resulting strain on the body and the mind, and has tended to focus on people in extreme situations, i.e. victims of war, rape, racism, poverty, serious illness. However, the everyday abuse suffered by an 'obese' person within a disapproving and hostile social landscape, whilst not being of the same order of magnitude as the above examples, can nevertheless result in marginalisation and stigmatisation for the individual, and this has rarely been examined in terms of 'trauma'. A possible explanation for this could be a social tendency to hold the 'fat' individual responsible for his/her condition as a result of alleged self-indulgence, over-consumption, moral weakness or lack of discipline.[293] For instance, Crandall documents the

---

[292] Ian Hacking, *Rewriting the Soul: Multiple Personality and the Sciences of Memory* (Princeton: Princeton University Press, 1995), p. 4.

[293] Christian S. Crandall, 'Prejudice Against Fat People: Ideology and Self-Interest', in *Journal of Personality and Social Psychology*, 66:5 (1994), 882-94; William DeJong, 'Obesity as a Characterological Stigma: The Issue of Responsibility and Judgments of Task Performance', in *Psychological Reports*, 73

prejudice against fat people recorded in the data he gathered from his 'antifat attitudes questionnaire'. Crandall noted that fat people are seen as 'unattractive, aesthetically displeasing, morally and emotionally impaired. They are denigrated by thin people, peers, potential romantic partners, their parents, and even by themselves.'[294] He also adds that female participants in his research scored notably higher on 'fear of fat' than men pointing to a gender-biased stigma attached to obesity, which counterpoints Mary Harris's 1982 study according to which the stigma affects men and women at the same level. William DeJong's 1993 research conducted on high school girls showed that 'obese' girls are more likely to be seen as 'having less self-discipline and being more self-indulgent.'[295] A close reading of these studies leads one to see the overweight person as suffering more from the social and psychological stigma attached to 'obesity' than the bare medical implications of the actual physical condition. These studies mostly engaged with the adult subjects of the weight stigma. However, as Leonard Taitz states, weight stigma causes more damage to children than adults. He points out that

> in a status-conscious society, being 'different' or merely at the extreme of the norm may exact a savage penalty. Whatever one might conclude about the long-term physical hazards of obesity, there can be no doubt about its psychological and social consequences for at least some fat children. Some are merely teased, others are bullied unmercifully and some are virtually ostracized.[296]

The cultural pressures considered here bear down in a cruel way on the children, in particular 'fat' ones, who do not fit the norm. Cramer and Steinwert's 1998 study on the social reception of fatness

---

(1993), 963-70, Mary. B. Harris, Richard. J. Harris, Stephen Bochner, 'Fat, Four-Eyed, and Female: Stereotypes of Obesity, Glasses, and Gender', in *Journal of Applied Social Psychology*, 12 (1982), 503-16.

[294] Crandall, p. 885.
[295] DeJong, p. 968.
[296] Leonard S. Taitz, *The Obese Child* (Oxford, London, Edinburgh, Boston, Melbourne: Blackwell Scientific Publications, 1983), p. 21.

amongst preschool children aged between three to five reaffirms 'the negative attitudes'[297] held by very young children toward their overweight peers which become more extreme as they get older. Arguably, these negative attitudes may potentially result in physical and mental oppression, and further lead to emotional trauma scarring the individual for life. Drawing upon Maria Root's conceptualisation of 'insidious trauma' as 'a distinct threat to psychological safety'[298], Laura S. Brown points out that 'there are traumatogenic effects of oppression that are not necessarily overtly violent or threatening to bodily wellbeing at the given moment but that do violence to the soul and spirit.'[299] It might be argued that Joan's relationship with her mother is a literary manifestation of this form of trauma where the mother's 'normal' and 'acceptable' hostility towards her daughter's 'excessive' embodiment leaves the latter with feelings of insecurity, lack of confidence, and even paranoia. Yet, Atwood offers a nuanced view of this dynamic allowing the negative and traumatic experience of the protagonist to metamorphose and re-emerge in creative endeavour. That is to say, her former 'excessive' embodiment, which is the repository of her unpleasant memories, functions as a catalyst for her transformation into a creative writer of romances and 'Lady Oracle' poems, where we read the history of her relationship with her mother.

Early in the novel, Joan reveals her mother's motive in naming her after the actress 'Joan Crawford' (42): she wanted her 'to be like the screen characters she played – beautiful, ambitious, ruthless, destructive to men' or because she wanted Joan 'to be successful' (42).

---

[297] Phebe Cramer and Tiffany Steinwert, 'Thin is Good, Fat is Bad: How Early Does it Begin?', *Journal of Applied Developmental Psychology*, 19:3 (1998), 429-51 (p. 430).

[298] Maria P.P. Root, 'Reconstructing the Impact of Trauma on Personality', in *Personality and Psychopathology: Feminist Reappraisals*, ed. by Laura S. Brown and Mary Ballou (New York: Guildord, 1992), pp. 229-67 (p. 241).

[299] Laura S. Brown, 'Not Outside the Range: One Feminist Perspective on Psychic Trauma', in *Trauma: Explorations in Memory*, ed. by Cathy Caruth (Baltimore: The Johns Hopkins University Press, 1995), pp. 100-13 (p. 107).

However, as Joan grows older and starts to expand in size, the mother regrets having named her daughter after the famous actress, and we hear Joan reflecting: 'Joan Crawford was thin' (42). As a little girl, Joan finds it hard to understand her mother's aggressive contempt for her, but in time she comes to realise that her mother's dislike towards her has been rooted in the physical comparison between Joan and her namesake. With her bulging body, Joan becomes a repository of shame for her parent: 'this is one of the many things which my mother never quite forgave me' (43). Her mother is an attractive woman who is obsessed with the cultural values about femininity, 'she had kept her figure, she had been popular in her youth' (68), and it is the contrast between the mother's slender body and Joan that is the source of friction between them. As Joan observes:

> The war between myself and my mother was on in earnest; the disputed territory was my body. [...] I reacted to the diet booklets she left on my pillow, to the bribes of dresses she would give me if I would reduce to fit them [...] – to her cutting remarks about my size, to her pleas about my health. [...] I swelled visibly, relentlessly, before her very eyes, I rose like dough, my body advanced inch by inch towards her across the dining-room table, in this at least I was undefeated. I was five feet four and still growing, and I weighed a hundred and eighty-two pounds. (69-70)

On the surface Joan seems perfectly at ease with her past to the extent that she can describe herself as '[rising] like dough', and yet by writing in this amusing and off-hand style one can see the humour functioning as a shield masking the ever-present emotional pain beneath her experience, and showing her reluctance to confront it at this stage in the novel. However, there is also an interesting tone of triumph over the mother as Joan speaks of growing 'inch by inch towards her across the dining-table', and the humour here serves to expose the futility of the position taken by the mother towards her child. This type of problematic mother-daughter relationship is explored by Carolyn Costin in her book *Your Dieting Daughter*: 'In trying to protect her daughter from becoming overweight or from being discriminated against, a mother may give an unclear message, making her daughter feel unacceptable the way she is, and thus doing more harm than good.'[300] Drawing upon Costin's observation, one can see that in the novel the mother's constant criticism of Joan's 'fat' body and her painstaking attempts to mould her daughter into an image of ideal femininity are doing Joan harm, and in this case further lay the ground for an unloving relationship which gradually evolves into a battle of power. As Jane Arthurs and Jean Grimshaw point out, 'women's bodies are entirely disciplined and constrained by the relations of power operating in society'[301], and typically the notion of power has often been explored in relations between opposite sexes. However, in *Lady Oracle*, the power struggle is between a mother and a daughter, and as such contains a different dynamic. Atwood has the mother attempting to assume a position of power over the daughter seeking to force Joan to fit into an image like her own: she tries everything to make Joan lose weight, but her efforts remain in vain as Joan 'refuses to take the pills or stick to the diets' (83). Joan's view of her mother at this stage is reflected by her words: 'she was to be the manager, the creator, the agent; I was to be the product' (67). She visualises herself in the eyes of her mother as 'the embodiment of her own failure and depression, a huge edgeless cloud of inchoate matter which refused to be shaped into anything for which she could get a prize' (67). Joan attributes her mother's frustration to her position as an unhappy woman trapped in a stifling marriage with an unwanted child, and stranded in a house which she describes as 'a plastic shrouded tomb from which there was no exit' (179-80). Even though later in her adulthood Joan feels sympathy for her mother's self-deprecation, the misery caused by the parent remains intact for a long time.

---

[300] Carolyn Costin, *Your Dieting Daughter* (New York: Brunner/ Mazel, 1997), p. 5.

[301] Jane Arthurs and Jean Grimshaw, 'Introduction', in *Women's Bodies: Discipline and Transgression*, ed. by Jane Arthurs and Jean Grimshaw (London and New York: Cassell, 1999), pp. 1-15 (p. 15).

From the mother's point of view, encouraging Joan to diet might arguably be considered a means to assist her daughter in achieving the recognition and power which she was unable to achieve. As Judith Ruskay Rabinor has stated, 'mothers do train their daughters to have access to the only power that exists: body power.'[302] However, Rabinor's assertive assumption about the attainment of female power via conforming to a socially acceptable body image is unjustified in this case, as this bodily power is not practically available to Joan's mother despite her well-preserved youthful physique. The reason behind this is that by making herself and Joan adhere to a kind of prescriptive femininity, the mother adopts a position of simple acceptance and submission to the externally imposed cultural ideals of femininity. However, that Joan initially resists her mother's efforts to 'feminise' her makes her the winner of this ongoing battle at this stage in the novel:

> I had developed the habit of clomping silently but very visibly through rooms in which my mother was sitting; it was a sort of fashion show in reverse, it was a display, I wanted her to see and recognize what little effect her nagging and pleas were having. (71)

Joan asserts her power and presence and negates her mother's expectations by becoming ample, taking as much space as possible. She eats 'to defy her' (78), and gets 'a morose pleasure from [her] weight'. Driven by antagonistic exchanges the relationship thus turns increasingly hostile. Her mother constantly attacks and humiliates her by throwing unpleasant remarks at every opportunity: 'nobody who looked like you could ever accomplish anything' (84). 'If I looked like you, I'd hide in the cellar' (88), 'Look at you, eat, eat, that's all you ever do. You're disgusting, you really are' (123-24). Her emphasis on the word 'look' is yet another indication of her preoccupation with

---

[302] Judith Ruskay Rabinor, 'Mothers, Daughters, and Eating Disorders: Honouring the Mother-Daughter Relationship', in *Feminist Perspectives on Eating Disorders*, ed. by Patricia Fallon, Melanie A. Katzman, Susan C. Wooley (New York: The Guilford Press, 1994), pp. 272-87 (p. 277).

appearance. Joan, in return for the mother's insults, preoccupies herself with a vengeful plot against her by exposing her 'excesses' as visibly as possible: 'I sought out clothes of a peculiar and offensive hideousness, violently coloured, horizontally striped' (87). Despite the mother's 'hopeless and passive' (88) cries, she enjoys her victory: 'I had defeated her. I wouldn't ever let her make me over in her image, thin and beautiful' (88).

Joan initially defines herself through hostile opposition to the mother. Marianne Hirsch describes the daughter's self-defence against the mother who threatens her integrity, which results in 'the elimination of the mother from the narrative.'[303] However, in Joan's case, when the mother's physical presence ceases, her spiritual presence takes over as a monstrous image haunting Joan's dreams, or as a ghost reminding her of her troubled memories from which she longs to escape. Joan comments on her dream of her mother as a three-headed monster as follows:

> This didn't frighten me, as it seemed merely a confirmation of something I'd always known; but outside the door there was a man, a man who was about to open the door and come in. If he saw, if he found out the truth about my mother, something terrible would happen, not only to my mother but to me.
> As I grew older, this dream changed. Instead of wanting to stop the mysterious man, I would sit there wishing for him to enter. I wanted him to find out her secret, the secret that I alone knew: my mother was a monster. (67)

In his *Interpretation of Dreams* (1911), Freud argued for the potential of dreams for providing a space for wish-fulfilment. He defined these dreams as accomodating 'pure and simple'[304] satisfaction and happiness. However, as opposed to the positive attribution of this kind of dream, there are also dreams that consist of 'justified worries, pain-

---

[303] Marianne Hirsh, *The Mother-Daughter Plot: Narrative, Psychoanalysis, Feminism* (Bloomington: Indiana University Press, 1986), p. 57.

[304] Sigmund Freud, *The Interpretation of Dreams* (1911), 'Chapter 7: The Psychology of Dream Processes: (C) The Wish-Fulfilment', trans. by A.A. Brill (New York: Macmillan, 1927), pp. 339-61, (p. 343).

ful reflections and distressing realisations.'[305] According to Freud, 'such dreams with a painful content may either be indifferent in feeling, or they may convey the whole painful affect, which the ideas contained in them seem to justify, or they may even lead to the development of anxiety.'[306] He further argues:

> Painful dreams may also be punishment dreams. It must be admitted that the recognition of these dreams adds something that is, in a certain sense, new to the theory of dreams. What is fulfilled by them is once more an unconscious wish – the wish for the punishment of the dreamer for a repressed, prohibited wish-impulse. To this extent, these dreams comply with the requirement here laid down: that the motive-power behind the dream-formation must be furnished by a wish belonging to the unconscious.[307]

Joan's dreams can be accounted for with a combination of Freud's theory of the painful and punishment dream as well as the wish-fulfilment dream. Her dream exposes the 'painful affect' of her relationship with her mother, but more importantly, it makes manifest her unconscious fear of becoming like the mother. She visualises her as a 'monster' which, on a psychic level, is an imaginary manifestation and a subconscious desire to situate the mother as the 'other', who has formerly marginalised the daughter.

Joan has the dream after watching her mother's beauty ritual in front of her vanity table, whose surface is full of 'cosmetics and implements: lipsticks, rouges, perfume in dainty bottles, bright red nail polish, little tweezers, nail files and emery boards' (65). Here, we see how the idea of her mother beautifying herself is transformed into Joan's desire to taint the mother's beauty as a vengeful retaliation for the suffering she inflicted on her when young. As a woman who values 'good looks', looking like a 'three-headed' (213) creature would be an appalling affront to her vanity. In her later years when Joan con-

---

[305] Ibid., p. 343.
[306] Ibid., p. 343.
[307] Ibid., pp. 343-44.

templates this particular dream, she wishes to let the stranger in, as she wants to make her mother's 'monstrosity' visible. Here, the mother embodies, in Atwood's words, the 'mother-monster'[308] who signifies a threat to the daughter.

In another dream Joan visualises her mother as negligent, careless and unaffectionate in matters concerning her daughter's life. In this dream, when Joan is half-way across a bridge, it starts to collapse:

> I would try to run but it would be too late, I would throw myself down and grab onto the far edge as it rose up, trying to slide me off. I called out to my mother, who could still have saved me, she could have run across quickly and reached out her hand, she could have pulled me back with her to firm ground. But she didn't do this, she went on with her conversation, she didn't notice that anything unusual was happening. She didn't even hear me. (65)

In her essay, 'Mothers and Daughters Revisited', Jane Flax has explored the conflict embedded in the relationship between mothers and daughters. She has pointed out how the mother's 'voice and touch pervade [the daughter's] senses and provide a bounded sense of space within which security and continuity become possible' but 'the same being is also the tormentor, source of denial and frustration as well as gratification.'[309] When Flax's argument is applied to Joan's relationship with her mother, it might be assumed that their relationship represents this conflicting territory of feelings. Joan's earlier dream mirrored her feelings for her mother based on fear and hatred, and the mother image was closer to the association of the mother with the 'tormentor', a rapacious, vengeful image haunting her. However, this dream represents Joan's longing for the feeling of security embedded

---

[308] Catherine Martens, 'Mother-Figures in *Surfacing* and *Lady Oracle*: An Interview with Margaret Atwood', in *American Studies in Scandinavia*, 16 (1984), 45-54 (p. 47).

[309] Jane Flax, 'Mothers and Daughters Revisited', in *Daughtering and Mothering: Female Subjectivity Reanalysed*, eds. Janneke van Mens-Verhulst, Karlein Schreurs and Liesbeth Woertman (London and New York: Routledge, 1993), pp. 145-56 (p. 148).

in motherly love and care. Here, the mother's hand arguably signifies a warm and tender touch that saves the daughter. Yet, in her dream the mother ignores the daughter's cry for help. As Melanie Klein argued, 'the conflict between love and hate plays an important role in the mother-daughter relationship'[310] which results in the 'splitting' of the mother as 'good' (as the source of pleasure), and 'bad' (as the source of frustration). As Klein explained, 'splitting is one way of preserving the good object and the good impulses against the dangerous and frightening destructive impulses which create retaliatory objects.'[311] In Joan's case, particularly in her childhood, the mother is mostly perceived as a persecutory figure. It is significant to note that Joan later replaces this image of the mother as a threatening object with a 'kind and placid [one] who died of a rare disease' (41). This romanticised relocation of the mother in the realm of the 'good' object could be read as Joan's desire to compensate for the mother's lack of love and care, with an idealised vision of an affectionate and protective mother who counterpoints the 'bad' mother. As she says: 'My mother seldom touched me. Her hands were delicate and long-fingered with red nails, her hair carefully arranged; no nests for me among those stiff immaculate curls' (89). Unable to earn the love of her mother, Joan, as Sarah Sceats suggests, 'feels nurtured by Aunt Lou in ways she never does with her own mother'[312], and she pretends that Aunt Louise is her real mother. As Margaret Atwood states: '*Lady Oracle* is all about motherfigures. [...] *Lady Oracle* is a search for "the real mother."'[313] The desire for the mother is made explicit in Joan's relationship with Aunt Lou who for Joan acts as a surrogate mother. Despite the fact that

---

[310] Melanie Klein, 'On Mental Health', in *Envy and Gratitude and Other Works 1946-1963* (New York: Delacorte Press, 1975), pp. 268-74, (p. 271).
[311] Ibid., p. 273.
[312] Sarah Sceats, *Food, Consumption and the Body in Contemporary Women's Fiction* (Cambridge: Cambridge University Press, 2000), p. 101.
[313] Margaret Atwood cited in Shannon Hengen, *Margaret Atwood's Power: Mirrors, Reflections and Images in Select Fiction and Poetry* (Toronto: Second Story, 1993), p. 66.

Aunt Lou does not have a long-lasting impact on Joan as her mother, she still satisfies her need for motherly love: 'My mother didn't hold me by the hand, there were her gloves to think of' (89), but Aunt Lou would hold her by the hand. She is, as Joan says, 'was soft, billowy, woolly, befurred' (89), and a lot less bitter and frustrated' (83) than her 'menacing and cold' (214) mother.

On another level, Joan feels closer to Aunt Lou in terms of physical resemblance, as Aunt Lou is also 'tall and heavy' (80). Furthermore the aunt has an air of freedom: she likes to decorate her voluptuous body with extravagant accessories which 'made her look even taller and fatter' (81), which she has never minded. For Joan the time she spent with her aunt has been 'among the happiest moments of [her] childhood' (81), and it is during this time that Joan develops an interest in the idea of romance. She is particularly interested in happy endings: 'I was a sucker for ads, especially those that promised happiness' (29), and this can be further traced in her fondness for the formulaic 1940s and 1950s Hollywood romance movies she watches with Aunt Lou. Yet, it might well be argued that watching these movies, which feature attractive, slender ladies in 'beautiful costumes' (82), lead to Joan's gradual dislike of her body and her increasing awareness of how far she is removed from the physical perfection of glamorous actresses such as 'June Allyson, Judy Garland, Eleanor Parker' (81) whom she admires passionately. She says: 'I was quite fat by this time and all fat women look the same, they all look forty-two. Also fat women are not more noticeable than thin women; they are less noticeable, because people find them distressing and look away' (82). Joan re-emphasises this in a further passage:

> If Desdemona was fat who would care whether or not Othello strangled her? Why is it that the girls Nazis torture on the covers of the sleazier men's magazines are always good-looking? The effect would be quite different if they were overweight. The men would find it hilarious instead of immoral or sexually titillating. (52)

The unifying factor in these images is the endearing vulnerability of the heroines, and here Joan observes that a fat woman is unable to fulfil this role in the eyes of the culturally conditioned observer. Her bigness presents a barrier to bringing out the feelings of protective sympathy from the viewer. Thus, Joan's dislike of her own image can be attributed to the strong influence that these cultural representations of femininity have on her. Consequently, her concept of what women should aspire to seems to be limited by those stereotypes that form the normative idea of beauty. The more she immerses herself in romanticised images of femininity, the more she realises the cultural fat/thin dichotomy, and the social tendency to render fat women invisible. However, Joan wants to retain her visibility. At a young age, she expresses a desire to perform on stage. First she aspires to be like 'opera singers' whom she thinks '[are] loved and praised even though they [are] fat' (78), and later, after watching *The Red Shoes* she wants to become 'a dancer' (82). Indeed, Joan does have some experience in dancing; however it turns out to be far from her ideal dance performance resulting in total frustration and humiliation and traumatising Joan for life. As an overweight child, she looks 'grotesque in the short pink skirt, with [her] waist, arms and legs exposed' (46). For Joan's mother and Miss Flegg (the teacher), both of whom are 'slender and disapproving' (43), Joan in the short pink skirt exposes the body's potential for chaos and excess, which for them have to be taken under 'control'. Finding Joan's 'grotesque' appearance unfit for the dance performance 'Butterfly Frolic', Joan is made to act as a 'mothball' (48) instead of her dream role as the butterfly. Even though Joan is not quite satisfied with her own image – 'it wasn't quite the effect I wanted. I did not look like a butterfly. But I knew the addition of the wings would make all the difference' (46) – she nonetheless did not think of taking off 'her cloudy skirt and spangles and put on one of the white teddy-bear costumes' (48), and wearing around her neck 'a large sign that said MOTHBALL' (48-49). Joan initially ascribes the humiliating transformation from the butterfly into the mothball to her mother's interference:

> As I was putting on my butterfly costume, I saw my mother standing beside [Miss Flegg].
> She was supposed to be out in the front row where I'd left her. [...] But now she was talking with Miss Flegg. Miss Flegg looked over at me; then she walked over, followed by my mother. She stood gazing down at me, her lips pressed together. 'I see what you mean', she said to my mother. [...] What they were both seeing was [Miss Flegg's] gay, artistic, *spiritual* 'Butterfly Frolic' being reduced to something laughable and unseemly by the presence of a fat little girl who was more like a giant caterpillar than a butterfly. (47)

Joan's dance of 'rage and destruction' (50) is interpreted by the audience as a comic entertainment to be applauded, however, this experience emotionally scars her, as she later expresses: 'I was wounded, desolated' (48). The traumatic effects of this experience later capture Joan's adulthood in which she is haunted by the image of 'a fat lady' in pink costumes whom she imagines as performing miraculous acts using her body, or as simply being reduced to the object of gaze, laughter and ridicule. However, the particular visibility that Joan renders to this 'fat lady' represents adult, slim Joan's compliance with her society's dislike of fat which she is painfully taught in her childhood. It is worth examining adult Joan's interpretation of the dance performance:

> I am reconstructing this from the point of view of an adult, an anxious, prudish adult like my mother or Miss Flegg; but with my jiggly thighs and the bulges of fat where breasts would later be and my plump upper arms and floppy waist, I must have looked obscene, senile, almost indecent; it must have been like watching a decaying stripper. I was the kind of child, they would have thought back then in the early months of 1949, who should not be seen in public with so little clothing on. No wonder I fell in love with the nineteenth century: back then, according to the dirty postcards of the time, flesh was a virtue. (46)

Joan's choice of words to describe her body such as 'jiggly', 'bulges', 'plump', 'floppy', 'obscene', 'senile', 'indecent', 'decaying stripper' counterpoints her earlier assertion, 'I like being fat' (83). As the above extract suggests, the adult Joan, after losing her excess, seems to sympathise with her mother and dance teacher's unflattering views of her 'fatness', which further affirms Joan's collusion with her present culture's norms of acceptable femininity, and her discontentment with her former 'fat' self. The extract can also be interpreted as a clash between Joan's present and past selves. Whilst the slim Joan is in complicity with her present society's views of 'fatness', which tends to associate 'fatness' with 'deviance', 'disorder' and 'chaos', the 'fat' Joan has a nostalgia for the past, in particular, for the nineteenth-century aesthetic, where fatness was usually regarded as a symbol of social status and wealth. It is interesting to contrast Joan's romanticised view of nineteenth-century attitudes towards obesity with the reality of this period. Whilst it is true that fatness was a 'culturally acceptable mode of embodiment'[314] during this period, some opinions were shifting towards intolerance. For instance William Banting's 1863 pamphlet *A Letter on Corpulence*[315] documents the ills of 'obesity', and can be regarded as an example of the changing Victorian attitudes toward embodiment. Yet, Joan's idealised view of this century does not acknowledge this emerging fat-phobia, and could therefore be regarded as a form of escapist fantasy. Furthermore, the adult Joan does not seem to understand 'fat' as a social construct. Even while she is narrating her painful and traumatic experience at the dance performance from the point of view of her adult self, she has a disinclination to acknowledge the powerful influence of her society on her understanding about her self-image. She does not seem to realise the

---

[314] Joyce L. Huff, 'A "Horror of Corpulence"', in *Bodies Out of Bounds: Fatness and Transgression*, ed. by Jane Evans Braziel and Kathleen LeBesco (Berkeley, Los Angeles, London: University of California Press, 2001), pp. 39-60 (p. 39).

[315] Banting's pamphlet opens with his statement: 'Of all the parasites that affect humanity, I do not know of, nor can I imagine, anymore distressing than that of obesity'. [*A Letter on Corpulence*: London: Harrison, 1864), p. 5].

mechanisms lurking beneath her traumatic experiences with her 'fat' embodiment at this stage in her narrative.

The humiliation of being the 'mothball' is not the only trauma Joan experiences because of her weight. The cruel attitude of her female friends in her early adulthood is yet another unpleasant experience that reinforces Shelley Bovey's argument that 'fat is not a feminist issue.'[316] Bovey argues:

> Other women are very often fat women's worst enemies. Whoever sets the standard of thinness as the ideal, it is women who rush to attain it at whatever cost and who often denigrate and patronise those of us who do not 'belong' in this way.[317]

Joan's experience with the Brownies, who take delight in punishing her for her deviation from 'feminine' behaviour, for 'skipping too heavily in the fairy ring', for 'having dirty fingernails', and for 'being fat' (59), exemplifies Bovey's observation. More importantly, the girls' uniform hostility towards Joan represents a microcosmic version of a society which makes deviation from prescribed femininity unacceptable. It is not a surprise that Joan later adopts a compensating personality as 'kindly aunt' (93), and 'a fat duenna' (94) to her female friends to eliminate stigma and humiliation, she says: 'No one shouted things at me on the street; no one who went to our school, at any rate' (94). However, by adopting a role for the sake of acceptance, she becomes her own tormentor, as she forces herself to behave in a certain way which is out of her personality:

> I was a sponge, I drank it all in but gave nothing out, despite the temptation to tell everything, all my hatred and jealousy, to reveal myself as the duplicitous monster I knew myself to be. I could just barely stand it. (95)

---

[316] Shelley Bovey, *The Forbidden Body: Why Being Fat is not a Sin* (London: Pandora, 1994), p. ix.
[317] Ibid., p. ix.

Being a fat girl in a social environment which is highly preoccupied with 'good looks', there are three options for Joan: she will either continue being the 'fat duenna', 'Miss Personality' (35) or risk being unfairly stereotyped as the other fat girls at her school, or lose weight. Aunt Lou's death and the statement in her will which is a promise of inheritance on the condition that Joan loses a hundred pounds fuels her decision to go on a diet despite her feelings of disappointment towards her aunt. About Aunt Lou's will, Joan says:

> How was I to interpret it? Did it mean she hadn't really accepted me for what I was, as I thought she had – that she too found me grotesque, that for her also I would not do? Or was it just pragmatism on her part, her realization that I would have an easier life if I were thinner? She's offered me the money to get away, to escape from my mother, as she knew I wished to do; but on terms that would force me to capitulate, or so it seemed. (121)

For Joan, the condition that Aunt Lou has set in her will brings about the idea of leaving one form of submission for another. Although she could use the money to get away from a bullying mother, this would also mean changing her image into a more acceptable one. More importantly, what wounds her above all is to see her own image in her confidante's eyes. She thinks Aunt Lou has found her 'grotesque'. Here, the word is used to denote repulsion and disgust, and it hardly resonates with Bakhtin's account of the grotesque, where the notion of excess means transgression and power. Joan uses her fleshy embodiment as a site of power only in her relationship with her mother:

> I would have welcomed the chance to embarrass her, strangers were different, they saw my obesity as an unfortunate handicap, like a hump or a club foot, rather than the refutation, the victory it was, and watching myself reflected in their eyes shook my confidence. It was only in relation to my mother that I derived a morose pleasure from my weight; in relation to everyone else, including my father, it made me miserable. But I couldn't stop. (74)

This extract explicitly relates Joan's 'obesity' as a purposeful act against her mother, however as she starts to internalise the cultural implications of 'excessive' embodiment which is often explained in terms of a physical and moral 'defect', she begins to express her discontent with her body in rather derogatory terms:

> I happened to glance down at my body. [...] I didn't usually look at my body, in a mirror or in any other way; I snuck a glance at parts of it now and then, but the whole thing was too overwhelming. There, staring me in the face, was my thigh. It was enormous, it was gross, it was like a diseased limb, the kind you see in pictures of jungle natives; it spread on forever, like a prairie photographed from a plane, the flesh not green but bluish-white, with veins meandering across it like rivers. (121)

Here, the idea of self-gaze is significant and can be explained in relation to its theorisation by Foucault. According to Foucault, 'an inspecting gaze' is 'a gaze which each individual under its weight will end by interiorising to the point that he is his own overseer, each individual thus exercising this surveillance over and against himself.'[318] Foucault's study, which is based on the idea of Panopticon as one way to establish and maintain social discipline in 'dealing with a multiplicity of individuals on whom a task or a particular form of behaviour must be imposed'[319], finds its resonance in the disciplining of the female body where the individual becomes 'the principle of [his/her] own subjection.'[320] As the above extract suggests, Joan's gaze over her body is a form of self-surveillance and is indicative of her desire to correct it. However, she does not come to view her body as 'gross' on the grounds of her personal judgement. According to Carole Spitzack, 'power mechanisms require women [...] to see themselves as they are seen through the eyes of the collective and normalising prac-

---

[318] Michel Foucault, 'The Eye of Power', in *Power/Knowledge: Selected Interviews & Other Writings 1972-1977*, ed. and trans. by Colin Gordon (Harlow: Longman, 1980), pp. 146-66, (p. 155).
[319] Foucault, *Discipline and Punish*, p. 205.
[320] Ibid., pp. 202-03.

tices within culture.'[321] Orbach further expands this notion of self-gaze performed as a way of conforming to normative regulations of femininity:

> John Berger's prescient statement that (bourgeois) women watch themselves being looked at has been transmuted into women assuming the gaze of the observer, looking at themselves from outside and finding that they continually fail to meet the expectations our pervasive and persuasive visual culture demands.'[322]

Drawing upon these observations, it might be argued that Joan's gaze is an interiorised reflection of her culture's judgement of her body. It is after this culturally-inflicted close gaze at her body that Joan starts to see her fatness as 'revolting' (122) and feels the urge to reconstruct herself in a slim body. However, through internalising the cultural gaze, she becomes the source of her own restriction, and thus takes up her mother's world of normative limitations. As Susan Bordo has argued, '"the slender body" has become a symbol of correct attitude, it means that one "cares" about oneself and how one appears to others, suggesting willpower, energy, control over infantile impulse, the ability to "make something" of oneself.'[323] With her decision to go on a diet, Joan in fact complies with this implication of the slender body seeking approval. She wants to make a new beginning with a new, socially acceptable image of herself. She takes fat pills, laxatives whose side effects cause 'blinding headaches, stomach cramps, accelerated heartbeat, an alarming clarity of vision, and fits of weakness' (122). She willingly accepts this self-inflicted torture as a penance for being fat. She desperately wants to bury her painful memories in which she has been teased, bullied and rejected because of her size. As soon as she starts to lose weight her battle with her mother moves to a different platform. Formerly, her enormous body has been a triumph

---

[321] Carole Spitzack, *Confessing Excess: Women and the Politics of Body Reduction* (New York: State University of New York Press, 1990), p. 47.
[322] Orbach, *Bodies*, p. 87.
[323] Bordo, 'Reading the Slender Body', pp. 94-95.

over her mother's desire to 'feminise' her. However, now that Joan is turning into her mother's desired image of the 'ideal' body the relationship between them gets even more tense and uneasy. One of the reasons beneath the mounting tension could be ascribed to the fact that the mother can no longer exert her control over her daughter's appetite, and she feels a sense of powerlessness against Joan's dedicated attempt to lose weight. As Joan says: 'She went on baking sprees and left pies and cookies around the kitchen where they would tempt me, and it struck me that in a lesser way she has always done this' (123). These actions are revealing in that they show how the power struggle between the mother and the daughter has been based around food and how Joan's fatness is a mechanism by which the mother can reproach her and thus maintain power over her. When Joan starts to lose weight this is removed, and we see the mother having lost all power over her:

> While I grew thinner, she herself became distraught and uncertain. She was drinking quite heavily now and she began to forget where she had put things. [...] At times she would almost plead with me to stop taking the pills, to take better care of myself; then she would have spasms of rage, a dishevelled piecemeal rage unlike her former purposeful fury. (123)

Another reason for the mother's loss of power can be attributed to her feelings of inefficacy. At first Joan puts on weight despite her mother's attempts to the contrary, but later she loses weight without her parent's enforcement and help. This gradually pushes the mother away from the battlefield where Joan's body has been the former 'disputed territory', and brings about a role-reversal. In the war against her mother, Joan moves away from her victimised position whilst her antagonist is left to confront defeat.

3.1.2 From 'Fat' to 'Thin': Reversals, Reconciliations, and Confrontations

Joan experiences a different role-reversal when her shrunken body starts to stimulate a kind of attention that is new to her: 'Strange men, whose gaze had previously slid over and around me as though I wasn't there, began to look at me from truck-cab windows and construction sites' (123). The more she loses weight, the more this gaze indicates sexual undertones. She says: 'Men didn't make passes at fat girls, so I had no experience' (140). This echoes Weldon's Bobbo in *The Life and Loves of a She-Devil*, who hypothetically thinks that Ruth could not be considered a 'natural rape victim'[324] because of her physical appearance. However, for Joan, 'plump unattractive women are just as likely to be tortured as thin ones. More so, in fact' (52). Here, Joan might be referring to the emotional strain resulting from the stigmatisation of the 'obese' female. From Joan's own experiences with her 'excessive' embodiment, we can see the destructive attitudes of those around her which have led her to suffer intense feelings of humiliation to the point that she felt she was tortured. However, there is a shift in Joan's persona after she slims down. She starts to collude with the assumption that fat is ugly and repulsive, and adopts the position of her former oppressors, most particularly her mother, towards her embodiment. By realigning herself with her former oppressors, Joan adopts a position which Paulo Freire has describes thus: 'the oppressed, instead of striving for liberation, tend themselves to become oppressors.'[325] Freire goes on to highlight the notion of this 'prescription' in this process:

> One of the basic elements of the relationship between oppressor and oppressed is *prescription*. Every prescription represents the imposition of one individual's choice upon another, transforming the consciousness of the person prescribed to into one that conforms with the prescriber's consciousness. Thus, the behaviour of the oppressed is a prescribed behaviour, following as it does the guidelines of the oppressor.[326]

---

[324] Weldon, *The Life and Loves of a She-Devil*, p. 33.
[325] Paulo Freire, *Pedagogy of the Oppressed*, trans. by Myra Bergman Ramos (New York, London: Continuum International, 2000 [1970]), p. 45.
[326] Ibid., p. 46-47.

Freire's conceptualisation of the interdependent dynamics between the oppressor and the oppressed could well be accommodated in the discussion of oppressive relationships that develop around 'excessive' embodiment, where the oppressed by 'following the guidelines of the oppressor' metamorphose into oppressors themselves. In this case, the oppressed is the inhabitant of bodily excess, and the oppressor is the one that makes the oppressed uncomfortable with her body. Joan's relationship with her mother exemplifies this structural relationship. Even though Joan resists her mother's oppressive attitudes to control her weight in her childhood, by reducing in size she conforms to her parent's ideals and internalises the image of the oppressor. Yet, in doing so, instead of repelling the oppressor, she becomes an oppressor of her former 'obese' embodiment herself. This is clearly shown as Joan describes her body in pejorative terms, for example as a 'fat mongoloid idiot' (180), 'single enormous breast' (99), 'gargantuan' (101). Her negative self-image is a projection of the mother's cultural conditioning which measures female corpulence in rather heterosexist terms viewing it against the mainstream standards of beauty. Her mother's cruel remark, 'who would think of marrying a mothball?' (51), and the psychiatrist's question, 'don't you want to get married'? (83), exemplify the pressures in Joan's social environment which considers fatness unattractive, and fat women less likely to marry.

The moment Joan starts to lose weight, and look more 'feminine' according to her culture's beauty norms, she begins to be more visible. Although in her formerly 'obese' state she harboured a yearning to be seen and noticed, in her later slim form she is not content with the kind of visibility she acquires: 'without my magic cloak of blubber and invisibility I felt naked, pruned, as though some essential covering was missing' (141). This gaze is different from what she has experienced in the past when she was the target of a sort of ambiguous gaze which was either avoiding or dismissive. Formerly she experienced two forms of the gaze. The first one involves her position as the object of the gaze at the dance performance, which made her visible as a cultural oddity or joke and which she viewed as a 'humiliation disguised as a privilege' (50). The second includes her imagined subject-position as the spectator of the 'Fat Lady' whom she subconsciously identifies herself with. Her first encounter with this woman happens at the Canadian National Exhibition, where Aunt Lou does not allow Joan to see the Fat Lady as she thinks that 'it's wrong to laugh at other people's misfortunes' (90). Joan recalls:

> I found this unfair: other people laughed at mine, I should get a chance too. But then, nobody regarded being fat as a misfortune; it was viewed simply as a disgusting failure of will. It wasn't fated and therefore glamorous, like being a Siamese twin or living in an iron lung. (90)

Here, Joan's views reflect a social tendency that attributes fatness to a personality defect, to over-indulgence. To retaliate against this social construction, Joan renders a stronger subject position to the 'Fat Lady', whom she imagines as an efficient, wilful woman who is not ashamed of her size, but who 'would rebel one day' (90).

Joan tends to identify herself with the 'Fat Lady', but after she slims down, she internalises cultural views about weight and her unconscious fears of excess start to haunt her through her other fantasies of the 'Fat Lady' in which she pictures her as an object of the gaze and ridicule. The fact that Joan herself has been a victim of the degrading stereotype does not hold her back from imagining the 'Fat Lady' in situations where she posits shame and humiliation. Her earlier fantasy of her as a rebellious woman is now replaced by an image as a reminder of Joan's troubled memories with her body. 'Fat' Joan disappears physically, however, as in Madeleine Davies words, her fat 'melts away to reappear magically as 'another kind of text'[327], a text that makes her unconscious speak and release the painful images re-

---

[327] Madeleine Davies, 'Margaret Atwood's Female Bodies', in *The Cambridge Companion to Margaret Atwood*, ed. by Coral Ann Howells (Cambridge: Cambridge University Press, 2006), pp. 58-71 (p. 65).

lated to her traumatic 'obese' childhood. It is not surprising that she visualises the Fat Lady as a dancer, figure skater or a tightrope walker, all of which allude to Joan's childhood dream of artistic visibility. However, her fantasies also manifest her fluctuation between individual fantasy and the social reality which she lives in. For instance, she pictures the Fat Lady as performing difficult acts, which opposes the idea of holding excess as an obstacle to such physical activities. However, at the end of her fantasies, Joan reduces her to a deplorable sight of ridicule, which implies her confinement to the strictures of her society that disapproves of 'excessive' embodiment, which she herself experienced first hand. We can clearly see her ambivalent view of the Fat Lady as both an object of admiration and derision in two of her fantasies where the Fat Lady is an ice skater and a tight rope walker:

> The Fat Lady skated out onto the ice [...] in a pink skating costume. [...] She smiled at the crowd, nobody smiled back, they didn't believe what they were seeing because she was whirling around the rink with exceptional grace, spinning like a top on her tiny feet, then the thin man lifted her and threw her and she floated up, up, she hung suspended. Her secret was that although she was so large she was very light, she was hollow, like a helium balloon, they had to keep her tethered to her bed or she'd drift away, all night she strained at the ropes. (273-74)

This image of the Fat Lady becoming a weightless figure is reminiscent of Winterson's constructions of the weightless, floating, dancing princess Fortunata, and the huge Dog Woman, who can be small and invisible at will. As I discussed in the previous chapter, in Winterson's representation of her female protagonists their large or weightless bodies transgress corporeal limitations and give visible form to an ideal, liberating position outside normalising cultural requirements. In Winterson, 'excessive' embodiment signifies power and is perhaps suggestive of an archetypal Mother Goddess image, an image that becomes an alter ego for the slim ecologist. However, in Atwood's text, excess carries a negative connotation and becomes indicative of a repressed other. As Joan points out, she could have identified herself with this idealised image of a huge Goddess[328] as an epitome of power, fertility and serenity in her former 'obese' state. However, Joan rejects this in her slim form: 'My ability to give was limited, I was not inexhaustible. I was not serene' (253). Thus, Joan's unwillingness to be associated with this image displays her contradictory insights. By refusing this image, she might be assumed to be expelling an idealised image of femininity that risks restricting her into an essentialist standpoint and reducing femaleness to women's capacity to bear children. For Marilyn Patton, Joan's reluctance to be associated with this image 'trivialises the powerful Goddess image, and takes power over her.'[329] Patton bases her argument in relation to Joan's perception of the Goddess, which, as Joan's narration exposes, is a combination of indifference and insignificance: 'I stood licking my ice-cream cone, watching the Goddess coldly' (253). Indeed, Joan can be assumed to be dismissing the Goddess as trivial by defining it solely as a symbol of fertility rather than recognising the power inherent in the image. She does not 'take power' over this idea of a strong and serene Goddess, rejecting an association with it on the grounds of the femininity she sees the image as representing.

The cultural implications that get written on the female body vary according to different social and historical contexts. However, one thing beyond dispute is the fact that even though the patterns of femininity change in time, there have always been ideal images, either fat and fertile, or slender and elegant, that women have been expected to fit. In Joan's social landscape, what was formerly considered as the ideal becomes a site of shame. She does not want to identify herself with this image of a fat lady as a Goddess, because she knows from her experiences that in her own social reality, 'fat' does not denote an ideal image of beauty or power. Thus, her anxiety of excess as repre-

---

[328] Here, the Goddess that Joan refers to is Diana of Ephesus, whose multiple breasts in the shape of grapes have often been associated with fertility.
[329] Marilyn Patton, '*Lady Oracle*: The Politics of the Body', in *Ariel*, 22:4 (1991), 29-48 (p. 38).

sented by her fantasies of the Fat Lady indicates an impasse between individual fantasy and social reality. This controversy is made explicit here:

> In this one I was sitting in a circus tent. It was dark, something was about to happen. [...] Suddenly a spotlight cut through the blackness and focused on a tiny platform at the top of the tent. Upon it stood the Fat Lady from the freak show at the Canadian National Exhibition. She was even fatter then I imagined her. [...] She was wearing pink tights with spangles, a short fluffy pink skirt, satin ballet slippers and, on her head, a sparkling tiara. She carried a diminutive pink umbrella; this was a substitute for the wings which I longed to pin on her. Even in my fantasies I remained faithful to a few ground rules of reality.
> The crowd burst out laughing. They howled, pointed and jeered; they chanted insulting songs. But the Fat Lady, oblivious, began to walk carefully out onto the high wire. (102-03)

This variation of her Fat Lady fantasy is again interrupted by Joan's understanding of a social reality which disapproves of excess. Here, she pictures the Fat Lady having the face of her class-mate Theresa, her 'despised fellow-sufferer' (103), who has been teased because of her weight. Even though Joan tries to avoid associating herself with this image of a fat girl as the object of the gaze and of laughter, the experience of the Fat Lady in her fantasy bears a resemblance to her painful childhood memory at the dance performance. Her fantasy of the Fat Lady further brings to mind Freud's explanation of the return of a repressed memory in relation to the uncanny. In his essay 'The Uncanny' (1919), Freud argued that

> the subject of the uncanny is undoubtedly related to what is frightening – to what arouses dread and horror; equally certainly, too, the word is not always used in a clearly definable sense, so that it tends to coincide with what excites fear in general. The uncanny is that class of the frightening which leads back to what is known of old and long familiar. [...] It may be true that the uncanny [*unheimlich*] is something which is secretly familiar [*heimlich–heimisch*], which has undergone

repression and then returned from it, and that everything that is uncanny fulfils this condition.[330]

In many ways, Joan's fantasy of the Fat Lady as a reminder of her traumatic memories of excess has parallels with Freud's theorisation of the uncanny as the revival of a fearful experience. Her fantasy of the Fat Lady performing in front of an audience, and her 'pink umbrella' as a substitute for the 'wings', is suggestive of her unrealised dance performance as a 'butterfly', which marks her utmost traumatic experience. In her fantasy, she posits the Fat Lady in a similar position where the Fat Lady becomes the object of laughter. That is one of the reasons why Joan gives Theresa's face to the Fat Lady, as she does not want to re-experience her former humiliation. She contemplates her husband Arthur analysing this fantasy and saying: 'how much better for me if I'd been accepted for what I was and had learned to accept myself, too' (103). However, the past is unknown to Arthur, and for Joan it is inescapable. As she writes:

> When I looked at myself in the mirror, I didn't see what Arthur saw. The outline of my former body still surrounded me, like a mist, like a phantom moon, like the image of Dumbo the Flying Elephant superimposed on my own. I wanted to forget the past, but it refused to forget me; it waited for sleep, then cornered me. (214)

For Joan, it is 'not so simple' (103) to come to terms with her former self. The fat that once was her weapon against her mother's slender femininity now represents a part of herself that she sees as incongruous with her present, socially acceptable image that she has constructed to please others. More importantly, underneath her fear of being found out is her fear of social exclusion, and being held in low regard because of her past image, a fear which also suggests a critique of weight stigma and its potentially destructive impact on one's self-esteem. Joan epitomises this fear of rejection and humiliation that may

---

[330] Sigmund Freud, 'The Uncanny', in *The Standard Edition of the Complete Psychological Works of Sigmund Freud*, trans. and ed. by James Strachey, 24 vols (London: Hogarth Press, 1966-1974), vol. 17, 217-256 (p. 237).

unfairly be inflicted on one because of one's embodiment. Her imprisonment in a traumatic past influences her present state of mind. She lives in constant fear and anxiety worrying and speculating about her image in people's eyes.

The source of her fears, as I have discussed, has its origins in the past in relation to her painful memories of her mother, who wanted everything in her life to be 'acceptable' (70), the dance performance and her relationships with her friends. The continual mockery due to her embodiment has taught her to endure being noticed only as a 'joke', despite her childhood desire to acquire visibility as a ballet dancer. She goes through a reverse dilemma in her adult life. That is to say, even though she loses her excess, and gains a socially acceptable image, she does not want to be visible or to be noticed. She starts to experience a self-inflicted repression that revolves around her painstaking attempts to repress her past memories. This can be attributed to the ill-treatment she experienced in her interpersonal relationships, which damages her self-image leading her to be in perpetual fear and anxiety about being recognized. When Arthur sees a picture of her, she immediately gets defensive and lies to him saying the woman in the picture is her Aunt Deirdre who, as Joan says, 'ate too much' (91). The fact that she relates her former fatness to 'overconsumption' is just another example of Joan's entrapment in cultural assumptions against fatness, which further exposes her fear of being stigmatised and rejected. That is why she becomes frantic every time she encounters someone from her former life. When she finds out that Leda Sprott, the spiritual medium, is the wedding minister, she panics: 'She looked me straight in the face, and I could tell she knew exactly who I was. I moaned and closed my eyes' (202). She begs her not to tell Arthur about her past 'shape', she cannot even say the word 'fat' (207). Although she had the courage to defy her mother, in her adulthood she becomes, in Margery Fee's words, 'a panic-stricken conformist'[331] who is frightened to lose the love of her man because of her past image. She reacts similarly when she meets Marlene, one of the Brownies who used to torment her. She hopes that her former tormenter does not remember her as a fat Brownie. It is ironic that even though ideally it should be Marlene who is ashamed of ganging upon Joan, it is Joan who feels shame because of her obese adolescence. Yet, the fact that Marlene does not remember Joan induces contradictory thoughts. On the one hand, Joan does not want to be recognised, on the other she feels resentment for not being remembered by Marlene. She says: 'It seemed very unjust that an experience so humiliating to me hadn't touched her at all' (230), which further reinstates Joan's former invisibility despite her visible embodiment.

Joan's entrapment in her past and her inability to reconcile it with her present identity becomes increasingly evident in her fantasies of the Fat Lady. As Freud stated in his essay 'Creative Writers and Day-Dreaming' (1908), 'a happy person never fantasizes, only an unsatisfied one. The motive forces of fantasies are unsatisfied wishes, and every single fantasy is the fulfilment of a wish, a correction of unsatisfying reality.'[332] Likewise for Joan, fantasy functions as a way of escaping a painful past. However, even in her fantasies, her longing to replace her past with 'a different, a more agreeable one' (141) remains futile, as her fear of excess is constantly erupted by the image of the Fat Lady.

> My old daydreams about the Fat Lady returned, only this time she'd be walking across her tightrope, in her pink tutu, and she'd fall in slow motion, turning over and over on the way down....Or she'd be dancing on a stage in her harem costume and her red slippers. But it wouldn't be a dance at all, it would be a striptease, she'd start taking

---

[331] Margery Fee, *The Fat Lady Dances: Margaret Atwood's Lady Oracle* (Toronto: ECW Press, 1993), p. 39.
[332] Sigmund Freud, 'Creative Writers and Day-Dreaming', in *The Standard Edition of the Complete Psychological Works of Sigmund Freud*, trans. and ed. by James Strachey, 24 vols (London: Hogarth Press and the Institute of Psycho-Analysis, 1966-1974), 9, pp. 143-54 (p. 146).

off her clothes, [...] but no one would whistle, no one would yell *Take it off baby*. (251)

In a related fantasy Joan imagines herself being kept in a cage, fattened up, and forced to wear black satin underwear:

> Would they charge admission to the men of the town, would I become one of those Fellini whores, gigantic and shapeless? [...] I didn't want to spend the rest of my life in a cage, as a fat whore, a captive Earth Mother for whom somebody else collected the admission tickets. (328-29)

Joan's fantasies of the fat lady are significant, as they not only reveal her fear of excess, but are also readable as a critique of the ways in which female embodiment is made the object of male control and a 'grotesque' spectacle for male voyeuristic interest. In this respect, the representation of the 'fat lady' in the novel does not only evoke a resistance to the social construction of femininity, but it also expresses an anxiety about the commodification of the 'excessive' female embodiment. Hence, the visibility of the female body in this fashion signifies yet another manipulative control mechanism over the female body which is constructed as an object for financial profit.

Viewed from another perspective, Joan's fantasy of the carnival Fat Lady in circus settings arguably evokes the 'gay parody of official reason'[333] that Bakhtin associated with the transgressive energies of the carnival. However, in Joan's case, her fantasies of the Fat Lady can hardly be considered liberating or subversive, as they are a constant reminder of her painful memories which she longs to forget. More importantly, for Bakhtin the carnival spirit incarnates the unconscious desire to violate rules and norms. However, as Kim Worthington suggests, 'subversive subconscious energies, by definition, remain below the level of consciousness, unharnessable towards the achievement of deliberately conceived revisionary ends.'[334] Atwood's con-

---

[333] Bakhtin, *Rabelais and His World*, p. 39.
[334] Kim L. Worthington, *Self as Narrative: Subjectivity and Community in Contemporary Fiction* (Oxford: Clarendon Press, 1996), p. 287.

struction of Joan as a woman who struggles to reconcile her subversive energies as represented in her past with her later conformist profile epitomises Worthington's challenge to Bakhtin's idealisation of the carnival as a subversive site. As we see, Joan is very much repressed by her social mask. Even her fantasies of the Fat Lady are repressed, as they embody the negative cultural construction of the obese female body which is reduced to being the object of the gaze and/or laughter. There is a constant struggle between the notion of conformity represented by Joan's slender image, and her unruly fat past, which she associates with pain and resentment, and which she avoids confronting. However, while she cannot confront her fat past in her social reality, the textual space provided by the act of writing enables her to do this. That is to say writing serves as an agent to bring Joan's unconscious fears to the surface (particularly the fear of excess and of the mother) and make them comprehensible to Joan.

It is no wonder that Joan resorts to the Gothic genre both as a reader and writer, as the emblematic fear within Gothic fantasy corresponds with her own psychology. According to Coral Howells, recurrent Gothic motifs include 'fear of ghosts, women's fear of men, fear of the dark, fear of what is hidden but might leap out unexpectedly, fear of something floating around loose which lurks behind the everyday.'[335] In many ways, Joan's writing, particularly her experiments in automatic writing which produce her 'Lady Oracle' poems, becomes a medium through which she projects her fears, those which unveil her fear of her mother, and the pressure to live up to her ideals. Interestingly, in her first experiment with automatic writing, Joan jots down the word 'bow' (220), which is suggestive of submission. Later in her 'Lady Oracle' poems, the idea of submission reappears:

> She is one and there
> The dark lady   the redgold lady
> the blank lady   oracle of blood,

---

[335] Coral Ann Howells, *Margaret Atwood* (Houndmills, Basingstoke, Hampshire, New York: Palgrave Macmillan, 2005 [1996]), p. 52.

she who must be
obeyed   forever (226)

Here, the notion of submission is ascribed to an image of a powerful woman who 'must be obeyed'. Joan's writing of this 'enormously powerful' (222) woman, it might be argued, bears some resemblance to Cixous's promotion of a feminine writing which 'surpass[es] the discourse that regulates the phallocentric system'[336], and thus reclaims women's power. For Cixous, this practice of writing plays a significant role in refusing the textual objectification of women. Joan's automatic writing initially operates on a similar motive. As opposed to her early Gothic Romances in which she creates her heroines compliant with normative regulations of femininity (that is they are sexy, demure, passive) prevalent in her culture, her 'Lady Oracle' poems point towards 'the male-female roles in [her] society' (227). However, Joan does not write her poems with a conscious impetus to critique gendered identities. As she explains to an interviewer: 'These words would sort of be given to me. [...] I'd find them written down, without having done it myself' (237). This practice of automatic writing serves a double purpose in the novel. First, it reveals the mother's story. Second, it manifests Joan's subconscious thoughts that represent the uncanny effect of the return of her unpleasant memories with her mother. As I discussed earlier, Cixous situated the mother as a stimulus to develop a feminine writing that incarnates feminine bodily rhythms. Joan's 'Lady Oracle' poems embody the mother, but in a less celebratory fashion than that of Cixous's conceptualisations. In Joan's poems the notions of fear and imprisonment that the mother evokes become a prevalent theme, which leads Joan to view her 'Lady Oracle' poems as a 'Gothic gone wrong' (232):

> It was upside-down somehow. There were the sufferings, the hero in the mask of a villain, the villain in the mask of a hero, the flights, the looming death, the sense of being imprisoned, but there was no happy ending, no true love. The recognition of this half-likeness made me

---

[336] Cixous, 'The Laugh of the Medusa', p. 253.

uncomfortable. Perhaps I should have taken it to a psychiatrist instead of a publisher. (232)

Joan's association of her poems with the Gothic genre operates on various levels. In the traditional Gothic plot as also employed in Joan's Gothic Romances, the heroine is a motherless (and often fatherless), 'passive and helpless'[337] young woman who, as Tania Modleski describes, 'suspects her lover or her husband of trying to drive her insane, or trying to murder her or both.'[338] As Shuli Barzilai points out, at the end of a gothic romance 'heroines find happiness in the embrace of a handsome, strong, nurturing, and oftentimes wealthy man.'[339] Even though Joan's romances are driven by this Gothic romance formula, her novels differ from the conventional genre, as they do not offer a happy ending. Notions of unhappiness and imprisonment also become an underlying motif in her 'Lady Oracle' poems. Yet, in these poems, the element of fear is not directed to a threatening male figure but to a feared, omnipotent mother figure whose very image re-awakens Joan's antagonistic memories of her.

Claire Kahane argues that at the centre of the Gothic novel 'is the spectral presence of a dead-undead mother, archaic and all-encompassing, a ghost signifying the problematics of femininity which the heroine must confront'.[340] Joan's poems in fact indicate 'the problematics of femininity' in the image of her oppressive mother, who tried to feminise her. Yet, viewed from another perspective, Joan's poems also tell the story of her mother. In this respect, by writ-

---

[337] Bouson, *Brutal Choreographies*, p. 74.
[338] Modleski, *Loving with a Vengeance*, p. 60.
[339] Shuli Barzilai, 'The Bluebeard Syndrome in Atwood's *Lady Oracle*: Fear and Femininity', in *Marvels & Tales: Journal of Fairy-Tale Studies*, 19:2 (2005), 249-73 (p. 249).
[340] Claire Kahane, 'The Gothic Mirror', in *The (M)other Tongue: Essays in Feminist Psychoanalytic Interpretation*, ed. by Shirley Nelson Garner, Claire Kahane and Madelon Springnether (Ithaca: Cornell University Press, 1985), pp. 334-51 (p. 336).

ing her mother's story through the process of automatic writing, Joan 'gives birth to the mother', to use a phrase by Kim Chernin:

> The familiar mother-daughter story of our culture tends to be drawn out between the ever-shifting emotional positions of blame and forgiveness. The bad, inadequate, failing, weak, abandoning mother of childhood is raged at and blamed for everything that once went wrong in the daughter's life. There are of course daughters who have never been angry at their mothers. Most women, however, know what it means to experience anger followed by a sense of reconciliation and forgiveness. Childhood is reimagined, insight or understanding of the mother's life as a woman is reached, the daughter feels that she has arrived at a resolution of her ongoing struggles with her mother. [...] In this moment, it becomes possible for the daughter to create the mother she feels she has always needed and deserved. She re-creates her real mother or she creates a symbolic mother to hold and foster her psychological and emotional development. That, to begin with, is what I mean by the phrase 'to give birth to one's mother'.[341]

One can see a similar structural relationship in Joan's interaction with her mother. Joan 'gives birth' to her mother in her Gothic poems by re-writing her mother's story which she has subconsciously internalised. She visualises this woman as powerful yet 'unhappy' (222). The fact that Joan imagines her as a powerful woman is suggestive of her long-lasting impact on Joan, whilst her unhappiness could be related to her frustrated life. As Joan later points out: 'She had been the lady in the boat, the death barge, the tragic lady with flowing hair and stricken eyes, the lady in the tower' (330). The imagery here seems to refer to Tennyson's 'The Lady of Shalott', where the imprisoned heroine is condemned to pursue a life both devoid of fulfilment of personal desires and given over to the pursuit of an obscure and unsatisfying task. Joan interprets her mother's drama in these terms seeing her as an unhappy, unfulfilled, dependent woman who is imprisoned in an unsatisfying marriage, and who renounces her ambitions in order to be

---

[341] Kim Chernin, *The Woman Who Gave Birth to Her Mother* (London: Penguin, 1998), pp. xii-xiii.

a wife and mother. As Joan states: 'Nobody did appreciate her, even though she'd done the right thing, she had devoted her life to us, she had made her family career as she had been told to do' (178). Her former view of her mother as a romanticised image of femininity collapses, as she comes to realise that her mother has been an unhappy woman who was denied the life she would have aspired to live. This affects her writing of romantic fictions as well. As she points out: 'I started a novel called *Storm over Castleford* – but the hero played billiards all the time and the heroine sat on the edge of her bed, alone at night, doing nothing' (181). She further exploits this idea of a discontented woman in her poems, where she imagines her as 'bent down under the power' (222), which can arguably be read as a critique of the patterns of domination and subordination that govern repressive femininity. Even though Joan avoids associating this woman with herself and speaks with certainty that the woman in her poem 'ha[s] nothing to do with [her]' (222), it is obvious that she identifies herself with various repressive images of femininity throughout her narrative.

As discussed, Joan is fascinated by cultural and literary stereotypes of women, and as a 'romantic' (143) she feels an 'intense empathy'[342] for the unhappy heroines. However, in her adulthood she comes to realise the ordeal that they have to go through because of their deviation from their prescribed roles. She says:

> I just drifted around, singing vaguely, like the Little Mermaid in the Andersen fairy tale. In order to get a soul you had to suffer, you had to give something up; or was that to get legs and feet? I couldn't remember. She'd become a dancer, though, with no tongue. Then there was Moira Shearer, in *The Red Shoes*. Neither of them had been able to please the handsome prince; both of them had died. I was doing fairly well by comparison. Their mistake had been to go public, whereas I did my dancing behind closed doors. It was safer, but.... (216)

---

[342] Rao, 'Margaret Atwood's *Lady Oracle*: Writing Against Notions of Unity', p. 145.

As the extract suggests, Joan believes that she is different from those heroines, since she is inventive enough to do her profession secretly. Yet, the motive that lies beneath this secrecy is her fear of rejection, which ultimately epitomises her entrapment in a socially constructed femininity that thwarts her from performing her desired preoccupations overtly in public and private realms. This might well be the reason why she writes her romantic fictions under a pseudonym and does her writing secretly, hiding it from her husband for fear that her career as a writer of romances would lead Arthur to take her for granted:

> Why did I never tell him? It was fear, mostly. When I first met him he talked a lot about wanting a woman whose mind he could respect, and I knew that if he found out I'd written *The Secret of Morgrave Manor* he wouldn't respect mine. (33-34)

In keeping her creative writing secret from her lover we can see Joan's fear of not being accepted, the root of which dates back to her childhood relationship with her mother. The internalised influence of the mother remains intact in Joan's relationships with male figures who impose upon her a similar form of femininity that she feels compelled to obey. For instance, in her relationship with Paul, her physique is of primary importance. Paul would tell her that 'the mystery of man is of the mind, whereas that of the woman is of the body' (166). In her relationship with the Royal Porcupine, she initially allows him to treat her like a sexual object, and worries about 'letting him down' (245). Finally in her marriage with Arthur, she lets Arthur 'control [her] life' (24): she dresses as he likes; she reads the books that he asks her to read. She even regrets having 'Lady Oracle' poems published as they have made Arthur 'displeased' (227). According to what Joan has seen in the fairy tales and the movies, particularly in the film adaptation of *The Red Shoes*, a woman has to sacrifice and repress her aspirations, artistic imagination and creativity for acceptance. Atwood comments on the film in *Second Words*, and states that 'the message was clear. You could not have both your artistic career and the love of a good man as well, and if you tried, you would end up committing suicide.'[343] Atwood's construction of Joan as a woman who is trapped in a prescribed feminine behaviour casts a critical eye on the impact of these manipulative cultural precepts that encourage conformity and female passivity, and hamper artistic imagination. The influence of these cultural texts on Joan is indisputable. She performs her art 'behind closed doors' for fear of losing the love of a man. However, she does not realise that, in doing so, she subconsciously conforms to role conditioning. Her incomplete sentence with her bleak 'but' arguably suggests her reluctance to accept her imprisonment within these cultural ideals of femininity.

Joan initially plots her Gothic Romances in the same pattern which rewards femininity and punishes disobedience. In her novel-in-progress *Stalked by Love*, she follows the conventional Gothic code by depicting Charlotte as the 'good, innocent virgin' and Felicia as the 'angry, dangerous' wife. She projects herself on to her own heroines. She feels empathy for Charlotte first, but as the plot progresses starts to identify herself with Felicia. Although Joan realises that sympathy for the wife is 'against the rules' and 'would foul up the plot' which demands wives to be 'eventually either mad or dead, or both' (319), she does not want to sacrifice Felicia for Charlotte: 'I was getting tired of Charlotte, with her intact virtue and her tidy ways. [...] I wanted her to fall into a mud puddle, have menstrual cramps, sweat, burp, fart' (319). Joan's appropriation of Charlotte from an ideal image of femininity to vulgarity can be considered as an indicator of Joan's gradual departure from stereotypical images of femininity. Previously, she depicted Felicia smelling like 'the edges of swamp', whilst Charlotte smelled like 'lavender' (318). Arguably, this might signify Joan's entrapment in cultural dichotomies, a state which, as Cixous has argued, associates 'good smell' with 'purity and desired femininity', and 'bad smell' with 'danger and diabolism.'[344] Joan's changing attitude towards her characters in this case can be read as her attempt to get

---

[343] Atwood, *Second Words*, p. 224.
[344] Cixous and Clement, *The Newly Born Woman*, p. 37.

beyond the confines of a one-dimensional construction of her heroines. She progressively gets irritated by Charlotte's 'firm young body' (30), and her socially scripted role of femininity: pure, chaste, passive, and selfless. She says: 'Wearing [Charlotte] was like wearing a hair shirt, she made me itchy' (319). More importantly, her reversed approach to her characters serves as a psychological device enabling Joan to resolve the conflict between her past and present selves, and eventually to come to terms with her repressed other. She does not let the rebellious Felicia die and be replaced by the 'thin and flawless' (342) Charlotte. She makes Felicia reappear while Redmond and Charlotte are busily engaged with their wedding plans. Felicia is now 'an enormously fat woman' (322), which gestures at Joan's gradual reconciliation with her fat self. As she says towards the end of the book:

> Below me, in the foundations of the house, I could hear the clothes I'd buried there growing themselves a body. [...] a creature composed of all the flesh that used to be mine and which must have gone somewhere. [...] It was the Fat Lady. [...] For a moment she hovered around me like ectoplasm, [...] my ghost, my angel; then she settled and I was absorbed into her. (320-21)

As the extract suggests, Joan's anxiety of excess leads to disturbing hallucinations about the 'fat lady', resurrecting from her flesh, an imagery which may suggest in Freudian terms the return of the repressed, and in Joan's case, the return of her troubling memories concerning her former embodiment. It is only by writing herself as Felicia that Joan eventually comes to realise her own narrative of selfhood trapped in the restrictive myths of idealised femininity. As she lets Felicia go into the 'maze', she confronts the unconscious patterns emerging in her writing, and realises, in Frank Davey's words, 'the secret transferences which have determined the course of her life.'[345]

---

[345] Frank Davey, *Margaret Atwood: A Feminist Poetics* (Vancouver: Talonbooks, 1984), p. 85.

This becomes explicit when Joan as Felicia figuratively encounters her multiple selves in the maze:

> Two of them looked a lot like her, with red hair and green eyes and small white teeth. The third was middle-aged, dressed in a strange garment that ended halfway up her calves, with a ratty piece of fur around her neck. The last was enormously fat. She was wearing a pair of pink tights and a short pink skirt covered with spangles. From her head sprouted two antennae, like a butterfly's, and a pair of obviously false wings was pinned to her back. (341)

In the maze Joan as Felicia sees her former and present selves. The woman with red hair and green eyes is obviously her present self, whilst the second woman might be her unruly other as a lover of Royal Porcupine and mistress of Paul. The middle-aged woman could be interpreted as Aunt Lou, her surrogate mother; and the fat lady in the pink costume represents Joan's oppositional self. According to Jerome Rosenberg, Joan's various personas portray 'something like multiple personality disorder, in which traumatic episodes initiated in early childhood trigger the formation of separate personalities which constitute distinct parts of the victim's psyche and exist side by side.'[346] The traumatic episodes that Rosenberg refers to are embedded in Joan's experiences as a 'fat' girl, memories of which Joan longed to escape in her later life. However, her entry into the 'maze' enables her to see her rejected and repressed selves, and ultimately helps her to be reconciled with her fat self. In her final experiment with automatic writing, she realises that the image which she has assumed to be her mother is her own 'reflection' (330). She recognises that 'it is she who writes the narrative of self-victimisation, guilt, and repression previously attributed to her mother.'[347] This further suggests that in her attempts to reject her mother, Joan has ironically turned into an image of femininity much like her mother. As Adrienne Rich observes, 'where a mother is hated to the point of matrophobia,

---

[346] Jerome H. Rosenberg, *Margaret Atwood* (Boston: G.K. Hall, 1984), p. 116.
[347] Worthington, p. 297.

there may also be a deep underlying pull toward her, a dread that if one relaxes one's guard one will identify with her completely.'[348] In Joan's case, even though she does not want to be identified with her mother, she realises that by becoming a woman in conformity with social expectations of femininity, she adopts her mother's persona, where the mother becomes both the self and the other. As she says: 'I carried my mother around my neck like a rotting albatross' (213), and her final realisation, 'She'd never really let go of me because I had never let her go. It had been she standing behind me in the mirror, she was the one who was waiting around each turn, her voice whispered the words' (329-30), makes manifest 'the psychological shaping presence'[349] of the mother from Joan's childhood to adulthood.

In *Pedagogy of the Oppressed*, Freire has pointed out that 'the "fear of freedom" which afflicts the oppressed may equally well lead [the oppressed] to desire the role of oppressor or bind them to the role of oppressed.'[350] Joan's case arguably exemplifies Freire's hypothesis, in that the underlying rationale behind Joan's inability to free herself from the mother can be attributed to her tendency to align herself more with her former oppressor – in this case her mother. However, the power struggle between Joan and her mother resolves itself when Joan starts to feel sympathy for the mother. During her mother's last astral appearance to her she wonders in a complete reversal of her previous hateful comments, 'could she see I loved her? […] I longed to console her. […] I would do what she wanted' (329). Joan's confession here implies her acknowledgement of her mistreatment of her mother, and it is after she realises her mother's story that she comes to see her differently and sympathises with her frustrations. Consequently, she confronts her unconscious fears of the parent which are related to her anxiety of living up to the mother's impositions of a so-

---

[348] Adrienne Rich, *Of Woman Born: Motherhood as Experience and Institution* (New York: Norton, 1976), p. 235.
[349] Worthington, p. 296.
[350] Freire, p. 46.

cially acceptable image of femininity. In the end Joan figures out that her mother's frequent appearance in her memory as well as in her imagination is a result of the unconscious patterns that permeated her life, and which she desperately tried to escape from. This indicates once more that her alibi of being an 'escape artist' (334) proves to be unsuccessful in suppressing her past trauma of excess inflicted by her mother. Whilst she takes refuge in writing as a form of escape, she confronts her fears and repressions, and this process forces her into reconciliation with her past. However, for Emma Parker, the ending of the novel in which we see Joan in the kitchen observing dried out 'cooked pasta and a yellowing bunch of parsley' (311) indicates 'the absence of proper, nourishing food', and, thus, Joan's failure to 'escape her old life and her old self.'[351] Yet, Joan's consent to tell the reporter her story implies that she eventually comes to accept her 'obese' past, and confront her traumatic memories. As she says in the final pages: 'I'll try some science fiction. The future doesn't appeal to me as much as the past, but I'm sure it's better for you' (345). Her last words, where she implies that she will not 'ever be a tidy person' (345) further gesture towards her potential liberation from the confines of feminine containment. As Atwood states, in the end Joan 'will be able to say "O.K. that's really who I am". Before she said: 'I will hide who I am because nobody will like who I am. They will not accept me. They will think I'm ridiculous. If I conceal myself then I will be safe". So she's gotten as far as saying, "I am who I am – take it or leave it."'[352]

The ending of the novel clearly reads as a warning that enables us to observe the repressive energies, the social codes that are passed from mothers to daughters, and the daughter's need to struggle to acquire a unique self uninfluenced by the mother who acts as an enforcer

---

[351] Emma Parker, 'You're What You Eat: The Politics of Eating in the Novels of Margaret Atwood', in *Twentieth Century Literature*, 41:3 (Autumn 1995), 349-68 (p. 357).

[352] J. R. (Tim) Struthers, 'Playing Around', in *Margaret Atwood: Conversations*, ed. by Earl G. Ingersoll (London: Virago, 1992), pp. 58-69 (p. 66).

of beauty norms. More importantly, it shows how writing the 'obese' body presents a narrative that challenges the idealisation of the female body in cultural scripts and theories. Atwood's engagement with this theme might lead one to see the representation of fatness in this text as a 'feminist issue' which, as Molly Hite has argued, 'becomes symbolic of female resistance to a society that wishes to constrict women to dimensions it deems appropriate.'[353] However, the temptation to analyse the representation of fatness as a purely feminist issue must be tempered by the consideration that it is the mother, a female character, who imposes the cultural bodily ideals, and colludes with them, a situation that could further be traced in *Sweet Death*.

3.2 'I know what I look like. It's all planned, calculated, willed': The Revenge Narrative of 'Excess' in *Sweet Death*

Claude Tardat's *Sweet Death* is another novel that investigates this ambivalent position of the mother. Here we see again the writing of 'excessive' female embodiment becoming a young woman's weapon to dismantle the cultural ideals of femininity as they are imposed and monitored by the mother. In *Sweet Death* the unnamed daughter's writing of her 'excessive' embodiment engages more explicitly with the unconscious motives in mother-daughter power relations, and her diary serves as a medium to record the daughter's gluttonous revenge on the mother.

Published over a decade after Atwood's *Lady Oracle*, Claude Tardat's *Sweet Death*[354] highlights the issue of female corpulence from the point of view of a nineteen-year-old, unnamed young woman

---

[353] Molly Hite, *The Other Side of the Story: Structures and Strategies of Contemporary Feminist Narratives* (Ithaca and London: Cornell University Press, 1989), pp. 131-32.

[354] The original title of the book is *Mort Sucrée*, and has been translated into English by Linda Coverdale. The book inspired the Australian composer Andrée Greenwell's chamber opera of the same title which premiered at the Melbourne International Festival of Fine Arts in 1991.

who records her gluttonous consumption and 'excessive' embodiment in her diary. The novel's translation from French into English has made it more accessible to a wider circle of readers, yet *Sweet Death* has not received the literary critical attention it deserves. Its intelligent and wry engagement with consumption and 'obesity' is also a conscious exploration of writing the 'obese' female body in a highly stylised and inventive narrative. This text offers a multi-faceted representation of female embodiment, where the protagonist's altering embodiment (her mission to eat herself to death) is driven by both conscious and subconscious motives. The subconscious drives behind the protagonist's ambition in particular allow Tardat to propose a nuanced view of embodiment that I shall be contrasting with Cixous's advocacy of writing the body in terms of feminine bodily pleasures.

In *Sweet Death* we see bodily pleasure as a significant drive, but Tardat's representation of this pleasure is centred on the satisfaction of non-sexual appetites, specifically the excessive consumption of sweets, which contrasts with Cixous's emphasis on feminine sexual pleasure, an idea contained in what she defines as *jouissance* or the Feminine Imaginary – 'the act that will "realise" the un-censored relationship of woman to her sexuality.'[355] The young woman does not write about the joys, drives or rhythms of female sexuality, instead she writes about the bodily rhythms and noises that are related to eating and digesting: i.e. 'deglutiton',[356] 'borborygm' (83), 'constant nibbling, my only music' (59), 'stomach working away tirelessly' (59), 'sugar's lengthy progress' (4), which she likens to 'noises of rotary engines' (4). The young woman views this digestive functioning of her body as more ecstatic than Cixous's conceptualisation of the joys of female sexuality and thus explores her femininity in terms of her 'excessive' embodiment: she is 'four feet eleven inches' (12) tall, weighing more than 'two hundred and twenty pounds' (96), '[her] fat

---

[355] Cixous and Clement, *The Newly Born Woman*, p. 97.
[356] Claude Tardat, *Sweet Death* (London: Pandora, 1989), p. 83. Further references to the novel will be given in brackets.

is stored mostly around [her] thighs and pelvis' (56). Another divergence from Cixous's conceptual stance results from Tardat's situation of her protagonist's body within a landscape where the constricting expectations of the Western bodily ideal weigh heavily (literally and emotionally) on the protagonist's conceptualisation of her own embodiment. It is the influence of her cultural landscape that defines her embodiment despite her efforts to rise above her situation, and this runs contrary to Cixous's idealistic notion of an empowered female 'voice' divorced from her cultural reality with the freedom to establish a sense of ontology that negates acculturation. Tardat's text thereby offers a controversial dialogue that engages with a young woman's resistance to cultural boundaries, whilst exploring the improbability of a complete denunciation of cultural influences.

As I emphasised earlier, there are striking similarities between Atwood's *Lady Oracle* and Tardat's *Sweet Death* with both works sharing a central motif of a young woman's experience with her fat body in the context of a disapproving mother, and in both works the resulting straits and tensions become the overriding factor in their troubled relationship. However, unlike *Lady Oracle*, in which Joan's inner journey starts with feelings of anger towards the mother resolving when Joan arrives at an appreciation of the mother's life as an unsatisfied woman, there is to be no reconciliation between the mother and daughter in *Sweet Death*: the mother's inability to accept the daughter's wilful fatness constitutes an impasse in this work. Kim Chernin's argument that 'the two seemingly antithetical emotional positions, blaming and forgiving, turn out to be the twin poles of the mother-daughter story'[357] can be seen to be challenged by Tardat's representation of the mother-daughter bond, where the strains existent in their relationship never alternate with reconciliation and forgiveness as the mother solely remains a source of frustration to the daughter. The feelings of frustration, here, become a key to understanding the impact of weight as a significant issue that underpins the mother-

---

[357] Chernin, *The Woman Who Gave Birth to the Mother*, p. xii.

daughter relationships represented in the novel in a framework of power relations that centralises the idea of maternal control and the daughter's resistance to it.

According to Paula J. Caplan, 'the mother of an "overweight" daughter feels inept because her daughter does not fit the current feminine ideal, so she thinks she ought to do something. [...] But her offers of advice only highlight the daughter's "failure" of self-control, increasing her self-loathing.'[358] As a result, 'the daughter gets caught in the conflict between her mother's need to have a "presentable" daughter and her own struggles to become independent and develop a sense of identity.'[359] In the section on *Lady Oracle*, I explored this conflict particularly with regard to Joan's attempts to develop her subjectivity both in her personal and professional life as a writer which get sabotaged by the internalised mother. However, in *Sweet Death*, this conflict operates on a different level. First of all, unlike Joan, who loses weight in the process of resolving her conflicting relationship with the mother, Tardat's narrator chooses to expand in size. This ultimately increases the tension with the mother as the daughter gradually develops her subjectivity outside the mother's ideals. Secondly, Tardat's protagonist's position as a writer in which she records her expansion in size becomes a possible realm which initially enables her to exercise her subjectivity against the mother. The daughter's journal becomes a key area through which to explore the ways in which the traumatic relationship between parent and child informs and influences the conscious and subconscious motives in the daughter's attempt to eat herself to death. The text not only opens up another subjective perspective to explore the tensions between the two that spring from the daughter's resistance to the disciplining of her body, but it also presents a highly distinguished and privatised writing of 'excessive' embodiment.

---

[358] Paula J. Caplan, *Don't Blame Mother: Mending the Mother-Daughter Relationship* (New York, London: Routledge, 2003), p. 202.
[359] Ibid., p. 202.

3.2.1 Accessing the Private through Writing of 'Excess'

In her 'Laugh of the Medusa', Cixous has envisioned writing the female body as a strategy of empowerment. She has said:

> Women must write through their bodies, they must invent the impregnable language that will wreck partitions, classes, and rhetorics, regulations and codes, they must submerge, cut through, get beyond the ultimate reserve-discourse, including the one that laughs at the very idea of pronouncing the word 'silence'.[360]

We see Tardat's protagonist using the medium of writing to break free from the prevailing constricting norms and initially proclaiming her embodiment in concordance with Cixous's proposition of eschewing a reserved and silent state. Early in the book we see the young woman's unapologetic acceptance of her physicality as she says: 'Now they can't pretend I don't exist. I am seen. Seen forever. Seen, my rudimentary femininity swathed in cellulite' (11-12). Here, the young woman's insistence on being visible arguably illustrates Cixous's promotion of a feminine writing that reclaims the body. As Cixous has stated:

> Feminine writing never stops reverberating from the wrench that the acquisition of speech, speaking out loud, is for her – 'acquisition' that is experienced more as tearing away, dizzying flight and flinging oneself, diving. Listen to woman speak in a gathering (if she is not painfully out of breath): she doesn't 'speak', she throws her trembling body into the air, she lets herself go, she goes completely into her voice, she vitally defends the 'logic' of her discourse with her body; her flesh speaks true. She exposes herself. Really she makes what she thinks materialize carnally, she conveys meaning with her body.[361]

Cixous envisions a new feminine writing that operates outside the boundaries of the phallic construction of language. For her, the articulation of meaning through the body is central to this feminine writing since this practice of writing, as Bray points out, 'is capable of trans-

---

[360] Cixous, 'The Laugh of the Medusa', p. 256.
[361] Cixous and Clément, *The Newly Born Woman*, p. 92.

lating those moments when language fails us and the body attempts to speak.'[362] Yet, Cixous's proposition of this ideal feminine writing has been subjected to critical scrutiny. For instance, Susan Sellers argued the improbability of 'liv[ing] our body experiences without disturbance from the numerous taboos, descriptions and images that surround us', further stating the impossibility of 'writing this experience without recourse to the language system in which such definitions are embedded.'[363] *Sweet Death* is a text that illustrates both of these critical stances. Tardat's protagonist's writing about her body can partially be interpreted by means of Cixous's conceptualisation of this new feminine writing. However, the young woman does not imagine her body in defiance of the language system, since for her there is hardly a way of writing and imagining her embodiment without the language which in effect defines this embodiment. There are several instances in the novel where she tends to describe her body in pejorative terms. Yet, it can well be argued that her negative attitude towards her embodiment projects her culture's approach to excess, which has a tendency to associate fatness with 'glutton[y]' (110) or 'physical and mental deformity' (104). Viewed in this context, the young woman's writing of her body arguably undermines Cixous's celebration of a new feminine writing that repudiates cultural and social inscriptions on the body. More importantly, her anatomised engagement with her body deviates from Cixous's idealisation of writing the body in that the act of writing for the young woman does not serve as an entirely empowering process, but as an act that surfaces her feelings of lack and emptiness, which is evident right from the onset of her narrative.

Thus, her journal opens and ends with feelings of lack and emptiness which she expresses over her body. At the very beginning she notes 'a profound emptiness in the stomach that all the sweets in the world couldn't fill' (1), and in her last words before her ultimate disintegration she conveys this same sense of emptiness: 'to be so heavy

---

[362] Bray, p. 37.
[363] Sellers, p. 9.

and yet so empty' (126). Here, the young woman imagines the notion of heaviness in metaphorical terms in that she associates it with a state of being fulfilled. Viewed within this context, her consumption of sweets initially recompenses this feeling of emptiness, rendering her a certain kind of satisfaction and fulfilment: 'I'm infinitely pleased with myself' (60), 'the thrill of excess' (97), 'I'm fascinated by myself' (121). She longs for a similar sense of pleasure out of her writing in that her conscientious selection of words with 'well-rounded loops and curves' (35) such as 'guava, nougat, halvah, loukoum, baklava' (43) primarily enables her to fill her emptiness: 'such pleasure to rediscover those ebony words, those succulent words traced in beautiful ink, so thick and oily' (36). She aspires for her writing to mimic her embodiment and when failing to achieve this effect she says: 'sad, this shrunken style of writing, such a contrast to […] the preceding pages. Today my writing doesn't look like me' (35). For the young woman, her distinctive writing initially functions 'to flee [her] image of another possible form of [her]self, an image traced by the thin and fragile trail of the ballpoint pen' (35). Here, she renders a symbolic meaning to embodiment, in that thinness comes to signify a state of vulnerability and absence, notions that she avoids identifying herself with. That is why she seeks for her writing to embody her actual physical form, as a means to imagine herself as 'well-rounded', both physically and emotionally. In this respect, the medium of writing functions as a form of shield to escape confronting her very needs and desires, yet, as she later says, 'writing doesn't relieve the pain of this unbearable craving' (43). What seems at first a physical craving in fact reads as her craving for acceptance and love - feelings that she tries to suppress underneath her literary façade and bravado. Hence, she hides her unmet desires beneath gorging words in 'an excess of facile grandiloquence' (66). Yet, despite this, it is the very ink with which she writes that unveils her buried memories and feelings.

Her memory of a dream in which some 'huge ink stains attack [her] on all sides' (37), is particularly significant as it initiates a deeper articulation of the young woman's confrontation with her unmet desires and needs: 'Ever since that dream, the ink stains on the floor have haunted me. While I digest, I fall into a kind of hypnotic state in which the stain invariably reminds me of a scorpion. I'm obsessed by the scorpion' (38). The evocation of the image of the scorpion that she sees in the 'ink stain' here is particularly important as it operates on psychological and mythical levels. Psychologically, the imagery alludes to the 'inkblot test', introduced by the psychiatrist Hermann Rorschach, to evaluate an individual's deep secrets and innermost feelings and thoughts through his/her spontaneous or unrehearsed responses to what s/he sees in the inkblot. In this case, the scorpion image in the ink stain, which haunts the young woman throughout her narrative, represents her ambiguous feelings for her mother ingrained in her memories. Mythically, the image in African legends has an 'ambivalent implication derived from [its] wounding and healing features.'[364] For the young woman, the scorpion image functions as a metaphor for her emotional wound inflicted by her mother. In line with Joan's 'fat lady' fantasies, which functioned as a reminder of her traumatic memories regarding her embodiment, the constant evocation of the scorpion image in the ink stain serves as a metaphor for her feelings of frustration and emptiness, the cause of which can be traced back to her memories of her long-drawn troubled relationship with her mother.

The significance of memories is brought to the fore when the young woman refers to Marcel Proust's semi-autobiographical work *Remembrance of Things Past*, in which the protagonist's experience of a madeleine serves as a stimulus to unlock his memory, thus allowing the past to be experienced as a simultaneous part of his present existence. Joan initially views the role of the madeleines described by Proust as rather elevated and bearing no resemblance to her own experience. For the young woman the madeleines are 'simply a wonder-

---

[364] Jack Tressider, *The Complete Dictionary of Symbols* (San Francisco, CA: Chronicle Books, 2005), p. 428.

ful drug', and they 'do not have any effect on [her] beyond exciting [her] taste buds' (67).

She seems to undermine the powerful effect that the madeleines have on Proust, calling his experiences 'affectations' (67) and suggesting that her own excursions with them operate on a pleasantly superficial level: 'I eat madeleines shamelessly by the one-pound bag, and sometimes I enjoy them so much that I double my consumption' (66). Yet, as her narrative unfolds, she has her own 'madeleine' in the form of the ink scorpion image which serves to draw her into a more profound and troubled experience of the past, the essence of which gradually accommodates her writing in an engagement with her suppressed memories:

> I was innocently asleep, a scorpion arrived out of nowhere, probably guided by the power of some evil eye, and began crawling along the netting to pay me a criminal visit. The room was pleasantly cool and bathed in soft light. My mother sat close to me in a rocking chair, absorbed in her own mysterious reverie. Zohra was elsewhere, busy with the delicate laundering that was her specialty.
>
> 'Then', she [Zohra] told me, 'a comb fell from my chignon, and I knew you were in danger. I ran, ran to you so quickly, there were too many passageways and stairs in that house, I left water everywhere, all over the rugs, because of my wet hands and feet, and I still ran, and I saw Madame in her chair, and Madame was looking at the scorpion, and her eyes weren't there, because Madame she was smiling at someone in her thoughts, and the scorpion was coming down the net, and it was there, right by your mouth. Then Zohra arrived in time to chase away the scorpion. And Madame said, 'Go back to your work, Zohra'.
>
> The old woman nodded her head and then she took up a basket of beans and began to shell them without a word. Conscientiously. As for myself, I buried my face in her neck for a very long time, it seems to me. (69)

This memory offers the young woman an explanation as to why she has had this agitated response to the splash of ink, which she calls 'a frightening story' (70) that she wishes she had never heard: 'I did try to wash the floor to make it go away' (70). Here, the memory signifies the transmutation of the actual fear of the scorpion crawling upon the young woman's infantile body into a more complex symbolic representation where the image in the ink stain becomes a constant reminder of her uncaring mother prompting the return of her repressed memories. As Michael Sprinker suggests, 'just as dream interpretation returns again and again to the navel of the dream, so [confessional narrative] must return perpetually to the elusive centre of selfhood buried in the unconscious, only to discover that it was already there when it began.'[365] The young woman's experience with the ink stain operates on similar grounds in that it enables her to confront her present feelings of lack and emptiness fostered by the scorpion image. According to Freud, 'a strong experience in the present awakens in the creative writer a memory of an earlier experience […] from which there now proceeds a wish which finds its fulfillment in the creative work.'[366] Clearly, the protagonist's present experience with the scorpion image serving as a gateway to her relevant earlier memories corresponds to Freud's hypothesis of the correlative influences between present and past experiences. However, the act of writing for the young woman counterpoints Freud's proposition of the process of writing as a medium for wish-fulfilment since writing here functions less as a means of fulfilment than as a springboard that reveals the young woman's unmet wishes and desires, particularly those concerning her relationship with her mother.

3.2.2 Tensions in the Mother-Daughter Dyad and Desire for Power

Mothering, as Sarah Sceats states, 'is widespread in literature, used both as an indicator of love and nurturing (or its lack), and to

---

[365] Michael Sprinker, 'Fictions of the Self: The End of Autobiography', in *Autobiography: Essays, Theoretical and Critical*, ed. by James Olney (Princeton, New Jersey: Princeton University Press, 1980), pp. 321-42 (p. 342).
[366] Freud, 'Creative Writers and Day-Dreaming', p. 146.

suggest burdens and disempowerment.'[367] For the young woman in *Sweet Death*, the mother is the source of her hunger, and the lack of nourishment characterises a maternal relationship that has been unsatisfying since her earliest infancy. Susie Orbach has argued that '[the daughter] turns to eating in the search for love, comfort, warmth and support.'[368] In line with Orbach's hypothesis, Tardat's protagonist's consumption functions as a way of filling the lack of maternal love and nurturance. Her constant reference to milky, creamy drinks such as hot chocolate and condensed milk and her selection of words like 'endless suckling' (73) illustrate her hunger for the mother's milk. Yet there are some instances in the book where she voices her dislike for milk: 'A revulsion for milk, unless it's sweetened with something. The sour odor of pap and yeast. Musty, animal smell. The taste of cool flesh and spongy breasts' (73). Here, the young woman's stated dislike for milk could be viewed as masking an actual yearning for the mother's milk, which is reminiscent of a psychological phenomenon Freud called 'reaction formation', a self-defence mechanism where the subject deludes him/herself by replacing unpleasant emotions with their opposites. However, for the protagonist, this self-preservation strategy is not entirely successful: 'My mother wasn't afraid of scorpions. She wanted to be a beauty queen, not a mammal' (73). The re-invocation of the scorpion image, which is associated with her infantile memory, and the implication of her mother's arguably deficient mothering within the same paragraph, is indicative of her unmet infantile desires such as the love embodied in the mother's milk.

In *The Psycho-Analysis of Children*, Melanie Klein argued:

> The baby, to whom the mother is primarily only an object which satisfies all his desires – a good breast, as it were – soon begins to respond to these gratifications and to her care by developing feelings of love towards her as a person. But this first love is already disturbed at its roots by destructive impulses. Love and hate are struggling together in

---

[367] Sceats, *Food, Consumption and the Body*, p. 12.
[368] Orbach, *Fat is a Feminist Issue*, p. 28.

the baby's mind; and this struggle to a certain extent persists throughout life.[369]

Klein points out that the repressed earliest images in our minds are part of us, and they 'are directed for the most part against the object of love and hate, the mother, because it is she who is most associated with this pre-Oedipal period.'[370] As Patricia Waugh argues,

> The mother is the person who gratifies or frustrates as she offers or withholds the satisfactions of the breast as the source of food and comfort. She is all-giving and all-punishing, an all-powerful being who contains within her the means of satisfying every desire (the phallic mother), and thus intensely idealized as the source of good and feared [...]. At the earliest stage, the mother is not an integrated person but a 'good' [the part-object first experienced as good] and 'bad' [the object which frustrates] breast.[371]

For Joan, the early experiences in relation to her mother, particularly the episode with the scorpion and the absence of maternal nurturing have a lasting influence on her which manifests itself in her writing. The fact that the mother fails to satisfy her physical and emotional needs leads the daughter to situate her more in the realm of frustration and emotional absence as opposed to idealisations of the mother as an ever-present nurturing 'love object.'[372] Yet, the mother here is also a source of literary inspiration for the young woman, since her suppressed emotions resulting from their troubled relationship act as a driving force for her writing. This pursuit of writing operates on two levels: first, it can be seen as a way of confronting the mother who deprived her of physical and emotional nourishment; second, it is an act of reclaiming her subjectivity from the mother, who sought to impose her ideals upon the daughter. This exemplifies the power struggle between mothers and daughters, a struggle Luce Irigaray encapsulates in

---

[369] Melanie Klein, *The Psycho-Analysis of Children* (London: Hogarth, 1932), p. 308.
[370] Ibid., 313.
[371] Waugh, pp. 64-65.
[372] Conley, p. 83.

her words: 'Once you have assimilated me into nourishment. We have again disappeared into this act of eating each other. [...] Farewell mother, I shall never become your likeness. [...] I'll live my life, my story.'[373]

In *Sweet Death* the protagonist's experience with her subjectivity has conflicting resonances: her journal where she records her deliberate weight gain can be interpreted as her way of challenging her slender mother. Yet, her constant reference to her unpleasant memories of her mother changes the course of her literary creation, causing her to deviate from the original model of replicating her embodiment in her writing. That is to say, the young woman initially intends to write about her embodiment perhaps from an elevated, proud and distinct viewpoint, one that celebrates 'excess', and challenges the prejudiced assumptions held against 'fat' people: 'contrary to received opinion, fat people are not protected by their obesity and don't withstand changes in temperature as well as thin people do' (14). Yet, following scorpion image in ink, a process of unlocking deeper insights into her relationship with her mother is initiated. At this point, her writing seems to take a less subjective turn and becomes partially informed by her mother's oppressive remarks towards her embodiment. Thus, the protagonist's increasingly derogatory depictions of her embodiment, e.g. 'a second-rate sideshow freak' (21), 'a lady dwarf swaddled in fat, a stump of a woman, repulsively ugly' (98), are influenced by her mother's embarrassment and discontent with the daughter's body: 'she's less worried about my health than she is about the nasty things people might say' (22). She recalls her mother asking: 'Well, daughter, when are you going to decide to become beautiful?' (30). As Orbach argues, 'fat expresses the tension in the mother-daughter relationship which has been allocated the feminisation of the female.'[374]

---

[373] Luce Irigaray, 'And the One Doesn't Stir Without the Other', trans. by Hélène Vivienne Wenzel, in *Signs: Journal of Women in Culture and Society*, 7 (1981), 60-67 (pp. 62-63).

[374] Orbach, *Fat is a Feminist Issue*, p. 29.

The mother-daughter relationship represented in Tardat's novel, in which we see the protagonist's mother engaging in this process with her bitter comments on her daughter's embodiment, illustrates Orbach's statement. The young woman writes:

> The glance she shoots me from beneath her long mascara-coated eyelashes is ferociously sharp. She has sized up my bulges without a word. From what she can see, I've gained even more weight. [...] When coffee was served, she slipped me the card of a friend of hers, a doctor.
> 'You can rely on him. Between now and our return from Madagascar, he will have managed to make you presentable again'. (22)

Her mother's remarks challenge the daughter's self-image, leading her to compare her embodiment with the slender form represented by her parent: 'mama's body doesn't make noise. It sings' (122); 'mama's perfumed realm. And me, the intruder therein, a beached whale with chronic acne' (6); 'was it I who caused her blood, her waters, her milk to flow?' (119). In the light of her mother's critical attitude we see her developing a heightened sense of her embodiment in relation to her female friends at school and university, who are preoccupied with their looks, carefully watching their weight by calculating 'every snack on a precise scale' (46). The daughter writes:

> My sisters, but not like me, not *mes semblables*. They chatter away lightheartedly, gossiping about their rendezvous; slender and trim with their flat stomachs, they sparkle gaily or revel in some great sorrow, then show off again, checking and comparing their hip measurements, lending each other fashion magazines. (32)

Despite her poignant awareness of her different embodiment which she claims to be 'the only specimen of advanced obesity in the entire university' (46), we do not find her aspiring to be like her friends; in fact she feels contempt towards the superficial image they delight in presenting and a dread of becoming like them: 'Must I set myself to become like them? To talk, dance, smile? Must I become that languid and cooing young woman leaning up against a man beneath my bedroom window?' (33). She resolutely refuses to conform to the idea of this embodiment and in fact maintains her body shape despite her growing dislike of it. The reason underlying this can be ascribed to her desire to establish a sense of autonomy by resisting her mother's constant attempt to impose her ideals on her at every opportunity. She recalls her mother's tutorials where she deliberately singles out relevant parts from Baudelaire's 'Des femmes et des filles' ('Women and Girls'), in which 'Baudelaire describes the rotund curves of adiposity, that hideous well-being of idleness' (25). Reading the essay, the young woman protests against his linking of excess with 'idleness' and directs her anger not towards the writer but to her mother 'for appropriating the poet's thoughts to judge [her]' (25). The growing struggle with the mother is heightened with this experience, leading the young woman to reconsider the notion of the beautiful body:

> The noble body. The body beautiful, to be molded in accordance with the rediscovered standards of antiquity. The athletic body, to be displayed in its perfect plasticity. The one Mama tried hard to impose on me through endless exercise classes and ballet lessons, given to me in private by one of Mama's friends as a favour to her. The disciplined, well-formed body that I will never have. The body as façade, as illusion. The body Mama has. (47)

The young woman's depiction points to the mother's practice of power in the form of attempting to regulate her daughter's weight. This brings to mind Foucault's theorisation of power, a phenomenon which he elucidated in relation to the exercise of control over bodies. Here, the 'noble', 'disciplined' and 'well-formed' body of the mother bears semblance to Foucault's theorisation of 'the docile body', which represents a body receptive to obedience and subjugation. Viewed in this context, the mother's imposition of normative regulations of femininity on her daughter is indicative of her advocacy of the restrictive norms that legitimise the slender embodiment (she leaves behind gifts of bathroom scales for her daughter). Analogous to Atwood's construction of her protagonist's mother, the exercise of power held by the mother thus points to the parent's disguised state of powerlessness in relation to socially constructed notions of the female embodiment. Set against the mother's 'docile body', the daughter's 'excessive' embodiment here represents the transgressive body that defies maternal authority and control.

Underneath this power struggle, the traces of a troubled mother-daughter relationship can be observed. Throughout her narrative the protagonist presents the image of a mother who is unaffectionate, negligent, critical and manipulative. Perhaps one of the most unpleasant memories of her mother is the one which she describes as 'a black hole in [her] memory' (82). It unfolds the mother's unjust treatment of her child when the protagonist at an early age finds out about her parent's illicit affair with the Spaniard, whom she later suspects is her biological father. The young woman writes:

> Mama shouted, 'Enough!' And everything stopped. The laughter, the giddiness, the horror. She took me in her arms and carried me back to my room, my head buried in her low-cut neckline. I could hear the stormy pounding of her heart. The pin of her brooch was scraping my cheek. She climbed the stairs almost in a rage, her silver bracelets jangling wildly. [...] I was strictly forbidden to enter the drawing room when my parents were entertaining. It was then, I think, that the little packets of sweets began appearing on my bedside table. [...] But I never tasted any of them. (79-80)

The emphasis on sweets here is significant as it brings a deeper insight into the motives behind the protagonist's later obsession with sweets. It is in the context of the mother's affair that they first appear, and it seems clear that she puts them by her bed as a bribe to buy her silence. At the time she rejects the sweets because she sees them as emblematic of her mother's 'impermanence and falsehood' (114), but it is interesting that in her later episodes of binge eating the very thing she consumes most is sweets. By excessively consuming sweets at this stage she is in effect taking the attempted bribe and throwing it back at the mother in the form that would be most hurtful to her by becoming bigger.

Anger plays a prominent role in the protagonist's feelings towards her mother, and the over-consumption gives expression to this. As Kim Chernin has argued, 'women who eat compulsively have made their bodies the recipient of feelings they cannot bear to hold in consciousness. Their rage is expressed through their mouths, their need for love and solace is experienced as a longing for food.'[375] Resonating with Chernin's observation, Tardat's protagonist's excessive eating signifies a strong sense of rage directed against the mother who fails to satisfy her daughter's need for love: 'When she stroked my cheek absent-mindedly, checking her reflection in the cheval glass, there were icy needles in her kid gloves' (15). Prompted by feelings of frustration and anger, the young woman uses her very embodiment as a medium to punish the secretive and unloving mother in that her 'conscious will' (3) to expand in size becomes her triumph over her mother's 'noble body': 'what I lose in health, I'll gain in ugliness. That will be my reward' (25-26). She fantasises about the ultimate end of her weight gain, her conscious intent to kill herself by excessive consumption, and reflects with satisfaction on the spectacle her body would present:

> In a year, within the walls of this mauve temple where the rites of maternal beauty are performed, my body will lie candied in a bathtub full of sugar-water, like a mottled iceberg, a bleached Maillol statue. The thighs stuck together. The arms welded to the breasts, and the breasts to each other. The fingers indistinguishable in the shapeless mess of my swollen hands. (24)

The exuberance with which the above passage is written suggests a great pride in this image of herself, and it is the abject nature of the image of her dead self that seems to delight her. As Sceats suggests, in

---

[375] Kim Chernin, *The Hungry Self: Women, Eating and Identity* (London: Virago, 1986), p. 136.

Kristeva's theorisation of abjection, the abject falls into three categories:

> Oral disgust, which enacts a rejection of the mother and thus refusal of life; repugnance towards the bodily waste, which suggests an inability to accept the body's materiality, its rhythms and mortality (the corpse itself being the ultimate example of bodily waste); and revulsion from signs of sexual difference, encompassing the taboo against incest and horror at menstrual blood.[376]

The young woman in Tardat's novel respects the materiality of her embodiment. She imagines using her corpse as a form of bodily waste to enact revenge on her mother. By becoming 'abject' herself, she taints the mother's 'clean and proper body'. The daughter's assumed embodiment often functions as a form of rebellion. Initially, this is directed solely at the mother, but as her narrative progresses we see her enjoying the rebellious nature of her embodiment in a wider context. She pictures making a spectacle of herself in a swimming pool:

> Mama's girlfriends would display their gleaming tans, svelte figures, and silken skin drenched in musky perfume. […] They would strike seductive poses on a close-cropped lawn as smooth as their shaved armpits. And on this velvety green carpet I would sit, buttocks squashed. My breasts would ooze down on either side of me like liquefied gelatine. […] The sunshine would filter through the milky cortex of my sickly skin, melting a multitude of fatty deposits until they sizzled and seethed in tiny bubbles bursting on the epidermis. I'd revel in the horrified stares of those women. […] Oil slicks from the melting of my very substance would stain the water's tranquil blue surface. (31-32)

As the above extract vividly displays, the young woman 'revels' in violating the narrow conventions of her mother's social group and takes great pleasure in visualising the effect of her 'own personal aesthetics' (63) on the 'svelte figures' around her. The idea of making a spectacle here brings to mind Mary Russo's exploration of 'the female

---

[376] Sceats, *Food, Consumption and the Body*, p. 69.

transgressor as public spectacle'[377] as a form of liberation against the limitations of the feminine containment. The young woman's experience at the Renoir exhibition clearly illustrates this position as she displays her non-conforming embodiment against women who represent the normative regulations of femininity:

> They draw back instinctively as I pass by, offended in their contemplation of grace by my embodiment of the exact opposite. I'm an insult to their race, what a thrill!
> I defy them, bare my nibbling teeth at them, scatter cookie crumbs all over their lambskin boots – ersatz spit, a childish pleasure, but oh, how deeply felt. (63)

For the young woman, the notion of making a spectacle out of herself has two motives: first, it is her refusal to 'keep [her] body in its place'[378]; second, it functions as a way of restoring her subjectivity through the gaze of others. The young woman recalls a bus trip in which she is exposed to the gaze of a little girl:

> I sat down across from her. Pulling out a handful of Cracker Jacks from a big cellophane bag, I offered her some while her mother looked on suspiciously. A game sprang up between us. At first it was tacitly understood that we would crunch the sweetened popcorn in the same rhythm before swallowing it with an exaggerated expression of pleasure. Then the child decided to turn the game into a real dialogue of clowns. We pummelled our cheeks, puffed out as far as they would go, using our fists instead of our teeth to grind up the popcorn inside. The little girl pretended to be choking and pressed her lips tightly together to keep from bursting into laughter. She was funny. Myself, grotesque. But I know it and this experience gave me a certain feeling of euphoria. No one suspects this: I find it amusing to be the object of awkward glances that would rather avoid me altogether. Hiding behind their newspapers, the travellers sought shelter in an uneasy and hypocritical silence that we filled with our laughter. A child's laughter is often contagious. But a monster who dares to have fun – that's inconvenient, that keeps people from letting go and enjoying them-

---

[377] Russo, *The Female Grotesque,* p. 61.
[378] Ibid., p. 16.

selves, that freezes laughter into a grimace on the lips. The mother resented me. Barely concealed distaste, just below the surface. (51-52)

Unlike Atwood's Joan, who turns the gaze to herself as a form of 'self-surveillance', Tardat's protagonist manipulates the gaze to her advantage as a means to restore her existence against people who avoid looking her 'in the face' (52). The young woman longs to be noticed and stared at, saying, 'I was pleased to think of the striking picture I would present to people out in the broad daylight' (3). She writes about her experience with the street photographer who 'knows how to approach [his potential customers] boldly and seductively to win them over' (98). Yet, the photographer simply ignores the young woman, not even considering the possibility of her wish to be photographed. Upon his dismissive attitude towards her, the young woman herself asks for his service and observes his 'embarrassment': 'What interests me is the provocation. And the proof that people pay more attention to me than they let on' (99). The idea she excavates here can be connected to a social tendency that renders fat bodies either invisible or too visible, two seemingly contradictory approaches to the notion of the gaze, conversely operating on a similar conjecture based on the condescending and antagonistic appropriations of fat (in terms of a physical and moral 'defect' mostly received by pity, disgust or laughter). The young woman rejects being the object of the invisible gaze (because she is aware that people tend to see her but prefer not to look at her) that is often reserved by 'able-bodied' people for people with disabilities. She defies this prejudiced and 'hypocritical' gaze that seems to pathologise her 'obesity'.

It is significant to note that the moment she exhibits her indulgences in public, the pitiful gaze which formerly allocated her an invisible state is replaced with a vivid, critical gaze of disapproval and disgust. Perhaps, the most striking example of this form of disturbing gaze takes place when two men stare at her with a cynical laughter, calling her 'right out of Diane Arbus!' (45). The young woman turns this experience into a positive appropriation of her self-image, seeing her embodiment as a 'masterpiece' (63). As Susan Sontag has pointed out, 'Arbus's work is reactive – reactive against gentility, against what is approved. It was her way of saying fuck *Vogue*, fuck fashion, fuck what's pretty.'[379] The young woman in her self-proclaimed 'obesity' is proud of her likeness to the subjects of Diane Arbus' photographs: 'that man was doing me the honour of lumping me with those Fat Ladies exhibited by shady characters and opportunistic Barnums, and whom Diane Arbus spent her life tracking down in their miserable lairs' (48). She further states, 'extraordinary photos, of course. But their beauty idealizes and destroys their subjects' monstrosity. Anesthetized, odorless, two-dimensional monsters' (86). The young woman's enthusiasm for Arbus's distinct photography picturing various forms of embodiment in their unaestheticised simplicity arouses the young woman's critical interest to explore the idea of aesthetics prevalent in her social climate:

> If I haven't been given discreet notice to leave the premises, it's thanks to my Dior blouse and a few judicious tips. Will I be obliged to place myself under the protection of haute couture to have the run of this earthly paradise? Shall I be forced to make an exhibition of myself in expensive tailored suits, even though I disgrace them utterly, in order to be accepted here on the same footing as those ridiculous representatives of the canine race. [...] That's the way of the world, which puts up with imperfection and deformity as long as they come wrapped in designer labels. (5)

Here, the young woman vividly criticises the eminent issues attending the hypocritical and conflicting attitudes held by her society. She points to the fact that her society tends to accept her 'excessive' form when it is aestheticised as people see it differently when it is shaped and placed differently. Arbus's photography arguably illustrates this social tendency, a tendency which shows fascination towards 'difference' as long as it is aesthetically presented. In the young

---

[379] Susan Sontag, *On Photography* (London: Allen Lane, Penguin Books, 1978), p. 44.

woman's experience with her embodiment we see her reluctance to perform this superficiality in the concept of clothing her body in a designer fashion as a means of making herself more acceptable. As her narrative progresses we see her getting weary of her fight against her pretentious social environment and moving into a stage of loneliness refusing to interact with people including the very person, the Student who has not been judgemental in his approach to her. She says: 'He doesn't belong to this grotesque lair, handsome as he is, the negation of what I am. He belongs to the carefree world of perfumed bowers, tennis courts, music' (125). At this stage, her thoughts of death become increasingly prevalent. Her citing from Mallarmé's poem 'Sea Breeze' (1865), 'The flesh is sad alas and I've read every book' (120), is significant as it points to her desire to escape from her troubled existence. Death is her redemption: 'only eternity will allow me to live my way, beyond all measure' (119). Her words towards her ultimate disintegration, 'and all because of an ink stain' (126), relates her death to her resentment for the unloving mother. Viewed from a different perspective, her death also conveys her subconscious desire for the past when she and her mother were closely connected.

'The future must no longer be determined by the past'[380], asserts Hélène Cixous ideologically in her 'Laugh of the Medusa', arguing that women should eliminate 'the effects of the past', and 'refuse […] to confer upon them an irremovability, the equivalent of destiny.'[381] However, as both *Lady Oracle* and *Sweet Death* explore, the effects of the past, in particular the early relationships between mother and daughter can hardly be removed since they become heavily embedded in the protagonists' personal and social experiences informing and influencing their attempt to reclaim their subjectivity from the mother.

---

[380] Cixous, 'The Laugh of the Medusa', p. 245.
[381] Ibid., p. 245.

Conclusion
'I am sorry I am so fat': A Narrative of 'Excess' in *Fat Girl: A True Story*

In the previous chapters, I explored heterogeneous representations of female corpulence in literary texts which offered a re-imagining of fatness as metaphorical and powerfully transgressive. In the course of my analysis, I have examined how fatness is constructed both as a challenge to homogeneous representations of, and assumptions about, female embodiment, and as a stimulus for literary creativity that points towards a new aesthetics of embodiment which celebrates the difference of the different. To conclude this study, I will now be looking at an autobiographical text, Judith Moore's *Fat Girl: A True Story* (2005), to explore the limits of extra-textual representation, the tensions arising from the unlivability of Moore's life and the ways in which she uses the expression 'true story' to give herself a set of stories: 'sometimes my whole life seems to be stories about fat'.[382] Compared to the literary works that I have engaged with in the previous chapters, where I explored the notion of female corpulence as metaphor and literary trope, in Moore's memoir, 'fat' reveals a particular, idiosyncratic identity – an identity that is not reducible to that of a 'fat girl' but an identity with specific appetites, a specific story, about a specific family. The writer assertively points out at the opening of her narrative that 'this will not be a book about how [she] had an eating disorder and how [she] conquered this disorder through therapies or group process or antidepressants or religion […] or the love of a good man or (woman)'. She 'will not write about fat people', she 'will tell [her] story', 'tell the story of [her] family' (1-2). The previous chapters explored the difference of the different in relation to the idea of 'excessive' embodiment; here the attention turns to the specificity of a story that is unique. Moore's memoir is a book that, like Carolyn Steedman's *Landscape for a Good Woman*, is about 'lives, lived out

---

[382] Judith Moore, *Fat Girl: A True Story* (London: Profile Books, 2005), p. 40. Further references to the book will be given in brackets.

on borderlands, lives for which the central interpretive devices of the culture do not quite work. [...] It is about the stories we make for ourselves, and the social specificity of our understanding of those stories.'[383] Such lives are, as Annette Kuhn remarks, 'ways of knowing and ways of seeing the world – rarely acknowledged, let alone celebrated in the expressions of a hegemonic culture.'[384] Portraying a woman's real experience with her 'excessive' embodiment in a fatphobic society, Moore's memoir thus acknowledges the specificity of her life. Whilst revealing the unhappiness of her experiences, her book also engages with the pleasures of writing. Her 'excessive' embodiment does not constitute a threat to record the sensuous pleasures afforded by food. At the very beginning of her narrative, she recalls dining with a man who told her that she was 'too fat to fuck' (5). If she 'is too fat to fuck', she is not too 'fat' to write about her experience with the texture and sensations of fast food in elaborate detail:

> I was eating a cheeseburger, holding the assemblage in both hands. Crisp around the edges, the bun was warm and squishy, squeezed between fingers and thumbs. It had been fried on the griddle, had soaked up meat grease, and my hands were getting greasy.
> I was glad that the meat and bun and cheese and lettuce and dill pickle and mustard and mayonnaise and chopped onion were inside my mouth. I was glad that I was chewing and that my mouth was full. The chewing and the taste of the cheeseburger mush that I pushed against the roof of my mouth with my tongue made me dreamy and forgetful. (5-6)

Being supposedly 'too fat to fuck' prompts the compensatory sensual pleasures of eating, and the writer absorbs herself in the act of eating, losing herself in the taste, texture, all the sensations of the sensual experience. With food serving as a compensation for the lack of

---

[383] Carolyn R. Steedman, *Landscape for a Good Woman: A Story of Two Lives* (New Brunswick, NJ: Rutgers University Press, 1987), p. 5.
[384] Annette Kuhn, *Family Secrets: Acts of Memory and Imagination* (London: Verso Books, 1995), p. 5.

love, desire and the unhappy family life, we see Moore's text existing at a kind of intersection with the extra-textual reality of being 'fat'.

In their edited collection *Extremities: Trauma, Testimony and Community*, Miller and Tougaw have suggested that autobiographical writing has generally been concerned with 'life lived in extremities', and 'certain kinds of extreme suffering from the annihilatory technologies of the Holocaust to the devastation of Aids.'[385] Judith Moore's memoir deviates from this definition in that she cannot be considered to be depicting a life lived in such extremity. Her story might be seen as mundane in comparison with the above examples, yet her work deals with the real sufferings that a fat-abhorrent society can inflict on a 'fat' individual. Autobiography of this type in its intimate portrayal of an 'ordinary' life allows for individuals in similar circumstances to develop a strong sense of empathy with the story. Viewed in this context, it can be argued that by writing his/her life, the autobiographer transfers his/her experiences onto a broader collective level, and thus his/her self-representation comes to represent larger social groups with similar experiences. As Leigh Gilmore has stated, 'autobiography criticism is often political. It offers writers the opportunity to promote themselves as representative subjects, that is, as subjects who stand for others.'[386] Miller and Tougaw expand this appreciation of autobiography saying, 'in complex and often unexpected ways, the singular "me" evolves into a plural "us" and writing that bears witness to the extreme experiences of solitary individuals can sometimes begin to repair the tears in the collective social fabric.'[387] Here, Miller and Tougaw add a social purpose to autobiographical writing and indicate the potential for this genre to play an important role in addressing problems within a society. In this respect, autobiog-

---

[385] Nancy K. Miller and Jason Tougaw, 'Introduction', in *Extremities: Trauma, Testimony and Community*, ed. by Nancy K. Miller and Jason Tougaw (Urbana and Chicago: University of Illinois Press, 2002), pp. 1-25 (pp. 6, 2).

[386] Leigh Gilmore, *The Limits of Autobiography: Trauma and Testimony* (Ithaca and London: Cornell University Press, 2001), p. 4.

[387] Miller and Tougaw, p. 3.

raphy potentially transforms the private into the public discourse and adds a political dimension to it. This interpenetration of the private and the public becomes a way of giving voice to the suffering of suppressed groups. Gayatri Spivak's definition of autobiography as the 'genre of the subaltern giving witness to oppression, to a less oppressed other'[388] clearly conveys this aspect of autobiographical writing. Life writing, is "a way of seeing",[389] says Marlene Kadar quoting John Berger's famous phrase. Drawing upon Kadar's definition it could be argued that life writing does not only tell the story of the writer but it could also voice an experience common to other people. In this respect, autobiography turns into a medium which performs, 'a personal and a cultural task at once.'[390] As Gilmore has pointed out, 'women, people of colour, gay men and lesbians, the disabled, and survivors of violence have contributed to the expansion of self-representation by illuminating suppressed histories and creating new emphases.'[391] The arising stigma attached to overweight people in current Western society are marking a new area of suppression, and Moore's autobiography can be considered one that speaks to this issue by exploring the ways in which social responses to one's embodiment affect one's sense of self. The text thus engages with the notion of an embodied self by articulating how the sense of self is shaped through one's experience with one's embodiment.

There has been a number of confessional narratives that explored the notion of embodiment in relation to personal experience with a particular focus on the difficulties experienced as a result of illness:

---

[388] Gayatri Chakravorty Spivak, 'Three Women's Texts and Circumfession', in *Postcolonial Theory and Autobiography*, ed. by Alfred Hornung and Ernspeter Ruhe (Amsterdam and Atlanta, GA: Rodopi, 1998), pp. 7-22 (p. 7).

[389] Marlene Kadar, 'Coming to Terms: Life Writing –from Genre to Critical Form' in *Essays on Life Writing*, ed. by Marlene Kadar (Toronto, Buffalo, London: University of Toronto Press, 1992), pp. 3-21 (p. 10).

[390] Christl Verduyn, 'Between the Lines: Marian Engel's *Cahiers* and Notebooks', in *Essays on Life Writing*, ed. by Marlene Kadar (Toronto, Buffalo, London: University of Toronto Press, 1992), pp. 28-42 (p. 29).

[391] Gilmore, p. 16.

for example, 'Audre Lorde's *The Cancer Journals*, Oliver Sacks' *A Leg to Stand On*, May Sarton's *After the Stroke*, Barbara Webster's *All of a Piece: A Life with Multiple Sclerosis*.'[392] The significant aspect of these works is that they are concerned with the body impaired by illness or disability, and in this respect they fall into a sub-genre that Couser has called, 'autopathography[393]' (that is 'autobiographical narratives of illness or disability'). Judith Moore's work does not seek to represent 'obesity' as an illness, as the difficulties encountered by the author are not a direct result of her body but rather her society's reactions to her embodiment, and furthermore she makes clear at the beginning of her narrative that her book will not be about an 'eating disorder'. It is the unapologetically blunt story of her unhappy, loveless family, her unhappiness about being fat, and the love-hate relationship with food. From a broader perspective, her book tells the story of her culture's responses to 'excess' within a time span of half a century starting with the author's life as a young girl in 1950s America revealing mordantly her experience with her 'excessive' embodiment. From the very first page Moore explains her motivations in writing her book: 'I wanted to write about what it was and is like for me, being fat' (1). She gives a further explanation in her essay 'Why I Wrote *Fat Girl*':

> I wrote *Fat Girl* because I had read books that other fat women wrote about how they were fat. Most fat women did not write the truth about fat. They did not write about fat thighs and how tender flesh on the inside of fat thighs rubs and rubs. [...] What people do want to write about is weight loss and how to lose it. They want to write about

---

[392] G. Thomas Couser, 'Autobiography: Women, Illness, and Lifewriting', in *Women and Autobiography*, ed. by Marine Watson Brownley and Allison B. Kimmich (Wilmington, DE: Scholarly Resources, 1999), pp. 163-75 (p. 164). Works such as Donna Williams' *Nobody Nowhere: The Remarkable Autobiography of an Autistic Girl*, Christy Brown's *My Left Foot* further exemplify Couser's conceptualisation of 'autopathography'.

[393] Ibid., p. 164.

self-esteem and how to gain it. *Fat Girl* makes no claims to do either. What *Fat Girl* does is tell my story.[394]

It might be argued that Moore writes out the very things that Atwood's protagonist Joan wants to do with her fantasy heroines – that the 'fat' body is 'imperfect', its 'abjections' are 'unfeminine', 'improper'. She writes from first-hand experience of what it means to be a 'fat' girl and woman in the real world and in this world the 'fat' female body becomes the focus of alienation and humiliation. She gives a vivid portrayal that does not hesitate to show in graphic detail the difficulties resulting from her size:

> Sometimes I get the pantyhose pulled up, but I am too big for them and a waistband won't go farther than my crotch. [...] By this time sweat has run down from under my arms and from between my breasts. I am angry by this time too, and ashamed, and disgusted for being such a grotesque and grunting hog. I am red in the face, wet with sweat and slightly sick to my stomach. (20)

Here, the word 'grotesque' is used in pejorative terms and speaks to the reader of her self-disgust. Moore's descriptions of her self-identified grotesqueness clearly point to her imprisonment in a body which she 'never can quite get out of' (31):

> I am a short, squad toad of a woman. My curly auburn hair is fading. Curls form a clown's ruff about my round face. My shoulders are wide. My upper arms are as big as those maroon-skinned bolognas that hang from butcher's ceilings. My belly juts out. The skin on my thighs is pocked, not unlike worn foam rubber. When I walk my buttocks grind like the turbines I once saw move water over the top of the Grand Coulee Dam. [...] But mostly I am fat. (7)

Here, Moore's description of her size is reminiscent of the Dog Woman's depiction of her physicality. Moore, like the Dog Woman,

---

[394] Judith Moore, 'Why I Wrote *Fat Girl*' (February 2005) <http://www.vachss.com/media/righteous/why_fat_girl_moore.html> [accessed 10 March 2006] (para. 1 of 12).

describes excess, reaching to the point of hyperbole: 'her buttocks grinding like turbines'. Then she returns to plain, unadorned statement when she ponders a fat woman's place in society: 'no one says out loud one word about how fat you are (unless they're drunk on cans of Budweiser and telling you how you are too fat to fuck)' (33).

As James Olney has suggested, 'memories and present reality bear a continuing reciprocal relationship, influencing and determining one another ceaselessly: memories are shaped by the present moment and by the specific psychic impress of the remembering individual, just as the present moment is shaped by memories.'[395] In accordance with Olney's argument, the author's negative self-image in the present of the narrative is formed by her past negative experiences related to her embodiment with people around her. That is to say, she has failed to represent the ideal feminine body of her culture. Cecilia Hartley has characterised this, suggesting that 'modern American standards require that the ideal feminine body be small. [...] This model of femininity suggests that real women are thin, nearly invisible.'[396] Viewed from this perspective, a 'fat' woman counterpoints this 'model of femininity':

> A fat woman stands out. She occupies personal territory in ways that violate the rules for sexual politics of body movement. [...] A fat woman has strong muscles from moving her weight around in the world. She clearly has fed herself. [...] Thus, for women to not break the rules, and for women to not be ugly, bad, and invaluable, women must fear fat, and hate it in themselves.[397]

---

[395] James Olney, 'The Ontology of Autobiography', in *Autobiography: Essays Theoretical and Critical*, ed. by James Olney (Princeton, New Jersey: Princeton University Press, 1980), pp. 236-267 (p. 244).

[396] Cecilia Hartley, 'Letting Ourselves Go: Making Room for the Fat Body in Feminist Scholarship', in *Bodies Out of Bounds: Fatness and Transgression*, ed. by Jana Evans Braziel and Kathleen LeBesco (Berkeley, Los Angeles and London: University of California Press, 2001), pp. 60-73 (p. 61).

[397] Brown, 'Women, Weight and Power: Feminist Theoretical and Therapeutic Issues', p. 65.

Moore is aware of the fact that fat is stigmatised in American culture, that a 'fat' woman is 'stereotypically viewed as unfeminine, in flight from sexuality, antisocial, out of control, hostile, aggressive'[398] Drawing upon her experiences with her embodiment, Moore seems to internalise her culture's responses to fatness: 'the fat woman is the elephant in the room, the subject about whom no one talks and entertains at least one thought' (33); '[fat people's] bodies provoke disgust, even from people who call themselves friends' (39). Despite her tendency to associate fatness with feelings of 'disgust and dismay' (125), we also see in her narrative her desire to undo prejudiced assumptions about it:

> I've rarely eaten fast foods. Thirty years have passed since I ate anything from McDonald's. (11)
> I know that people talk about how since I quit smoking I gained so much weight. I know they do. They take for granted I gulp down soft drinks and wear out my arm dipping ridged potato chips into sour cream and onion dip. They feel sure that I don't walk farther than from couch to refrigerator. They are wrong. (32-33)

Here, Moore aspires to dismantle the stigma attached to overweight people that tends to relate their size to a combination of a number of factors such as over-consumption, unhealthy eating practices, lack of willpower and leading a sedentary life. She responds to this by saying:

> When I put myself onto a weight-loss regime, I am my own strict mistress. I stick to my diet. I eat not a crumb that isn't assigned me. Not one. But for all that I starve and for all that I walk an hour and ride miles to nowhere on the exercise bike, my fat holds on. (18)

It might be argued that the implicit apologetic voice that the author inhabits here is repeated later in her narrative when she says 'I am sorry I am so fat' (120). This penitent statement could be regarded as her

---

[398] Marcia Millman, *Such a Pretty Face: Being Fat in America* (New York, London: W. W. Norton & Company, 1980), p. xi.

way to seek sympathy from the reader for her failing attempts to lose weight. Thus, her occasional efforts to challenge the antifat rhetoric prevalent in her society are weakened by her frequent expressions of discontent about being fat: 'I am trying to get rid of pounds of my waddling self' (7), 'I want those fat lumps of me gone, gone, gone' (16), 'I fantasize rapid weight loss' (19), 'I like to imagine that I am having liposuction' (19). The underlying reason behind her negative self-image thus can be attributed to her living in an appearance-conscious culture –'print ads, television commercials promote trim, cheerful blondes' (18) – that is hostile towards fatness, a position which the author experienced both in and out of the household. For instance, the boys at school called her names like 'pig' (32), 'fatso' (47), 'hill-billy' (82), 'fat girl' (89) and 'pig face' (116) – a commonplace situation that mirrors a prevailing tendency in contemporary Western society where the 'fat' child is the victim of bullying that begins with name-calling. For the young Moore, being called a 'pig' perhaps is the insult that she is accustomed to hear most often: 'this was not the first time in my life that somebody had called out to me, "Sooey, sooey, pig"' (32). It is significant to note the recurrence of pig imagery throughout the book; Moore pinpoints the ambivalence adhering to the image. She compares the pigs represented in children's stories, in particular in her favourite story 'The three little pigs' (86), with 'real'(87) ones: 'the clean pink picture-book pigs were nothing like real pigs that grunted in their pen on my grandmother's farm. I dwelt on the difference between the book pigs and my grandmother's filthy swine' (86). She further states: 'rather than the squinting eyes from which real pigs looked at you meanly, book pigs had wide blue Shirley Temple eyes. Real pigs, if you fell down in their pen and no one was around, would eat you alive' (86-87).

In *The Politics and Poetics of Transgression*, Peter Stallybrass and Allon White offer, as in Angela Stukator's words, a 'social semiotic of the pig',[399] exploring the image 'at the intersection of a number of important cultural and symbolic thresholds.'[400] According to Stallybrass and White the pig has been a marginal creature since the Middle Ages when 'it resembled a baby, lived next to and with humans, and ate similar food, yet, at the same time, it was perceived as a greedy scavenger fit only to be devoured.'[401] The symbolic meaning of the pig, as Angela Stukator argues, 'has since been transformed because of a number of social and economic changes, most notably urbanization, after which the pig became a hated object of disgust lacking any appeal.'[402] The pig imagery in Moore's story represents these multiple and contradictory notions, evoking pleasant and unpleasant feelings. Moore tends to identify herself particularly with the negative connotation as a result of the humiliation that she is subjected to because of her 'fat' body. This leads her to develop a 'compensating personality'[403] almost as if she deserves to be punished for her appearance. For instance, she does not blame her peers who took delight in hurling nasty comments about her weight: 'these mean boys hurt my feelings. But I agreed with them. They were correct. I was fat' (119). Moore then internalises this attitude and continues it in her adult life. When her dog grabs a slender woman's 'grease-besotted sack of Kentucky Fried Chicken' (35), Moore compensates for her 'fat' dog's appetite by paying more than the actual cost of the damage, providing another illustration of her 'compensating personality'. She reacts similarly to her mother's insults that she is a 'goddamn pig' (113), who is 'eating [her mother] alive' (83).

---

[399] Angela Stukator, 'Comedy, Carnivalesque, and Body Politics', in *Bodies Out of Bounds: Fatness and Transgression*, ed. by Jana Evans Braziel and Kathleen LeBesco (Berkeley, Los Angeles, London: University of California Press, 2001), pp. 197-213 (p. 204).

[400] Peter Stallybrass and Allon White, *The Politics and Poetics of Transgression* (Ithaca, N. Y: Cornell University Press, 1986), 44-45.

[401] Ibid., p. 47.

[402] Stukator, p. 204.

[403] Bovey, p. 80.

Moore's sympathy with her parent – 'I understand that she felt devoured by me' (83) – offers a further insight into her acculturation of the degrading image of herself whilst outlining her troubled relationship with her mother caused by her weight. There are many instances in her memoir where Moore presents the tensions between herself and her mother in length and detail, which obviously parallels *Lady Oracle* and *Sweet Death*. For instance, Moore's mother, like the mothers in *Lady Oracle* and *Sweet Death*, is very elegant and slender with 'a pear's waist, rounded hips, [and] voluptuous bosom' (80). As opposed to her mother's 'dainty and petite' (80) figure, Moore is 'the spitting image of [her overweight father]' (84) whose '"self-indulgence" with food and physical laziness' (66) has triggered the collapse of his marriage. Moore's physical resemblance to her father enhances the mother's hostility towards her criticising her 'excess' weight at every instance: 'when I stood close to her so she could measure my waist or pin up the hem to my dress, she pinched me hard and flicked me with her fingernail and hissed again and again how disgusted she was' (85-86); 'she said nobody wanted to be friends with a fat girl' (86). When Moore tells her mother that she wants to be 'a ballet dancer' (93), she is subjected to a kind of humiliation arguably worse than Joan's early experience with dancing in *Lady Oracle*, in that her mother responds to Moore's aspiration with an immediate ridicule calling her 'baby elephant' (93). Being ashamed of having a 'fat' daughter saying 'you make me sick, just to look at you' (94), the mother feels the urge to keep her daughter's weight under control by forcing her onto various diets, and when young Judith does not lose weight she whips her. The young Moore responds to her mother's attempts to control her with acts of unruliness, for instance, by repeatedly breaking into her beloved neighbour's home to empty her refrigerator. Her choice of rebellion by overeating seems to be motivated by her need to fill a strong sense of emptiness left by an absence of parental love:

In my case you might have learned that I was someone whose mother, for her own reasons, could not love me, and whose father, for his reasons, had gone far away. I was getting love any way I could. I was one of those three little pigs who built a house of fat to keep from the door the ravening wolf from whose long teeth dark blood dribbled. [...] I became my own wolf. You would have watched me eat at my fingers, rip off cuticle and chew and smile. (194-95)

As the extract suggests, Moore is so full of self-loathing that she would abjectly cannibalise herself in order to make herself disappear. Being exposed to many harsh insults because of her 'fat' body, she is made to believe that she is unlovable. She blames herself for her father's leaving home, and for her mother's inability to love her. She writes: 'If I hadn't had fat arms like an old lady's maybe my mama would not have beaten me at all. Maybe she could have looked at me and purred, "I love you, darling. I love you"' (98). The motive behind her eating to excess, reminiscent of the young girl in *Sweet Death*, is her longing for love: 'food [...] is the mother, the father, the warm-hearted lover' (9); 'to me, food was love' (37). She writes: 'I wanted to say to the ice-cream, "I love you". I wanted to say, "You are my mother"' (13). Here, the ice-cream (similar to the young woman's indulgence in milky, creamy sweets in *Sweet Death*) can be interpreted as the author's way to compensate for her longing for the mother's milk.

The abusive relationship with her mother leads Moore to develop problems with her embodiment which turns into self-hatred, leading her to see herself as someone too fat to be loved and someone who ought to be punished for being fat. The body of the 'fat' woman, as Jane Arthurs has argued, is often assumed to be 'the repository of projected shame and guilt.'[404] This is evident in *Fat Girl*, where Moore projects the shame and guilt of having a fat body onto herself:

---

[404] Jane Arthurs, 'Revolting Women: The Body in Comic Performance', in *Women's Bodies: Discipline and Transgression*, ed. by Jane Arthurs and Jean Grimshaw (London and New York: Cassell, 1990), pp. 137-64 (p. 151).

Conclusion 181

> I hate myself. I have almost always hated myself. I have good reasons for hating myself, but it's not for the bad things I've done. [...] I hate myself because I am not beautiful. I hate myself because I am fat. (7)
> I am heavy, I am ashamed and I am resigned to my shame. (23)

Moore's feelings of self-hatred are reinforced through the gaze of herself or others: 'every time you feel pretty, the spell is broken, either you see yourself in a mirror or some boy screams "Pig Face"' (125). Her experience at the church, with regard to her photograph, vividly depicts her anxiety about her embodiment:

> I was happy. I'd lost forty pounds. I fit into my dress. I liked my hat [...]. I smiled and even preened a bit as the photographers shot photos.
> The next Sunday, [...] I stood at the bulletin board outside the sanctuary [...]. I saw me with Lily, and my knees – literally – went weak.
> My happy smile had made my mouth crooked; my eyes were slightly unfocused and I appeared frantic and theatrically crazy, as if I were the heroine in a silent film desperate to escape a mustachioed villain. My black hat, out from whose brim my curls poked, looked bizarre. The hat was a bad idea. The bare arms were a bad idea too. The worst was that the black linen dress pulled across my hips and the way my stomach bulged out I might have been six months pregnant.
> [...] I grabbed my purse and fled out the door and snatched that photo off the bulletin board and walked home fast as I could. (41-42)

Here, the author's detailed graphic portrayal of her embodiment through her own gaze brings to mind Foucault's notion of the 'inspecting gaze.'[405] However, unlike Foucault's contextualization of this form of gaze as a medium for self-disciplining of the body, here Moore's critical self-gaze is in fact implicative of a social gaze that represents her culture's views on 'excessive' embodiment. That is to say, her story diverts the act of the gaze, which we see initially projected onto her embodiment, towards her culture's regulations of the female embodiment. Viewed in this respect, her inspecting gaze,

---
[405] Foucault, *Power/Knowledge*, p. 143.

which we read as the index of her dislike of her body, acquires a broader significance by turning into a critique of contemporary American culture's bodily ideals.

We can interpret all the works considered in this study as criticising similar values that cause a preoccupation with appearance and hold up prescriptive ideals of female embodiment such as 'slender but voluptuous shapes, faces unmarked by the passage of time, and, most of all, an appearance in keeping with the acceptable norms of femininity'.[406] Even in *Sexing the Cherry*, which may not be considered at first glance as a response to these issues, we find the Dog Woman conscious of her embodiment and finding herself 'hideous' despite her power and strength. While these texts differ in their representation of time and place and in their literary strategies, they above all vary in their treatment of their subject matter: as Moore tells us, 'everybody fat has her own fat story' (7). In these highly stylised texts, fatness, which is often regarded as 'unaesthetic', is not only legitimised, but has also become aesthetic. Within this aesthetic realisation of the body lies the potential for new meanings which challenge modern pervading notions of fatness as a moral or physical disease/defect. In the light of the growing 'obesity epidemic' and the accompanying media-driven anti-fat rhetoric in Western culture, it will be interesting to see how the representation of fatness develops in the literature of the future.

---

[406] Davis, 'Remaking the She-Devil: A Critical Look at Feminist Approaches to Beauty', p. 25.

Bibliography

Primary Sources

Atwood, Margaret, *Lady Oracle* (London: Virago, 1976)
___, *Second Words: Selected Critical Prose* (Toronto: Anansi, 1982)
Moore, Judith, *Fat Girl: A True Story* (London: Profile Books, 2005 [2004])
Tardat, Claude, *Sweet Death*, trans. by Linda Coverdale (London, Sydney, Wellington: Pandora, 1989)
Weldon, Fay, *The Life and Loves of a She-Devil* (London, Sydney, Auckland, Toronto: Hodder & Stoughton, 1983)
___, *Letters to Alice: On First Reading Jane Austen* (London: Coronet, 1985 [1984])
___, 'Is Thin Better?', *FEMINA: Fashion and Beauty File*, April 1995, 66-67
___, *What Makes Women Happy* (London: Fourth Estate, 2006)
Winterson, Jeanette, *Fit for the Future* (London and Hendley: Pandora, 1986)
___, *The Passion* (London: Vintage, 1996 [1987])
___, *Sexing the Cherry* (London: Vintage, 2001 [1989])
___, *Art Objects: Essays on Ecstasy and Effrontery* (London: Jonathan Cape, 1995)
___, *Lighthousekeeping* (London, New York, Toronto and Sydney: Harper Perennial, 2005)
___, *Weight* (Edinburgh, New York, Melbourne: Canongate, 2006 [2005])

Secondary Sources

Andermahr, Sonya, ed., *Jeanette Winterson: A Contemporary Critical Guide* (London, New York: Continuum, 2007)
Arnold, Matthew, *Culture and Anarchy,* in *The Works*, vol. 6 (London: Macmillan, 1903)

Arthurs, Jane, and Jean Grimshaw, eds, *Women's Bodies: Discipline and Transgression* (London and New York: Cassell, 1999)

Bakhtin, Mikhail, *Rabelais and His World*, trans. by Helene Iswolsky (Bloomington: Indiana University Press, 1984 [1968])

Banting, William, *A Letter on Corpulence* (London: Harrison, 1864)

Barr, Helen, 'A Conversation between Jeanette Winterson and Helen Barr', *The English Review* (Oxford), 2:1 (1991), 30-33

Barreca, Regina, ed., *Fay Weldon's Wicked Fictions* (Hanover and London: University Press of New England, 1994)

Barzilai, Shuli, 'The Bluebeard Syndrome in Atwood's *Lady Oracle*: Fear and Femininity', *Marvels & Tales: Journal of Fairy-Tale Studies*, 19: 2 (2005), 249-73

Becker, Howard S., *Outsiders* (New York: Free Press, 1963)

Belsey, Catherine, 'Postmodern Love: Questioning the Metaphysics of Desire', *New Literary History*, 25 (1994), 683-705

Bengston, Helene, ed., *Sponsored by Demons: The Art of Jeanette Winterson* (Denmark: Scholars' Press, 1999)

Bentley, Nick, ed., *British Fiction of the 1990s* (London, New York: Routledge, 2005)

Bordo, Susan, and Alison M. Jaggar, eds, *Gender/Body/Knowledge: Feminist Reconstructions of Being and Knowing* (New Brunswick and London: Rutgers University Press, 1989)

Bouson, J. Brooks, *Brutal Choreographies: Oppositional Strategies and Narrative Design in the Novels of Margaret Atwood* (Amherst: The University of Massachusetts Press, 1993)

Bovey, Shelley, *The Forbidden Body* (London: Pandora, 1994 [1989])

Bray, Abigail. *Hélène Cixous: Writing and Sexual Difference* (Basingstoke: Palgrave, 2004)

Braziel, Jane Evans, and Kathleen LeBesco, eds, *Bodies Out of Bounds: Fatness and Transgression* (Berkeley, Los Angeles, London: University of California Press, 2001)

Brown, Laura S., 'Women, Weight and Power: Feminist Theoretical and Therapeutic Issues', *Women and Therapy*, 4:1 (1985), 61-71

Brown, Laura S., and Mary Ballou, eds, *Personality and Psychopathology: Feminist Reappraisals* (New York: Guilford, 1992)

Brown, Rosellen, 'Fertile Imagination', *Women's Review of Books*, 7 (1990), 9-10

Brownley, Marine Watson, and Allison B. Kimmich, eds, *Women and Autobiography* (Wilmington, DE: Scholarly Resources, 1999)

Brownmiller, Susan, *Femininity* (London: Hamish Hamilton, 1984)

Butler, Judith, *Bodies that Matter: On the Discursive Limits of 'Sex'* (New York and London: Routledge, 1993)

___, *Gender Trouble* (New York and London: Routledge, 1999)

Campos, Paul, *The Obesity Myth: Why America's Obsession with Weight is Hazardous to Your Health?* (New York: Penguin, 2004)

Caplan, Paula J., *Don't Blame Mother: Mending the Mother-Daughter Relationship* (New York, London: Routledge, 2003)

Carr, Helen, ed., *From My Guy to Sci-Fi* (London, Winchester, Sydney, Wellington: Pandora, 1989)

Carter, Angela, *Nights at the Circus* (London: Vintage, 1994 [1984])

Caruth, Cathy, ed., *Trauma: Explorations in Memory* (Baltimore: The Johns Hopkins University Press, 1995)

Chen, Eunice Y., and Molly Brown, 'Obesity Stigma in Sexual Relationships', *Obesity Research* 13 (2005), 1393-97

Chernin, Kim, *The Obsession: Reflections on the Tyranny of Slenderness* (New York: Harper & Row, 1981)

___, *The Hungry Self: Women, Eating and Identity* (London: Virago, 1986)

___, *The Woman Who Gave Birth to Her Mother* (London: Penguin, 1998)

Cixous, Hélène, and Catherine Clement, eds, *The Newly Born Woman*, trans. by Betsy Wing (Manchester: Manchester University Press, 1986)

Clark, Robert, and Piero Boitani, eds, *English Studies in Transition* (London and New York: Routledge, 1993)

Clayborough, Arthur, *The Grotesque in English Literature* (Oxford: Clarendon Press, 1965)

Colin Trodd, Paul Barlow, and David Amigoni, eds, *Victorian Culture and the Idea of the Grotesque* (Hants: Ashgate, 1999)

Conboy, Katie, Nadia Medina, and Sarah Stanbury, eds, *Writing on the Body: Female Embodiment and Feminist Theory* (New York: Columbia University Press, 1997)

Conley, Verena Andermatt, *Hélène Cixous: Writing the Feminine* (Lincoln and London: University of Nebraska Press, 1984)

Cooper, Charlotte, *Fat and Proud: The Politics of Size* (London: The Women's Press, 1998)

Costin, Carolyn, *Your Dieting Daughter* (New York: Brunner/Mazel, 1997)

Cramer, Phebe, and Tiffany Steinwert, 'Thin is Good, Fat is Bad: How Early Does it Begin?', *Journal of Applied Developmental Psychology*, 19:3 (1998), 429-51

Crandall, Christian S., 'Prejudice Against Fat People: Ideology and Self-Interest, *Journal of Personality and Social Psychology*, 66:5 (1994), 882-94

Creed, Barbara, 'Horror and the Monstrous-Feminine – An Imaginary Abjection', *Screen* 27:1 (1996), 44-70

Cullivan, Ceri, and Barbara White, eds, *Writing and Fantasy* (London and New York: Longman, 1999)

D'Arcy, Chantal Cornut-Gentille, and José Ángel García Landa, eds, *Gender I-deology: Essays on Theory, Fiction and Film* (Amsterdam, Atlanta, GA: Rodopi, 1994)

Davey, Frank, *Margaret Atwood: A Feminist Poetics* (Vancouver: Talon Books, 1984)

Davis, Kathy, 'Remaking the She-Devil: A Critical Look at Feminist Approaches to Beauty', *Hypatia* 6:2 (1991), 21-43

___, *Reshaping the Female Body: the Dilemma of Cosmetic Surgery* (New York and London: Routledge, 1995)

DeJong, William, 'Obesity as a Characterological Stigma: The Issue of Responsibility and Judgements of Task Performance', *Psychology Reports*, 73 (1993), 963-70

De Zordo, Ornella, 'Larger than Life': Women Writing the Excessive Female Body', *Textus* (Tilgher, Genova), 13:2 (2000), 427-48

Diamond, Nicky, 'Thin is the Feminist Issue', *Feminist Review*, 19 (Spring 1985), 45-64

Diamond, I., and G. F Orenstein, eds, *Reweaving the World: The Emergence of Ecofeminism* (San Francisco: Sierra Club Books, 1990)

Douglas, Mary, 'The Social Control of Cognition: Some Factors in Joke Perception', *Man*, 3 (1968), 361-76

___, *Purity and Danger: An Analysis of Concepts of Pollution and Taboo* (London and New York: Routledge, 2002 [1966])

___, *Natural Symbols: Explorations in Cosmology* (London: Barrie & Rockliffe, 1970)

Dowling, Finuala, *Fay Weldon's Fiction* (London: Associated University Presses, 1998)

Dubino, Jeanne, 'The Cinderella Complex: Romance Fiction, Patriarchy and Capitalism', *Journal of Popular Culture* 27:3 (1993), 103-18

Eakin, Paul John, *How Our Lives Become Stories: Making Selves* (Ithaca and London: Cornell University Press, 1999)

Fallon, Patricia, Melanie A. Katzman, and Susan C. Wooley, eds, *Feminist Perspectives on Eating Disorders* (New York: The Guilford Press, 1994)

Faludi, Susan, *Backlash: The Undeclared War Against Women* (London: Vintage, 1992)

Farwell, Marilyn R., *Heterosexual Plots and Lesbian Narratives* (New York: New York University Press, 1996)

Featherstone, Mike, Mike Hepworth, and Bryon S. Turner, eds, *The Body: Social Process and Cultural Theory* (London, Newbury Park, New Delhi: Sage, 1991)

Fee, Margery, *The Fat Lady Dances: Margaret Atwood's Lady Oracle* (Toronto: ECW Press, 1993)

Fiedler, Leslie, *Freaks: Myths and Images of the Secret Self* (Middlesex: Penguin, 1981 [1978])

Foucault, Michel, *Discipline and Punish: The Birth of the Prison*, trans. by Alan Sheridan (New York: Vintage, 1977)

___, *Power/Knowledge: Selected Interviews & Other Writings 1972-1977*, ed. and trans. by Colin Gordon (Harlow: Longman, 1980)

Freeman, Hadley, 'Thinking Big as Women's Waists Expand', *The Guardian*, 28 August 2006

Freire, Paulo, *Pedagogy of the Oppressed*, trans. by Myra Bergman Ramos (New York, London: Continuum International, 2000 [1970])

Freud, Sigmund, *The Interpretation of Dreams*, trans. by A.A. Brill (New York: Macmillan, 1927)

___, *Standard Edition of the Complete Psychological Works of Sigmund Freud*, trans. by James Strachey (London: Hogarth, 1953-74)

___, *Three Essays on the Theory of Sexuality* (New York: Avon Books, 1962 [1905])

___, *New Introductory Lectures on Psychoanalysis* (London: Hogarth Press and the Institute of Psychoanalysis, 1974)

Gardiner, Michael, *The Dialogics of Critique: M. M. Bakhtin and The Theory of Ideology* (London and New York: Routledge, 1992)

Garner, Shirley Nelson, Claire Kahane, and Madelon Springnether, eds, *The (M)other Tongue: Essays in Feminist Psychoanalytic Interpretation* (Ithaca: Cornell University Press, 1985)

Gilmore, Leigh, *The Limits of Autobiography: Trauma and Testimony* (Ithaca and London: Cornell University Press, 2001)

Goffman, Erving, *Stigma: Notes on the Management of a Spoiled Identity* (Englewood Cliffs, New Jersey: Prentice-Hall, 1963)

Gorra, Michael, 'Gender Games in Restoration London', *New York Times Book Review*, 29 April 1990

Grice, Helena, and Tim Woods, eds, *Postmodern Studies 25 ('I'm telling you stories': Jeanette Winterson and the Politics of Reading)* (Amsterdam, Atlanta, GA: Rodopi, 1998)
Hacking, Ian, *Rewriting the Soul: Multiple Personality and the Sciences of Memory* (Princeton: Princeton University Press, 1995)
Haffenden, John, *Novelists in Interview* (London: Methuen, 1985)
Haraway, Donna, *Simians, Cyborgs and Women: The Reinvention of Nature* (London: Free Association Books, 1991)
Harpham, Geoffrey Galt, *On the Grotesque: Strategies of Contradiction in Art and Literature* (Princeton: Princeton University Press, 1982)
Harris, Mary. B., Richard. J. Harris, and Stephen Bochner, 'Fat, Four-Eyed, and Female: Stereotypes of Obesity, Glasses, and Gender', *Journal of Applied Social Psychology*, 12 (1982), 503-16.
Harris, Paul, '"Fat is Fabulous" insist Anti-Diet Protesters', *Guardian*, 8 August 2004
Hebert, Ann Marie, 'Rewriting the Feminine Script: Fay Weldon's Wicked Laughter', *Critical Matrix: The Princeton Journal of Women, Gender and Culture*, 7:1 (1993), 22-40
Hengen, Shannon, *Margaret Atwood's Power: Mirrors, Reflections and Images in Select Fiction and Poetry* (Toronto: Second Story, 1993)
Hirsh, Marianne, *The Mother-Daughter Plot: Narrative, Psychoanalysis, Feminism* (Bloomington: Indiana University Press, 1986)
Hite, Molly, *The Other Side of the Story* (Ithaca and London: Cornell University Press, 1989)
Horner, Avril, and Sue Zlosnik, 'Agriculture, Body Sculpture, Gothic Culture: Gothic Parody in Gibbons, Atwood and Weldon', *Gothic Studies*, 4:2 (2002), 167-77
Hornung, Alfred, and Ernspeter Ruhe, eds, *Postcolonial Theory and Autobiography* (Amsterdam and Atlanta, GA: Rodopi, 1998)
Howard, Jacqueline, *Reading Gothic Fiction: A Bakhtinian Approach* (Oxford: Clarendon Press, 1994)

Howells, Coral Ann, *Margaret Atwood* (Houndmills, Basingstoke, Hampshire, New York: Palgrave Macmillan, 2005 [1996])

___, ed., *The Cambridge Companion to Margaret Atwood* (Cambridge: Cambridge University Press, 2006)

Hutcheon, Linda, *A Poetics of Postmodernism: History, Theory, Fiction* (New York: Routledge, 1988)

___, *The Canadian Postmodern: A Study of Contemporary English-Canadian Fiction* (Oxford and Toronto: Oxford University Press, 1988)

Hyde, Lewis, *Trickster Makes This World: Mischief, Myth and Art* (New York: Farrar, Straus and Giroux, 1998)

Hynes, William J. and William G. Doty, eds, *Mythical Trickster Figures: Contours, Contexts and Criticisms* (Alabama: University of Alabama Press, 1997)

Ingersoll, Earl G., ed., *Margaret Atwood: Conversations* (London: Virago, 1982)

Irigaray, Luce, *This Sex Which Is Not One*, trans. by Catherine Porter and Carolyn Burke (Ithaca: Cornell University Press, 1985)

Jacobus Mary, Evelyn Fox Keller, and Sally Shuttleworth, eds, *Body/Politics: Women and the Discourses of Science* (New York and London: Routledge, 1990)

Jensen, Emily, 'Margaret Atwood's *Lady Oracle*: A Modern Parable', *Essays on Canadian Writing*, 33 (Fall 1986), 29-49

Jung, C. G, *The Archetypes and the Collective Unconscious*, trans. by R.F.C. Hull (Princeton: Princeton University Press, 1990 [1959])

Kadar, Marlene, ed., *Essays on Life Writing* (Toronto, Buffalo, London: University of Toronto Press, 1992)

Kauffman, Linda, ed. *Gender and Theory: Dialogues on Feminist Criticism* (Oxford: Basil Blackwell, 1990)

Kay, Jackie, 'Unnatural Passions': Interview with Jeanette Winterson', *Spare Rib*, 209 (1990), 26-29

Kayser, Wolfgang, *The Grotesque in Art and Literature*, trans. by Ulrich Weisstein (Indiana: Indiana University Press, 1963)

Kennedy, Maev, 'Only Sing When You're Slimming', *The Guardian*, 8 March 2004

Kenyon, Olga, *Women Novelists Today: A Survey of English Writing in the Seventies and Eighties* (Sussex: Harvester Press, 1988)

Klark, Katerina and Michael Holquist, *Mikhail Bakhtin* (Cambridge, Massachusetts, London: Harvard University Press, 1984)

Klein, Melanie, *The Psycho-Analysis of Children* (London: Hogarth, 1932)

___, *Envy and Gratitude and Other Works 1946-1963* (New York: Delacorte Press, 1975)

Kristeva, Julia, *Powers of Horror: An Essay on Abjection*, trans. by Leon S. Roudiez (New York: Columbia University Press, 1982)

Kroker, Arthur, 'Body Digest: theses on the disappearing body in the hyper-modern condition', *The Canadian Journal of Political and Social Theory*, 11:1-2 (1987), i-xvi

Kuhn, Annette, *Family Secrets: Acts of Memory and Imagination* (London: Versa Books, 1995)

Langland, Elizabeth, 'Sexing the Text: Narrative Drag as Feminist Poetics and Politics in Jeanette Winterson's *Sexing the Cherry*', *Narrative*, 5:1, (January 1997), 99-107

Lauter, Estella and Carol Schreier Rupprecht, eds, *Feminist Archetypal Theory: Interdisciplinary Re-visions of Jungian Thought* (Knoxville, Tenn.: University of Tennessee Press, 1985)

LeBesco, Kathleen, *Revolting Bodies? The Struggle to Redefine Fat Identity* (Amherst and Boston: University of Massachusetts Press, 2004)

Lodge, David, *After Bakhtin: Essays on Fiction and Criticism* (London and New York: Routledge, 1990)

Markert, John, 'Romance Publishing and the Production of Culture', *Poetics*, 14:1-2 (April 1985), 69-93

Marks, Elaine, and Isabelle de Courtivron, eds, *New French Feminisms* (Brighton: Harvester, 1980)

Martens, Catherine, 'Mother-Figures in *Surfacing* and *Lady Oracle*: An Interview with Margaret Atwood', *American Studies in Scandinavia*, 16 (1984), 45-54

Martin, Sara, 'The Power of Monstrous Women: Fay Weldon's *The Life and Loves of a She-Devil* (1983), Angela Carter's *Nights at the Circus* (1984) and Jeannette Winterson's *Sexing the Cherry* (1989)', *Journal of Gender Studies*, 8:2 (1999), 193-210

McElroy, Bernard, *Fiction of the Modern Grotesque* (New York: St. Martin's Press, 1986)

McLeish, Kenneth, 'Larger than Life: Sexing the Cherry', *The Times* (London), 10 September 1989

Mens-Verhulst, Janneke van, Karlein Schreurs, and Liesbeth Woertman, eds, *Daughtering and Mothering: Female Subjectivity Reanalysed* (London and New York: Routledge, 1993)

Metzger, Linda, and Deborah A. Straub, eds, *200 Contemporary Authors: Bio-bibliographies of Selected Leading Writers of Today with Critical and Personal Sidelights* (Detroit: Mich Gale Research Company, 1986)

Michie, Helena, *The Flesh Made Word: Female Figures and Women's Bodies* (Oxford: Oxford University Press, 1987)

Miller, Nancy K., Jason Tougaw, eds, *Extremities: Trauma, Testimony and Community* (Urbana and Chicago: University of Illinois Press, 2002)

Millman, Marcia, *Such a Pretty Face: Being Fat in America* (New York: Norton, 1980)

Modleski, Tania, *Loving with a Vengeance: Mass-Produced Fantasies for Women* (New York, London: Routledge, 1990 [1982])

Nicholson, Colin, ed., *Margaret Atwood: Writing and Subjectivity* (Houndmills, Basingstoke, Hampshire, London: Macmillan, 1994)

Oliver, J. Eric, *Fat Politics: The Real Story Behind America's Obesity Epidemic* (Oxford, New York: Oxford University Press, 2006)

Oliver, Kelly, 'Julia Kristeva's Feminist Revolutions', *Hypatia*, 8:3 (Summer 1993), 94-114

Olney, James, ed., *Autobiography: Essays Theoretical and Critical* (Princeton, New Jersey: Princeton University Press, 1980)

Orbach, Susie, *Fat is a Feminist Issue: The Anti-Diet Guide for Women* (London: Arrow Books, 2006 [1978])

___, *Bodies* (London: Profile Books, 2009)

Palmer, Paulina, 'Foreign Bodies: The Grotesque Body in the Fiction of Jeanette Winterson', *Gramma*, 11 (2003), 81-93

Parker, Emma, 'You're What You Eat: The Politics of Eating in the Novels of Margaret Atwood', *Twentieth Century Literature*, 41:3 (Autumn 1995), 349-68

Patton, Marilyn, '*Lady Oracle*: The Politics of the Body', *Ariel*, 22:4 (1991), 28-49

Puhl, Rebecca M., and Kelly D. Brownell, 'Psychosocial Origins of Obesity Stigma: Towards Changing a Powerful and Pervasive Bias', *Obesity Reviews*, 4 (2003), 213-27

Radford, Jean, ed., *The Progress of Romance: The Politics of Popular Romance Fiction* (London: Routledge, 1986)

Radin, Paul, *The Trickster: A Study in American Indian Mythology* (London: Routledge & Kegan Paul, 1956)

Rao, Eleonora, *Strategies for Identity: The Fiction of Margaret Atwood* (New York: Peter Lang, 1993)

Reesman, Jeanne Campbell, ed., *The Trickster Lives: Culture and Myth in American Fiction* (Athens, Ga., London: University of Georgia Press, 2001)

Rich, Adrienne, *Of Woman Born: Motherhood as Experience and Institution* (New York: Norton, 1976)

Richardson, Stephen A., Norman Goodman, Albert H. Hastorf, and Sanford M. Dornbusch, 'Cultural Uniformity in Reaction to Physical Disabilities', *American Sociological Review*, 26:2 (1961), 241-47

Rosenberg, Jerome H., *Margaret Atwood* (Boston: G.K. Hall, 1984)

Ruoff, A., LaVonne, and Jerry W. Ward, Jr, eds, *Redefining American Literary History* (New York: The Modern Language Association of America, 1990)

Russell, Lorena, 'Dog-Women and She-Devils: The Queering Field of Monstrous Women', *International Journal of Sexuality and Gender Studies*, 5:2 (2000), 177-93

Russo, Mary J., *The Female Grotesque: Risk, Excess and Modernity* (New York: Routledge, 1995)

Sage, Lorna, 'Weightlessness and a Banana', *The Observer*, 10 September 1989

Sceats, Sarah, *Food, Consumption and the Body in Contemporary Women's Fiction* (Cambridge: Cambridge University Press, 2000)

___, and Gail Cunningham, eds, *Image and Power* (London and New York: Longman, 1996)

Schur, Edwin M., *Labelling Women Deviant: Gender, Stigma, and Social Control* (Philadelphia: Temple University Press, 1983)

Schwartz, Hillel, *Never Satisfied: A Cultural History of Diets, Fantasies and Fat* (New York: Free Press, 1986)

Sellers, Susan, *Hélène Cixous: Authorship, Autobiography and Love* (Cambridge: Polity Press, 1996)

Showalter, Elaine, ed., *The New Feminist Criticism: Essays on Women, Literature and Theory* (London: Virago, 1986 [1985])

Smith, Patricia Juliana, 'Weldon's *The Life and Loves of a She-Devil*', *The Explicator*, 51:4 (1993), 255-57

Smith, Jeanne Rossier, *Writing Tricksters: Mythic Gambols in American Ethnic Literature* (Berkeley and Los Angeles: University of California Press, 1997)

Sontag, Susan, *On Photography* (London: Allen Lane, Penguin Books, 1978)

Spitzack, Carole, *Confessing Excess: Women and the Politics of Body Reduction* (New York: State University of New York Press, 1990)

Stallybrass, Peter, and Allon White, *The Politics and Poetics of Transgression* (Ithaca, N. Y: Cornell University Press, 1986)

Steedman Carolyn R., *Landscape for a Good Woman: A Story of Two Lives* (New Brunswick, NJ: Rutgers University Press, 1987)

Stern, Mark E., and Robert B. Marchesani, eds, *The Inhabitants of the Unconscious: The Grotesque and the Vulgar in Everyday Life* (New York, London and Oxford: The Haworth Press, 2003)

Strachey, James, ed., *The Standard Edition of the Complete Psychological Works of Sigmund Freud*, 24 vols (London: Hogarth Press, 1966-1974)

Sullivan, Ceri, and Barbara White, eds, *Writing and Fantasy* (London, New York: Longman, 1999)

Taitz, Leonard S., *The Obese Child* (Oxford, London, Edinburgh, Boston, Melbourne: Blackwell Scientific Publications, 1983)

Thomson, Philip, *The Grotesque* (London: Methuen, 1972)

Tressider, Jack, *The Complete Dictionary of Symbols* (San Francisco, CA: Chronicle Books, 2005)

Trodd, Colin, Paul Barlow, and David Amigoni, eds, *Victorian Culture and the Idea of the Grotesque* (Hants: Ashgate, 1999)

Turner, Bryan S., *The Body and Society* (London, Thousand Oaks, New Delhi: Sage, 1996)

Vice, Sue, *Introducing Bakhtin* (Manchester and New York: Manchester University Press, 1997)

Vizenor, Gerald, 'Trickster Discourse', *American Indian Quarterly*, 14 (Summer 1990), 277-87

Walker, Nancy A., *The Disobedient Writer: Women and Narrative Tradition* (Austin: University of Texas Press, 1995)

Wallace, Honor McKitrick, 'Desire and the Female Protagonist: A Critique of Feminist Narrative Theory', *Style*, 34:2 (2000), 176-87

Warhol, Robyn R., and Diane Price, eds, *Feminisms: An Anthology of Literary Theory and Criticism*, ed. by Herndl (Houndmills, Basingtone, Hampshire: Macmillan, 1997)

Waugh, Patricia, *Feminine Fictions: Revisiting the Modern* (London and New York: Routledge, 1989)

Werlock, Abby H.P, *British Women Writing Fiction* (Tuscaloosa and London: The University of Alabama Press, 2000)
Wide, Alan, '"Bold, but not too Bold": Fay Weldon and the Limits of Poststructuralist Criticism', *Contemporary Literature*, 29:3 (1988), 403-19
Wiget, Andrew, ed., *'Dictionary of Native American Trickster* (New York: Garland Publishing, 1994)
Williams, Anne, *Art of Darkness: A Poetics of Gothic* (Chicago: Chicago University Press, 1995)
Wilson, Sharon Rose, *Margaret Atwood's Fairy-Tale Sexual Politics* (Jackson, MS: University Press of Mississippi, 1993)
Wolf, Naomi, *The Beauty Myth: How Images of Beauty are Used against Women* (London: Vintage, 1991 [1990])
Woolf, Virginia, *A Room of One's Own* (London: Penguin, 2000 [1929])
Worthington, Kim L., *Self as Narrative: Subjectivity and Community in Contemporary Fiction* (Oxford: Clarendon Press, 1996)

Internet Resources

Alicandro, Erin, 'Fay Weldon on Writing and Feminism', University of Connecticut, *Creative Writing Program*, Spring 2006 <http://long river.uconn.edu/cw/cw_newsletter2006.pdf>
BBC News, 'Call for Fertility Ban for Obese', 30 August 2006 <http ://news.bbc.co.uk/1/hi/health/5296200.stm>
Borkoles, Erika, 'Obese Women Can Get Healthier without Diets' *Reuters* Health (London), 05 December 2006 <http://www.nlm. nih.gov/medlineplus/news/fullstory_42107.html>
Burne, Jerome, 'Obesity: Size Isn't Everything', 21 June 2005 <http://www.size-acceptance.org/uk/ >
Cable, Simon, 'British Woman Banned from Entering New Zealand', *The Daily Mail*, 17 November 2007 <http://freerepublic.com/fo cus/f-news/1927165/posts>

Cochrane, Kira, 'Too Fat for a Family', *Guardian*, 31 August 2006 <http://www.guardian.co.uk/society/2006/aug/31/health.medicineandhealth>

Freeman, Hadley, 'Thinking Big as Women's Waists Expand', *Guardian*, 26 August 2006 <http://www.guardian.co.uk/society/2006/aug/26/health.food>

Harris, Paul, '"Fat is Fabulous", insist Anti-Diet Protesters', *Observer*, 8 August 2004 <http://www.guardian.co.uk/world/ 2004/aug/08/usa.health>

Higgins, Charlotte, '"Too Fat" Opera Star Makes Slight Return', *Guardian*, 04 April 2007 <http://www.guardian.co.uk/uk/2007/apr/05/classicalmusic.artnews>

Hoggard, Liz, 'Why We're Beautiful Now?', *Observer*, 9 January 2005 <http://www.guardian.co.uk/uk/media/2005/jan/09/advertising.comment>

Holt, Leslie, 'China Toughens Adoption Standards' <http://www.icue.com/portal/site/iCue/flatview/?cuecard=35300>

Hull Daily Mail/ East Riding Mail, 15 January 2008 http://www.thisisyourmail.co.uk/posts/your_patch/view/1805-how-did-doctors-miss-my-cancerous-tumour>

Kennedy, Maev, 'Only Sing When You're Slimming', *Guardian*, 8 March 2004 <http://www.guardian.co.uk/uk/2004/mar/08/arts.artsnews>

Moore, Judith, 'Why I Wrote Fat Girl', February 2005 <http://www.vachss.com/media/righteous/why_fat_girl_moore.html>

NAAFA, 'But Isn't it Unhealthy to Be Fat?' <http://www.naafa.org/documents/brochures/naafa-info.html#whatis>

Politt, Katha, 'New Fiction', *New York Times* (Books), 26 September 1976 <http://partners.nytimes.com/books/00/09/03/specials/atwood-oracle.html>

Rérolle, Raphaëlle, 'Interview with Jeanette Winterson', *Le Monde* (English), April 2002 <http://www.jeanettewinterson.com>

The Food Museum Online Exhibit <http://www.foodmuseum.com/ exfatCulture.html>

UK Health Select Committee, 'Obesity Report', *Health Committee Publications*, 27 May 2004 <http://www.publications.parliament.uk/pa/cm200304/cmselect/cmhealth/23/2303.htm>

Walezak, Emilie 'They lived happily ever after, or did they? The Rewriting of Grimms' *The Twelve Dancing Princesses* in Jeanette Winterson's *Sexing the Cherry*' <http://conferences.univ-lyon2.fr/index.php/reprise/paper/view/58/108>

STUDIES IN ENGLISH LITERATURES

Edited by Koray Melikoğlu

ISSN 1614-4651

1   *Özden Sözalan*
The Staged Encounter
Contemporary Feminism and Women's Drama
2nd, revised editon
ISBN 3-89821-367-6

2   *Paul Fox (ed.)*
Decadences
Morality and Aesthetics in British Literature
ISBN 3-89821-573-3

3   *Daniel M. Shea*
James Joyce and the Mythology of Modernism
ISBN 3-89821-574-1

4   *Paul Fox and Koray Melikoğlu (eds.)*
Formal Investigations
Aesthetic Style in Late-Victorian and Edwardian Detective Fiction
ISBN 978-3-89821-593-0

5   *David Ellis*
Writing Home
Black Writing in Britain Since the War
ISBN 978-3-89821-591-6

6   *Wei H. Kao*
The Formation of an Irish Literary Canon in the Mid-Twentieth Century
ISBN 978-3-89821-545-9

7   *Bianca Del Villano*
Ghostly Alterities
Spectrality and Contemporary Literatures in English
2nd, revised editon
ISBN 978-3-89821-714-9

8   *Melanie Ann Hanson*
Decapitation and Disgorgement
The Female Body's Text in Early Modern English Drama and Poetry
ISBN 978-3-89821-605-5

9   *Shafquat Towheed (ed.)*
New Readings in the Literature of British India, c.1780-1947
ISBN 978-3-89821-673-9

10   *Paola Baseotto*
"Disdeining life, desiring leaue to die"
Spenser and the Psychology of Despair
ISBN 978-3-89821-567-1

11 Annie Gagiano
    Dealing with Evils
    Essays on Writing from Africa
    ISBN 978-3-89821-867-2

12 Thomas F. Halloran
    James Joyce: Developing Irish Identity
    A Study of the Development of Postcolonial Irish Identity in the Novels of James Joyce
    ISBN 978-3-89821-571-8

13 Pablo Armellino
    Ob-scene Spaces in Australian Narrative
    An Account of the Socio-topographic Construction of Space in Australian Literature
    ISBN 978-3-89821-873-3

14 Lance Weldy
    Seeking a Felicitous Space on the Frontier
    The Progression of the Modern American Woman in O. E. Rölvaag, Laura Ingalls Wilder, and Willa Cather
    ISBN 978-3-89821-535-0

15 Rana Tekcan
    The Biographer and the Subject
    A Study on Biographical Distance
    ISBN 978-3-89821-995-2

16 Paola Brusasco
    Writing Within/Without/About Sri Lanka
    Discourses of Cartography, History and Translation in Selected Works by Michael Ondaatje and Carl Muller
    ISBN 978-3-8382-0075-0

17 Zeynep Z. Atayurt
    Excess and Embodiment in Contemporary Women's Writing
    ISBN 978-3-89821-978-5

FORTHCOMING (MANUSCRIPT WORKING TITLES)

Kevin Cole
Levity's Rainbow
Menippean Poetics in Swift, Fielding, and Sterne
ISBN 3-89821-654-3

Fatma Tuba Terci
Postmodern Goddesses in Contemporary Chicana Feminist Novel
Peel my Love Like an Onion, Caramelo, or, Puro Cuento: A Novel and Face of an Angel
ISBN 978-3-8382-0023-1

Geetha Ganga
Historicizing Somalia through Literary Narrative
The Fiction of Nuruddin Farah
ISBN 978-3-8382-0083-5

Busuyi Mekusi
Negotiating Memory and Nation Building in New South African Drama
ISBN 978-3-8382-0232-7

Gianluca Delfino
Time, History and Philosophy in the Works of Wilson Harris
ISBN 978-3-8382-0265-5

Series Subscription

Please enter my subscription to the series **Studies in English Literatures**, ISSN 1614-4651, as follows:

- ❐ complete series   OR   ❐ English-language titles
- ❐ German-language titles

starting with
- ❐ volume # 1
- ❐ volume # ___
  - ❐ please also include the following volumes: #___, ___, ___, ___, ___, ___,
- ❐ the next volume being published
  - ❐ please also include the following volumes: #___, ___, ___, ___, ___, ___,

- ❐ 1 copy per volume   OR   ❐ ___ copies per volume

Subscription within Germany:

You will receive every title on 1st publication at the regular bookseller's price incl. s & h and VAT.

Payment:
❐ Please bill me for every volume.
❐ Lastschriftverfahren: Ich/wir ermächtige(n) Sie hiermit widerruflich, den Rechnungsbetrag je Band von meinem/unserem folgendem Konto einzuziehen.

Kontoinhaber: _____ Kreditinstitut: _____
Kontonummer: _____ Bankleitzahl: _____

International Subscription:

Payment (incl. s & h and VAT) in advance for
- ❐ 10 volumes/copies (€ 319.80)   ❐ 20 volumes/copies (€ 599.80)
- ❐ 40 volumes/copies (€ 1,099.80)

Please send my books to:

NAME _____ DEPARTMENT _____
ADDRESS _____
POST/ZIP CODE _____ COUNTRY _____
TELEPHONE _____ EMAIL _____

date/signature _____

Please fax to: **0511 / 262 2201 (+49 511 262 2201)**
or mail to: *ibidem*-Verlag, Julius-Leber-Weg 11, D-30457 Hannover, Germany
or send an e-mail: ibidem@ibidem-verlag.de

ibidem-Verlag
Melchiorstr. 15
D-70439 Stuttgart
info@ibidem-verlag.de

www.ibidem-verlag.de
www.ibidem.eu
www.edition-noema.de
www.autorenbetreuung.de